JUNGIAN ANALYSTS:
Their Visions
&
Vulnerabilities

OTHER BOOKS BY J. MARVIN SPIEGELMAN

MYSTICISM, PSYCHOLOGY AND OEDIPUS
by Israel Regardie, Christopher S. Hyatt and J. Marvin Spiegelman

The Jungian Psychology Series

BUDDHISM AND JUNGIAN PSYCHOLOGY
by J. Marvin Spiegelman Ph.D. and Mokusen Miyuki, Ph.D.

HINDUISM AND JUNGIAN PSYCHOLOGY
by J. Marvin Spiegelman, Ph.D. and Arwind U. Vasavada, Dr. Litt.

CATHOLICISM AND JUNGIAN PSYCHOLOGY
Edited by J. Marvin Spiegelman

JUNGIAN ANALYSTS: Their Visions and Vulnerabilities
Edited by J. Marvin Spiegelman, Ph.D.

JUNGIAN PSYCHOLOGY AND THE PASSIONS OF THE SOUL

THE TREE

THE QUEST

THE NYMPHOMANIAC

A MODERN JEW IN SEARCH OF A SOUL
Edited by J. Marvin Spiegelman, Ph.D. and Abraham Jacobson, Ph.D.

Inquiries into the availability of these and numerous other titles are welcomed by Falcon Press □ 3660 N. 3rd St. □ Phoenix, AZ 85012, USA.

JUNGIAN ANALYSTS:
Their Visions
&
Vulnerabilities

EDITED BY:
J. Marvin Spiegelman, Ph.D.

CONTRIBUTORS:
Dr. Med. Fritz Beyme
Dr. Phil. Gustaf Dreifuss
Michael Fordham, M.D.
Dr. Med. Adolf Guggenbuhl-Craig
Baroness Vera von der Heydt
Dr. Phil. Mario Jacoby
Joe McNair, Ph.D.
Andrew Samuels
Dr. Phil. Sonja Marjasch
Robert M. Stein, M.D.
Arwind U. Vasavada, Dr. Litt.
Joseph B. Wheelwright, M.D.
Dr. Med. Alfred Ziegler

1988
FALCON PRESS
PHOENIX, ARIZONA, USA

ISBN: 0-941404-66-8

First Edition 1988

Cover Design — D. Curtis
Typesetting Design — Cate Mugasis

FALCON PRESS
3660 N. 3rd Street
Phoenix, Arizona 85012, U.S.A.
(602) 246-3546

Manufactured in the United States of America

Table of Contents

Preface

It is with pleasure (and with appreciation to the contributors) that I present this book to those readers who might welcome it as a glimpse into the sincere reflections of experienced analysts. It is the kind of book that I wish had been available to read when I first began doing psychotherapy in 1951 or even when I began doing analysis under supervision, during the "control" phase of training, in Zurich in 1957. Every neophyte psychotherapist is anxious to "do it right"— whatever that means—and is uncertain as to how to proceed, no matter how much personal analysis he or she has had or how many training courses. The reason for this is that psychotherapy, in contrast with Behavior Modification, has to do with the soul. It is an art and a sensitivity to individuals, not a technique nor a science. All that one learns—history of symbols, mythology and religion, case studies, psychiatry and psychology, the arts, and from physical and biological sciences—is only background for the moment when one is confronted with the individuality of that suffering person who presents himself for therapy or analysis. All one's training helps, but it is of great benefit—even essential—to get the accumulated wisdom of one's senior colleagues, how they have approached the work and what they have learned through experience. It is in this way that the new therapist can glean hints, can supplement his own inner work with the comparative information that he longs for. To learn an art, one needs to examine the art of others. And that is what this book is about: a dozen senior Jungian analysts responded to the question as to how they go about doing what they do and what they have learned about it over the years.

The book began when I was writing about my own approach to analysis, realizing that it would be useful to compare the experience of others. To try and get the insights of senior Jungian analysts on paper, therefore, I took the membership list of the International Association of Analytical Psychology in 1959—the year that I joined the Association and the second-to-last year when Jung was still alive—and sent out an announcement of the task at hand to approximately 50 of the 150 members then listed, along with two others who graduated from the C.G. Jung Institute Zurich shortly afterward. I knew that these analysts had experienced Jung directly (a desideratum of selection), and that most of the others had not, or had died. To be sure that no one who was qualified to be included would be missed, I also placed an announcement in the current (1985) bulletin of the International Association of Analytical Psychology, which went to some one thousand members. No further response resulted from this announcement, but of the fifty notices sent personally, fourteen sent regrets; I was informed that two others had died; and sixteen agreed to participate. Eighteen, or 36%, did not respond at all. At last, a dozen analysts submitted papers and these are herein presented. In order to make this work of more use to people in training, I asked Dr. Joe McNair, a particularly able candidate in the Los Angeles training program, to read the papers, raise questions and make comments. His and my remarks were then sent to the contributors, who were kind enough to respond. Since McNair and I are still involved in the training process, I asked Fordham and Samuels of England to comment on my paper also. The results follow. At the end of the contributions there is an "Epilogue," in which Dr. McNair describes his experience in doing this work. I think that readers, particularly people in training, will enjoy his overview of his experience of this "opus."

Finally, there is a brief autobiographical section at the conclusion of the book, wherein the contributors were asked to describe their educational background and the nature of their contact with Jung.

I am impressed with the seriousness and depth of the presentations of my colleagues. All but two (von der Heydt and Ziegler) were known to me personally; many of them were also students during my own years at the C.G. Jung Institute Zurich in the late 1950s. All the same, the fact that this dozen hail from three continents, five countries, and at least eight cities, suggests that there is considerable difference among them. Three of them (Fordham, von der Heydt and Wheelwright) are "first-generation." All twelve experienced Jung in some way; yet the reader may be startled and pleased (as was I) at their differences as well as their similarities. I think that Jung would be delighted to see that individuation has been served.

I wish to thank these colleagues for their generous response to the project, and to Falcon Press for seeing the value of its publication. I also want to acknowledge the permission of the C.G. Jung Institute of San Francisco to reprint Dr. Wheelwright's contribution, which appeared as part of his own book, *ST. GEORGE AND THE DANDELION,* published by them. A summary version of my paper was presented at a national Jungian meeting in Boston in the fall of 1985. I hope that other colleagues will be inspired to similar endeavors. Advancement in our "art" will surely be enhanced by the sincere and reflective reportage of those who have been devotedly committed to its practice. Finally, I wish to express my appreciation to those analysts, teachers and colleagues who have contributed to my own growth in the field. As a bare minimum among these, I want to mention C.A. Meier, Marie-Louise von Franz, Liliane Frey, Rivkah Kluger and, in memoriam, Max Zeller, Bruno Klopfer, Hilde Kirsch, and Margaret McLean. If I add, as teachers, Barbara Hannah, Jolande Jacobi and James Kirsch, I mention only a minimum and neglect many others. To this august list, I would add, also in memoriam, the name of the secretary of the Institute during my years in Zurich, Alice Maurer, helper and good friend. Above all, the name of C.G. Jung—whose genius has been a beacon and even a life-saving gift to so many—is rightfully acknowledged in the title itself.

J. Marvin Spiegelman
Studio City, California
Winter 1987-1988

How I Do It

by

BARONESS VERA VON DER HEYDT

I found it difficult to write about "how I do it" because so much of it is in the past. I stopped analysing formally when I was eighty years old; now I am eighty-five. I still see a few patients, once a week, once a fortnight, once a month. I am asked to speak and teach. Finally, I realised that I was complicating matters because I am consulted by people who are looking for an analyst.

I thought of the mistakes I had made, of the opportunities I had let slip by; I thought of the people who had discovered their creative potential, and of those who had succeeded in accepting their limitations with good humour. I had also been thinking about technique and theoretical knowledge I had acquired over the many years I had been analysing. Of course I know more after a good forty years of working than I did when I started. However, my basic approach to people who put themselves in my care has remained the same.

My psychological upbringing occurred at a time when the line between analysis and therapy in Analytical Psychology was not rigidly defined as it is now, so that an analyst was more flexible and freer in his way of conducting the analytic treatment. This kind of undogmatic approach was expected of me at a Clinic which had been founded by a Freudian and was run predominantly on Freudian lines; the one other Jungian analyst was the co-medical director.

One of the very important questions for me was the subject of fees. At the Clinic, I had nothing to do with it; I was simply told how much I should charge, as careful enquiries about family commitments and the general financial situation had already been made. Later, when I had to make such decisions myself, I found it occasionally a knotty problem. I had had the experience of being treated with consideration and generosity; no doubt this coloured my attitude when charging a patient an appropriate sum of money. I was always careful about letting anyone pay for someone else, particularly in the case of young people, even with regard to parents for their children, because of the additional emotional conflict it can arouse. When this became apparent, I discussed the situation with my patient and worked out a feasible arrangement with him which might have meant a small or token fee for a while. Then I spoke to the parents with the full knowledge of my patient, and explained the situation to them.

My superior function is sensation; I watch and observe a patient from the moment he comes into the room until the end of the session. This does not mean that I look at him, directly all the time; I sit in such a way that a patient need not feel raped or invaded. There is space between him and me, but no piece of furniture; he is close enough to be able to stretch out a hand when overcome

5

by fear or grief. There is a couch in my room, but no one ever wanted to lie on it. I listen to the tone of the voice as much as to words spoken and I try to hear what lies behind them. This, I found, was usually fairly straightforward with matters from the instinctual and moral spheres, and aspects of the shadow could be easily detected. But this is much more complicated and complex to uncover in the spiritual area. I am a Roman Catholic and so I know about doubts and difficulties, and how they can be hidden and kept secret from prying or uncomprehending eyes. This applies to everyone who belongs to any religious system as well as those who do not. I have known for a long time that religion and spirituality are affected by a neurosis just as much as sex and relationships are. My patients have known of my religious framework and this—curiously enough—gave believers as well as unbelievers a sense of security; I was able to investigate those areas in which superstition, intolerance and infantile assumptions live, without causing offense.

Dreams were often a help: crumbling Churches or other religious buildings were viewed with dismay by the dreamer, or with satisfaction; teachers from the past appeared who had instilled fear, and they aroused anxiety yet again; these images stated facts which could be discussed. For instance, what was crumbling, belief or faith? Or what did the fear refer to: death, hell, being unloved? I made use of dreams as much as I could. The nature of their content, the way they presented conflict or a problem and a possible solution fascinated me. However, I realised that some patients are open to manifestations from the unconscious and experience them to be part of themselves, others never feel that a dream is in any way connected to them. Sometimes this turns out to be a defense mechanism. I respect resistances. But when a patient continues to tell me dreams without any comment, I remain silent and wait for what is going to emerge.

Soon after the war, I went to Zurich; Dr. Jung had agreed to see me on a regular basis. One day, I asked Jung about the transference. The transference is a disturbing notion, particularly when it is presented under the heading "this or that is nothing but the transference." This makes it sound as if all feelings of affection and gratitude as well as all anger and resentment against the analyst were artifically induced and worthless. Jung spoke at length about the "nothing but," and the healing element of acceptance. Finally, he said: *"Sie muessen es ihnen vormachen"*; "You have to show them what it is about."

I have never forgotten that hour with Jung; I understood that I had to get across to a patient that, yes there are feelings connected with the transference and also emotions, but "nothing but . . . ", no; those feelings are valid, they have value. What the patients have to give is acceptable and their lives meaningful— even if, for a while, they have to trust me before we can discover their trust in themselves. This was the only way I could work, treating every patient as an individual, reacting to him as the troubled human being he is, aware of his special needs as I can be.

COMMENTS BY SPIEGELMAN

Three different images present themselves about Baroness von der Heydt, whom I have never met, unfortunately, but who evoked in me memories of my own years in Zurich, memories which are richly nostalgic for the peculiarly European, and, particularly, "continental" attitude.

The first image is from the film, *Matter of Heart* (produced by Dr. Suzanne Wagner of Los Angeles), in which many of Jung's earlier students speak about him and his work. Baroness von der Heydt appears briefly and with great dignity and beauty. She looks far younger than her birth year of 1899 would suggest. When asked about Jung's relation with Toni Wolff, she responded quite matter-of-factly, to the effect: "Do not affairs also occur in the United States?" I loved her for this down-to-earth statement, given with charm.

The urbanity of the first image is contrasted with the second, which is much more religious in tone. I recall reading a description, or statement, or view, about a meeting of the Baroness with Jung in which her Catholic religious feelings were strongly at issue. I can not find that material now, but I retain a memory of a person who was deeply Catholic, deeply tolerant, totally psychological, and quietly committed to both tradition and individuality. This depth is particularly satisfying to one who saw its opposite so much while growing up a Jew in less tolerant Christian surroundings.

The third image is one that is available to all of us, as is given by her paper for this volume. Here, again, atmosphere is as important as content. But now, in contrast to urbanity and religious depth, we see the gentle, receptive and precise discrimination of a committed analyst. As a sensation type, she is one of a minority in the Jungian field, and one does experience the unspoken, the sensitivity to the peripheral as well as the central, the factual and precise yet fully imaginal capacity of a person who is differentiated in that typology. I have the feeling, as I rarely do, that it would have been a rare experience for me, an introverted intuitive-thinker-turned-feeler, to undergo analysis with this woman: patrician, continental, Catholic, and urbane. Her attitude about money shows that this in no way made her patients feel "less than" or were they put in some mold by the presence of the "title." Furthermore, the imagery presented in her brief comments about dreams immediately tell one that this is a person who connects in a specific manner with the unconscious. For example, dreams of crumbling churches cause her to question: "What was crumbling, belief or faith?" Here is precision sorely needed, particularly with people who love and need their religious tradition, yet need to develop individuality, as well.

I am at a loss for questions, but would like to just hear more from and about her. Is that possible? I should think that our colleagues and students would like this too. My own father just turns 85 this year and I, approaching 60, have had long talks with him about life, his life, and am struck that his (and her) generation have seen as many changes as could be possible in one century.

COMMENTS BY McNAIR

I suppose we all imagine, sometimes, the end of our career; I know I have. She writes " . . . so much of it is in the past . . . " To be looking back at the end, all things considered, must be a very rich moment. An image of being on a mountain top high in the Sierras, looking out over endless trees and mountains, comes to my mind. Yet I cannot see the memory of the beginning of my career, and she makes me realize that at 39, I am somewhere in the "soup" of it all.

I am moved by her phrasing, or "soundings," perhaps. She seems to convey the plasticity and patience of life itself—no urgency: "I thought of the past . . . "; "I attempted to bring about a transformation of attitudes . . . " Rilke's poem *Autumn* comes to mind:

> *And yet there is someone,*
> *whose hands infinitely calm,*
> *hold up all this falling.*

This letter-response has been very moving and gently inspirational for me. There is a quality of relationship, a "tone" in attitude that feels gentle, confident, dedicated, and appreciative of limits: "discovering their creative potential . . . " and " . . . accepting their limitations with good humour." This statement brought a free breath back; I can often lose the humorous perspective amidst the suffering or the struggle.

There is a constant sense of feeling and sensation throughout her letter—my thinking-intuitive apparatus was befuddled in the first two readings. Then I recalled, having read her book for help in working with an ex-priest, that she had said, " . . . I apprehend and comprehend from a centre other than mind." Aha! Relief.

She heightened my sense-awareness with phrases like "I watch and observe. . ."; she is able to "stretch out a hand" in the seating arrangement, listening for the "tone" behind a person's words, and "my psychological upbringing." These statements have a "touching" quality, and made a lasting impression upon me.

My lone question would address her perspective over a life's career: How did her perception of herself vis-a-vis her work transform at the different ages (i.e. at 50, 60, 70)?

Once upon a time . . .

REPLY TO COMMENTS BY SPIEGELMAN AND McNAIR

I was born in Berlin in December 1899; I had an older sister and a younger brother. I had parents who cared for each other and cared for us. My father was a Jew in whom Western Judaic sophistication mingled with the darker Eastern tradition and its Chasidic elements. He converted to Protestantism in his teens. My mother was half Nordic, Hanseatic Lutheran, half Celtic Irish Roman Catholic; her mother renounced her faith when she married. My father was an internationally well-known merchant and banker; he was frequently used as a troubleshooter by the German Foreign Office and the Kaiser. My mother was lovely, elegant, high-spirited. Underneath this light side lay problems and unconscious conflicts of too many opposing components which I was aware of from a very early age onwards.

I read a great deal, and in a vague way I thought a great deal about many things. When I was twelve years old, I asked my headmaster if he believed in the immortality of the soul. He told me to read Moses Mendelssohn. *WILHELM MEISTER* was the first book I bought for myself. Then the medieval mystics came my way. These books, so far beyond my world, were important to me, but I knew that I had to keep that kind of knowledge to myself. I married young; my husband introduced me to Far Eastern art, thought and religion. My marriage ended after nine years; I met Dr. Jung during the most difficult period of the break-up, but the idea of going to Zurich or to speak to him about myself never entered my head.

I returned to my parents, getting more and more restless and dissatisfied, but also frightened by the political developments. In 1933, I realised that I had to leave Germany. I chose to go to London. It was a complete break from life as I had known it till then. It was a new chapter; it was the beginning of the individuation process. In London I joined the Roman Catholic Church. I earned my living as a research worker and reader for British and American film companies. I learnt a method of hand analysis and my teacher exhorted me to have a Jungian analysis. I achieved this during the war, in Oxford. John Layard was my first analyst and he started me on my path of being an analyst myself. At the end of my training with him, Dr. Rushforth, Medical Director of the Davidson Clinic in Edinburgh, asked me to join her staff. The Clinic was a wonderful place to get clinical experience, and to learn about Freudian and neo-Freudian concepts and techniques as, with one exception, I was the only Jungian. Furthermore, the Clinic was a place where tolerance and respect of one another's psychological and religious allegiances were practised.

As soon as the war was over, I got a British passport and spent a holiday in Ascona for one of the Eranos meetings. Dr. Jung was present and I saw him twice. The second time he told me that he would see me in Zurich on a regular basis if I could arrange it. Dr. Rushforth gave me leave of absence for as long as I would need it.

The first time I sat in Dr. Jung's consulting room I was slightly apprehensive; this was justified because something happened which I had not foreseen. Dr. Jung quite automatically spoke German to me and I obviously answered him in German. Curiously enough, I had not noticed this in Ascona, but when I started to tell him dreams and experiences in my own language, which I had never done before, emotions welled up and came to the surface which I had ruthlessly repressed: the terror, the cruelty inflicted and endured, and the shame. The split I did not want to know about. Jung enabled me to integrate my German heritage as being part of my prima materia which had to be and could be transformed.

My time in Zurich came to an end. I went back to Edinburgh for a short while and then returned to London from where I had started my most intensive journey. Since 1951, London has been my home and in spite of difficulties and disillusionments, a happy place surrounded by helpful and friendly colleagues.

How I Do Analysis

by

MICHAEL FORDHAM, M.R.C.P., M.D.

The question about what analysts do is recurrent and is curious. There is a large literature on the subject: Freud described in his case studies how he treated his patients and Jung tried much the same in his essays contained in volume 16 of the *COLLECTED WORKS*. There has since developed a large literature on the subject, especially from those who have deviated or have developed the supposedly recognized techniques.

That the question arises in the minds of the lay public is not surprising but that it arises in analysts themselves, and not only some young ones in training, is curious. They have all submitted to a personal analysis and presumably received some instruction on the subject of how to treat patients analytically.

It arose at the Society of Analytical Psychology in London in the 1940s but latterly the question has ceased to be asked. That Society was in the forefront of Jungian Societies and Institutes in both analysing the transference and in training students by asking them to take cases under supervision. Concurrently, papers were written on technique and method by Society members. That policy has not always been pursued by other Societies and Institutes. It is my impression that only by undergoing supervision with an analyst that poses the question of how he proceeds can one get a good impression of what he actually does and for that the London Society provided opportunity.

Apart from these inconclusive reflections, the question of what an analyst does has two facets: (1) There are methods that can be acquired from training analysis and supervision, plus reading and seminars. These can be described and are available in the literature. Some may have to be discarded as useless to any particular candidate. (2) There are irregularities which can be described but which are difficult to generalise, though once an irregularity has been detected it may prove fruitful and can later become generalised to become part of a revision of method. It may not do that, however.

Here is an example that I would not like to generalise: I see a male patient at eight o'clock in the morning twice a week and once at eight o'clock in the evening after dinner at which I have drunk wine. I am regularly more talkative in the evenings than in the morning interviews. That my patient notices and decides that "You are an after-dinner man." Of course it might be interesting to investigate the effects of analyst's eating and drinking habits in relation to his analytic work but I would not recommend my behavior as a matter for general practice. My intention here is to introduce the idea that the life of an analyst outside his work influences what he does in his practice.

11

There have been several stable features of my life as an analytical psycho-therapist which need to be stated before saying what I do when seeing a patient. In the first place I have always had a supervisor in my wife, Frieda Fordham, and can scarcely imagine how an analyst gets on without somebody to talk to about his patients, especially those who cause him distress or puzzle him. I talk about patients in seminars, of course, and in other discussion groups and, although that is also helpful, it is not in the same intimate and "hot" way. Then there is writing: I do not often write notes, only when something has struck me as important and then only after interviews, but writing in a generalised way is also necessary and is an obligation so that others may know what I am doing at any particular time.

All these activities help to heal myself: analytic practice involves introjecting parts of various people and it may not be possible to find the means of digesting and projecting these parts back into the patients. That is particularly difficult when there is much projective identification. When that predominates, my identity may become threatened, boundaries become insecure, and I may be put in the position of "fighting for my life." That discovery, which I recorded in *DEFENSES OF THE SELF*, opened the doors for me to the treatment of patients as a whole, and seeing it as a precarious operation for any analyst who opens himself to patients so as to individualise his analytic endeavours.

I find I usually have a special interest I am pursuing at any one time. At present I have that in a patient who spends his time denigrating "analysis"; what you say is said to have no effect or is made the subject of ridicule, even if what you say is recognised as correct—then you are met with the defiant "so what?" I have also written about this and listed the countertransference responses which such behaviour is liable to evoke. So it is a long term interest as well. Now it is different from what happened originally, because I am no longer vulnerable to such patients—I have learned from them.

That brings me to the point of saying how difficult it is to describe what one is doing with patients because of the changes that are taking place, for the shape of any analysis is made as much by the patient as the analyst. That is in line with Jung's idea that the analyst is as much in the analysis as the patient, though I do not agree that he needs analysis in the same way as the patient; what he needs is supervision, including that provided by his patients.

With the same class of patient, I may make an interpretation which is new to me though I have come near to it before. A specific patient, as part of his view of analysis, stated: "I do not understand a word you are saying." To that I made the following interpretation, which I have never made before: "I don't think that matters but it is important that you continue to believe I know what it is all about even if you do not." I follow this up with an amplification; saying that what he experiences is like that of a baby to whom it is very important that his mother talks to him though he can not possibly understand the words. Here I had for the first time incorporated the memory of an observation on mother-infant interaction. That development can be reflected upon as part of a technique for detecting very infantile manifestations easily dressed up in argumentation. I think that these remarks go in very well with Jung's claim to being unsystematic by intention. Indeed I now try to do just that within the analytic frame. My effort to be unsystematic can also be gleaned from the attempt I make to meet a patient at each interview as if I had never seen him before. I empty my mind, as far as I can, of thought, memories and understanding. That makes it difficult to pursue a policy from interview to interview though a continuity in the analytic process may emerge—it arises as it were from between myself and my patient. Proceeding thus gives space for the patient who can bring to the fore the state of affairs which predominates in his mind in the present, i.e. today.

To further describe what I do as an analyst and therapist it may be helpful if I look back and survey what I have done and how I changed. These retrospective reflections highlight the skills I have acquired and used, digested and discarded or gone beyond, as it seems to me.

Early on, I observed children and did whatever I could. I was taught passive technique in which one did almost nothing. Then I heard about Melanie Klein and tried talking to child patients about their play as much as she did but fumblingly, as I now know. Much of that has stuck; much has been digested and altered as experience grew.

In adult analysis, I did my best to persuade patients to write down and work on their dreams as I had discovered how to do in my two analyses. I also wanted them to make pictures and paint, which a few could do but most could not or if they did their productions were not especially revealing.

During this first period I tried to apply methods and develop technique—Jung had said that it was required. I read what was available and found psychoanalysts much more explicit than my Jungian colleagues. Feeling at a loss with patients that neither dreamed nor painted, I listened much more carefully and was greatly helped in discovering more about how to listen in Theodore Reik's book, *LISTENING WITH THE THIRD EAR*. I consider this change in technique has been invaluable for I discovered much better how to listen to what a patient did not say as well as what he did say. I was, however, being "unsystematic"—not, as Jung says, "by intention," but out of ignorance and confusion.

I then attacked the problem of transference with renewed vigour. I had noted that, in my view, my first analysis ended because the transference was not analysed, nor was I supported in working on it; my second analysis ended on an enacted countertransference. When I had developed sufficient skill and, I may say, had learned from my patients, I wrote the paper on transference which, to my great delight, was highly praised by Jung.

In that paper, I introduced the term syntonic countertransference. At the time, analysts in London were asking the question: "What do analysts really do?" It was often met with a silence which was justified and enshrined in the alchemical notion of the enclosed vessel which must be kept sealed lest the spirit escape. In London, supervision of students' cases was carried out and that did not have any bad effect on the analyses; indeed, the reverse seemed true. It might be that analysts' reticence was somehow due to the lack of a framework within which to talk about the patient's effect on them. If that effect could be made respectable, it might help—it was as primitive as that.

The idea of a syntonic countertransference was derived from the discussions amongst colleagues and the hints that Jung had given: for instance, about induced psychosis in therapists treating psychotic patients and having dreams about them which were as relevant to the patients as to the therapist.

The next step was to try and interest analysts in technique, which, I believe, had been wrongly understood. I used to—and still do—have quite acrimonious arguments with Jo Wheelwright who, when he talked about his ingenious use of type theory, seemed to me the arch-exponent of technique whilst declaiming against it! Analysts, especially beginners, need to learn a technique and to digest it as much as is possible, throwing out what they can't use. So, I wrote "Technique and Countertransference," which included a further development in that I used the concepts of projective and introjective identification to include unconscious interactions between analyst and patient.

The paper also indicated changing views on transference and countertransference which occupied me more and more so that I came to realise that the unconscious processes involved were the equivalent of a dream or an active imagination. I therefore paid much less attention to nighttime dreams, though I continued to be pleased if patients brought one along. I liked it best if it elucidated the transference and it usually did.

As I have already inferred, as a patient I had found painting pictures, dreaming, remembered mostly only if I wrote them down, holding "internal" conversations with "inner figures" all too easy and so I began by expecting patients all to do as I had done. Some could, but most could not and then I discovered transference analysis; it was the instrument that went far to solve the problem.

It took me a very long time to understand that, in many if not all of these transferences, the patients were trying to get me to analyse their childhood. That was galling because I wanted these transferences to develop as Jung had described them but they did not. Progress only became possible if their infantile nature was worked on. I got no help from Jungian analysts in this discovery and it was inferred—and I was occasionally told—that I was too Freudian.

Though I had read much Freud, it was not from him that I gained most help but from the writings of Melanie Klein, which were invaluable. My work with children was greatly helped, not so much by her theories as the way she talked to her cases. I tried to use her methods and found that I could come into much closer contact with children even with my very fumbling efforts. In any case, I worked best in the inner world of children and here Klein was producing an extra dimension: she was the first psychoanalyst that entered into their inner life from a different vertex to Jung but many of her findings were analogous and some of her theories were identical. So I began to understand more and more about children and that helped with my adult patients. The essential nature of many, perhaps all transferences became increasingly apparent and I had the means of dealing with them. Only in the last few years did I include infancy with any confidence, thanks to the collaboration of Gianna Henry from the Tavistock Clinic in London.

Much of what I do is reductive analysis and I am reproached for it. I can now say, having divested it of its plethora of reproaches, that it is beautiful and productive. So I am not abashed by derogatory comments about it. I believe that my conclusion is due to a different meaning that attaches to the term: I have come to realise that the analysis of childhood, of infantile sexuality and violence, includes and assimilates aspects of patients which have been neglected by Jungian analysts and a good many others that I have known with interests in developmental lines and spiritual life. That made them unable to work in the area of sexuality and childhood at all adequately—they manifestly preferred dreams and fantasy so that their work became often seriously disembodied. That statement may suggest a reaction formation on my part but I do not think that the word "beautiful" is to be explained and dismissed in that way because I am looking not for causes but for additional meanings of the person's "inner world." It is a completion which prevents fantasy from becoming fantastic, and in this way, idealising processes are placed in their right proportion.

LISTENING AND LEARNING FROM PATIENTS

Listening to patients has to be acquired, but the idea and method of so doing was greatly facilitated by Jung's admonition not to know beforehand. Having scientific interests, I was struck when I read that Claude Bernard wrote that when he went into his laboratory he left his theories outside with his overcoat. An additional and more recent support for my ideas came from Bion who recommended that an analyst divest himself of memory, desire and understanding. I currently express my attitude to students as follows: I tell them that it is true that I and they are there to acquire knowledge but that generalisations have to be left outside the interview room and locked up in a "filing-cabinet." I do not deny that sometimes the knowledge in my filing-cabinet (and probably theirs also) gets out—that can be productive but too often it is used defensively: one feels safe at last because the interpretation is familiar, it is a "stock interpretation." When I do that, I suspect that I have stopped listening. If you listen, there is much less likelihood that your interventions will be "stock" but will have that element of originality, spontaneity, and surprise which indicates not only listening but learning.

THE USE OF MYTHS

Though I have spent much time reading myths and enjoying them, and though I used to use them in analytic interviews, I now scarcely ever do so. A powerful element in this change has been that I gradually discovered, mostly from my own experience, how to create interpretations about the inner world.

These were quite often mythical in nature and are in a sense original creations in as much as they grow out of my reflections on what a patient tells me—they often have no relation to reality and are mainly concerned with the interrelation between inner objects.

I will invent an intervention of this kind; it is like one that I have given but have somewhat idealised it for the sake of clarity. Suppose a patient has a mass of fragmentary thoughts in his head which he can't use and he complains that he gets nothing from his analyst. I will interpret as follows: He feels helpless like a baby when there is no breast. The absent breast is felt, owing to his hunger, to be a bad breast inside him and he tries to convert that into thoughts which fragment because they get attacked as representations of the bad breast. I would probably not say anymore but subsequently I add that the bad breast became violent at the attempted transformation and squirted sperm-thoughts into his mind, thereby disorganising what was being arranged by creating too many.

I will now refer to my filing cabinet: (1) The aspiring element makes me think of Prometheus (my patient is a forethinker with gifts he can not realise). (2) The trickster archetype. Much of this is contained in my interpretations. (3) From Alchemy, a quotation: "What is below is like what is above, that the miracle of the one thing may be accomplished." (4) Bion: no breast equals a bad breast inside. One way of evacuating this is to create thoughts which mitigate pain. (5) Bion: Attacks on linkage of thoughts. (6) The Kundalini Yoga.

From this list of headings which were immediate associations, I could now add many more so that it seems perhaps inappropriate even to make it. I only do so because I want to illustrate why I do not bring that material directly into the analysis. Nevertheless, all that and much more has, I think, to be digested before I could make the interpretations (somewhat idealised) that I did.

COMMENT BY SPIEGELMAN ON FORDHAM'S CONTRIBUTION

Dr. Fordham has written just the kind of essay that I had hoped for, combining both transpersonal and personal material, with his own history as an analyst and examples of how he works. The combination of general information and what he calls "irregularities," in my opinion, is just what helps the analyst come to his individual attitude and style of work. He then truly finds the "art" of therapy, as a consequence of the union of "science" (available literature, other analysts) and "practice" (his experience of patients). Fordham has done just this, and my remarks will be in connection with words of his that effect me particularly.

1. Healing one's self since "analytic practice involves introjecting parts of various people and it may not be possible to find the means of digesting and projecting these parts back into patients." And, further, one's identity can be threatened for "the analyst who opens himself to patients so as to individualise his endeavors."

My response is, Yes, indeed! Writing, etc. surely helps, but I also found that telling the patient of his/her effects on me, including body reactions and imagery (rather than interpretation at this point), and then dealing with the joint archetypal condition, helps even more! More on this later.

2. "My effort to be unsystematic can also be gleaned from the attempt to meet a patient at each interview as if I had never seen him before."

Here, here! But what about the analyst's own myth? In the previous example, Fordham clearly employs an interpretation based on a myth of mother-infant interaction, where nothing that has been said demands it as such. It may be "correct," but other myths could be used, too. Does Fordham think that his is the "true" interpretation?

3. Fordham's description of his attempt to be a "good Jungian" and get patients to write down dreams, do active imagination, paint, etc. is very helpful. Most of us have had to deal with this issue on our way to individualize our attitude or method. The openness that he later describes is just what Jung had, and I suppose, all of us have been compelled to do that also. I, too, the first few years after Zurich, tried to be "classical" as I had learned it, and came home exhausted each night. I, too, had to "attack" the transference situation differently than I had experienced it. But Fordham emerged with the archetype of the infant and child, and I emerged with the "conjunctio" and archetypal mutuality. It is just this patient experience that challenges us, of course, and the question is, how much is it patient and how much our own myth?

4. "Analysts' reticence was due to lack of a framework within which to talk about the patient's effect on them."

Yes, yes! Even in supervision, this is sometimes difficult, for various reasons. But it is possible that the analyst can tell the patient about these effects, too, encouraging the patient to give his true responses to this, thereby jointly discovering the archetypal situation that exists between them.

5. "I came to realise that the unconscious process involved (in the transference relationship) were the equivalent of a dream or active imagination . . . "

So did I, yet for me the "infantile nature" was more that of archetypal images and impulses, not the literal "child" alone. Fordham's encounter and use of Melanie Klein made a bridge to psychoanalysis and, no doubt, that myth of childhood has general significance, but my own myth led to bridges between Jungian psychology and various religions. Fordham's, like the psychoanalysts', has more general currency, apparently, but where does this lead, in terms of the development of the spirit and depth psychology generally? I suspect that both kinds of bridges are needed.

6. Fordham points out that many Jungians are unable to work in the area of sexuality and childhood, and thus become seriously "disembodied."

This is a legitimate criticism, and one that I have applied to myself, too. I told Fordham, once, that his work was brilliant, but often depressed me. He replied that I probably was "too high" and had to "come down." He was right. But I had to come down into the body, to reporting physical and instinctual reactions in analytic work, rather than in the focus upon childhood that Fordham felt required to do. (I have to add here, afterwards, and without Fordham having a chance to respond, that I, too, had to seek elsewhere for "body" and found it in eight years of Reichian body therapy. That kind of compensation helped a lot for both my healing and deepening, but, unlike Fordham's experience of Klein, the Reichian work contributed rather little to either theory or practice of an original nature, unless one considers an enhanced general world-view so contributory.)

7. Fordham's invented interpretation of the patient with fragmentary thoughts and complaint that he gets nothing from the analyst is very helpful, including the many possibilities from his "filing-cabinet" of knowledge and association.

I would add, as a contrast, that even if I felt this issue of "absent" or "bad" breast, my comment, I suspect, would be something like this: "As you say that I give you nothing, I feel as if I am a mother with empty breasts, and feel hurt and guilty. No matter how I try I can not satisfy you. How does my reaction effect you?" His response, such as guilt, anger, etc. would lead us into the mutual realization of the empty, suffering mother and hungry, suffering child archetype, right there in the relationship. Interpretation is participatory rather than from "outside." I am suspicious of the latter and it is this disconnection which "brings me down." It is here that I am also critical of the psychoanalytic attitude. What does Fordham think about that? Is it that I have the "coniunctio" myth and he another? Or my objectivity includes being "in" the transference?

My fantasy: Fordham and I spend some sessions in which he does "childhood" and I do "mutual process." What kind of 'coniunctio' would that be?

Conclusion: Fordham's paper is the best I have seen which enables a deeper understanding of differences between the focus on childhood and other Jungian approaches. It is just what I had hoped that the present book would contribute to our field, a presentation of commonality and individuality in more precise ways.

FORDHAM'S REJOINDER TO SPIEGELMAN'S COMMENTS

I want first to thank Spiegelman for his appreciative comments of my sketchy essay; it is condensed and could lead to unnecessary confusion, some of which I will try to dispel now.

1. I believe that I could make out a case for mutuality and the conjunctio lying near the centre of my analyses. That was suggested, I think, in a paper called "Technique and Countertransference," although I did not there use either term. I would not implement my experience in the way Spiegelman illustrates his— one must allow, however, for variations in the styles and idioms of expression from analyst to analyst. A clear difference between Spiegelman and myself is that I do not give raw emotional responses, when I have one, which is not often, but transform them into an interpretation.

2. As to the truth of an interpretation: I assume that the aim of any analysis is to arrive at the truth and so any interpretation I give is intended to serve that end.

My interpretation given at the end of my paper is liable to create more incredulity than is necessary because the context is omitted. I will add some of that: My patient had been in analysis for over ten years—nine years with another analyst. Other attempts to understand his communication had signally failed. In addition, I have not made it clear that months of work together was directed more specifically to try and understand what it was all about. Neither are recorded because I do not know how to compress it into reasonable space, nor is my memory good enough to record sufficient detail. I will, however, mention a feature of our work which was influential: once out of my room, interpretations become useful and he could benefit from many of them. The presence or absence of my body was therefore important. In addition, we had found that interpretive reconstructions about infancy in other contexts were meaningful whereas others were not.

3. The psychoanalytic attitude and method: a difficult question to answer, largely because psychoanalysts are too often bogies to criticise and not psychoanalysts as they are. I have, however, written more at length about how I conceive the analytic attitude and I fancy that some psychoanalysts would not disagree much. I can not decide whether Spiegelman wants to be "brought down" or not! [Spiegelman: to the body, yes! Psychoanalytically, no!]

4. There are some phrases that grate. I am not happy with the idea that I "do" childhood. I analyse patients and when data arise that require the understanding I have gained, and that is not only about childhood and infancy, I use it. I can not agree that I have come up with an archetype. I have gained knowledge about development. I would regard my original work under the heading of a historical study. In that study, archetypes emerge but there is more to history than archetypes.

Conclusion: I am not at all sure how much Spiegelman and I disagree essentially —I suspect not much. The difference is more in the matter of how our rather different special knowledge is implemented. I hope neither of us thinks there is only one way to analyse patients and I would like to point out that I am not uninterested in religion whilst I hope he is not uninterested in childhood and infancy.

McNAIR'S COMMENTS ON FORDHAM

I really enjoyed this paper. I appreciated Fordham's comment about the analyst's "eating and drinking habits" and the "life of the analyst outside his work." This is of great interest and concern for me. I don't hear a lot about it, most papers have not referred to it. But I know from personal experience that this factor is extraordinarily important.

As in other professions, I suppose, being an analyst becomes a way of life, a very demanding, comprehensive condition. How an analyst lives his/her life is, to me, the true application of the wisdom gleaned from the work, and, one hopes, results in a fuller life. It always concerns me if my professional life somehow becomes detrimental to my personal life. This has been very difficult at times.

I must admit to feeling chagrined at Fordham talking to his wife about patients. Although she is a colleague, this seemed utterly foreign to me. I was trained to keep the "vessel" sealed, and such a "break" would be a significant reflection of the relationship's tension. I tend to absorb and submit difficulties to a compression until they yield an image or emotion. Beyond that, I rely upon active imagination while running over the horse trails near my home. A more complete surrender has been to go out to the woods and let Mother Nature prevail. This is in addition to sharing with the patient, as often as possible, the immediate existential impact the analysand and our relationship is having upon me. Discussing it with my wife? Not likely. I have, for years, found consummate support within the dialogue known as supervision. I prefer to keep mine there.

I liked hearing about having a special interest at any one time. That is the creative pulse in my professional and personal life. That is also a primary attraction of being with colleagues—not the Platonic "how do you do it," but an Aristotelian "how are you doing it?" . . . The growing edge of one's therapeutic consciousness.

The notion of the patient "providing supervision" is great. The feedback loop is so sensitive to mutual conditioning or guiding that I've learned to trust it more as the years go by.

I am always fascinated by interpretation. When I come across a reasonably consistent framework like Fordham's mother-child, or Jung's alchemical, or Hillman's archetypal, I am intrigued. Each has his own myth—fingerprint. Some I find interesting and/or move me further along my own. I suppose we can all meet at Jung, but an individually developed perspective of interpretation is always good reading for me. Alas, I am never sure what it really does for the patient beyond observing that we have such a thing. The vision must be idiosyncratic and the words come from our own language system, so perhaps the feeling-tone gives it the life it needs. People like Lacan can give the words a purpose! An epiphany to context?

I have always felt a deep value in Fordham's transference papers. I still struggle with the sorting-out process and, as yet, am not the recipient of an archetypal/myth template. One day perhaps.

I appreciated hearing his very sturdy defence on his own behalf. True enough. Looking for additional meanings rather than causes has a warm, open-minded feeling to it. I enjoyed hearing how he was compelled by patients to analyse their childhood. What a difference from the reverse! His work took on a new dimension for me.

I would like to hear an "elder/sage" figure perceive themselves as having attained a level of consciousness that permits them to say: "divest . . . of memory, desire and understanding"—and do homage to the numerous years of one-point meditation that made it a possibility!

How I Do It

by

DR. PHIL. GUSTAV DREIFUSS

My first reaction to this question is of course that I don't DO it, that I let it happen. The more I want to do or try to do, the less happens. This is only a half-truth because by receiving the analysand, sitting opposite him, relating to him, I already DO something!

In order not to write from my head only, I asked myself how I could express my analytical work through my body. I saw myself standing with my arms wide open, the analysand opposite; I was smiling but did not move. I looked at the analysand and knew that my next move was entirely dependent on him. If he moved I would also move to where my body would move me. Backward or forward, to the side, closing my arms a bit and opening them again, and so forth. I felt entirely related to my body, giving space and freedom of choice to the analysand. I could encourage the analysand to move with me, I could follow him, I could accelerate the movements or slow them down.

And where was I, what did my body express? I felt my feet going down, down into earth and my hands going up, up towards heaven. I felt a movement to the right, going outward, being active, and a movement to the left, going inward, being passive. I felt pulled in different directions yet at the same time in tune with them. I felt the opposites, expressed them in my body and at the same time felt my body as one. I started dancing in my fantasy. I expressed the suffering of being torn and suddenly felt elated in being able to express myself in the body. And then, another strong impulse overcame me: I stopped moving entirely, felt as if I were immobilized, heavy, dead, and then back to life, moving with joy, light, happiness.

What I expressed in my body corresponds somehow to Jung's theory of opposites and their union. The above fantasy started with the image of my relationship to the analysand, standing opposite to him, and it developed into a fantasy about myself. These two aspects, the relationship to the other and to myself are—for me—the two central aspects of my work.

With regard to the analysand, the following words come to mind: love, empathy, feeling, giving space, to be aware of and wonder about the diversity of human beings and of the Self expressing itself differently in every human being. Then I asked myself which colours could best express the way I work? A red, warm and soothing, at times fierce and enthusiastic, came as a first choice. (Of course, the feeling function, my inner analyst commented!) But then, brown and green followed: earth, grounding, roots and vegetation, vegetative life, plants, natural growing. And only now followed blue: cold, interpretative, analysing, yet also detached, spiritual, meaningful.

But let me go back to my years of studying in Zurich at the beginning of the 1950s. To my mind come two statements of Jung himself during a talk with the diploma-candidates of the Jung Institute. The one is his well-known statement: my method is no method. The second is: how good that I am Jung and not a Jungian! I took this to mean that I have to find my own way of working, to free myself, to a certain extent, from Jungian theory. It meant, for me, to relate to the patient more from the heart and the belly and less from the head. This was very difficult to achieve because of the normal insecurity of the young therapist in the encounter with the analysand. One needed to know where the patient was with regard to his pathology, according to what I had learned. In those early days, my analyst and control-analysts were most helpful in my finding my own way. I saw four or five different analysts for control and sometimes I brought the same material of the analysands to different analysts. The difference in their approach to the material, to dreams, gave me lots of headaches and forced me to come to my own conclusions.

Now I want to relate one of my first experiences as an analyst in Israel. After a first interview, a woman—a victim of the Holocaust—said that I was the first therapist who had NOT made notes DURING the interview, and I was her tenth therapist! (I usually note an important dream or development after the hour to help my memory.) From this I learned how important it is for me to listen empathetically to what is said and to have it "sink into me" before making any commentary or interpretation. I have to be in a state of being open, of listening from the Self, from the center of my personality, from the "belly," and not from the head.

At the beginning of my professional career as an analyst, I used Jungian jargon too much and especially too early in analysis. I became aware of this when talking to analysts of other schools. I remember frustrating panel discussions where everybody remained in his theoretical approach and no communication was possible. In private discussion with colleagues of other schools, not only did I learn to appreciate their work, but I found that beyond all the differences in theory, there was very often a common ground which one could name, perhaps, the "human" approach. I learned to formulate without professional jargon, with patients and colleagues. On the other hand, in discussion with Jungian colleagues, using, for instance, the concepts of animus or anima helps or furthers the process of mutual understanding. Yet it can also be limiting: NAMING the complexes can take the essence out of the person and very often takes a turn to the negative (e.g. animus = negative animus!) By naming a complex we say very little about the unique person we are talking about, and very often we analysts are ourselves unaware of our own complexes when talking about those of others!

The following is an experience with an analysand which was encouraging in finding my personal way in therapy: A patient who had previously been in treatment with a colleague remarked in one of his sessions how good he felt that could talk to me about things which happened to him during the week. In his former treatment the accent was on dreams and he often left the session with a lot of frustration and in great tension as he had not been able to "let off steam," to express his anger and despair about things that had happened to him and to which he did not get to in the emphasis on dream-analysis. Although I also work a lot on dreams, I put much emphasis on what we call outer reality, not only by interpreting material of the unconscious in terms of the inner situation, but also in relationship to outer events. I also understand outer reality from an inner point of view. One can easily get lost in one of the two extremes: to work only on inner reality, dreams, and active imagination or to work only on outer reality. I choose a middle course, with the accent more on inner or outer according to the patient's condition.

I remember a 35 year-old analysand who was immersed in an inner world of fairy tales. I could relate to this with empathy, avoiding interpretations. This non-judgmental attitude, my acceptance of her inner world, gradually brought her to develop a healthier attitude towards "earthly" values, which in her case were especially problems with money.

A woman with early disturbances (negative mother-complex) was for years entangled in a severe marriage problem. She had tried to find meaning in her life by studying art and Jewish philosophy at the University. In the course of our work, I slowly came to the conviction that analysis could not help her very much. She was already involved with artistic work and I felt that she should stop putting more intellect into her head, that she could leave her studies at the University and the preoccupation with her marriage problem and to serve the spirit in her creative work. I thus freed myself from the belief that analysis, working on one's self, is a must for everybody. If the creative spirit wants to express itself through the artist, I, like a midwife, have to help to bring forth the baby, the work of art.

With a woman patient in her mid-forties, I had a deeply moving experience which taught me to be very sensitive to whatever intuitions I had when seeing a patient for the first time. I was reminded of my late mother—a similar figure, an almost identical way of walking when I looked at her as she went in front of me to the consulting room. I then did not go further into the question of what this could mean. This woman had been sent to me by a medical doctor because of obesity and hysterical symptoms which were confirmed by the results of a Rorschach test, administered by a well-known psychologist. A psychiatrist had diagnosed depression one year prior to her first visit with me. A chirological test suggested the presence of non-specific physical illness. I started therapy with one session per week. She was constantly under medical observation. About eight months after beginning therapy, she suffered from an attack that was diagnosed by a psychiatrist as an epileptic fit, and he ordered an EEG to be made. Soon after this she related a dream in which, while her mother was present, she killed three pigeons and took their brains out of their heads. Two weeks later she was operated on to remove a brain tumor (not malignant), but died one day later without regaining consciousness. Not only could I now understand the dream, but I also connected my first impression of the patient's resemblance to my mother: both died of a brain tumor. My patient had died because the pressure in the brain had damaged it. Had the tumor been diagnosed earlier, she probably could have been saved. I learned to take my feelings and intuitions seriously.

As a newly-baked analyst, I had difficulty in dealing with "love" whenever it came up during the hour. I tried to explain the feeling with the help of the concept of the transference. What was the difference between transference, relationship, and love? A turning point in my attitude came when a young analysand, moving restlessly in his chair, muttered, "I love you." I answered, unhesitatingly, according to my real feelings: "I love you too." I was somehow surprised that the analysis went on after this! Thus I was freed also in the treatment of woman patients from my inhibition in answering the same "I love you" when I really felt so. In my paper on "Empathy," I formulated these experiences. [See appendix at the end of this paper.]

With regard to the victims of the Holocaust, I found empathy of paramount importance. I freed myself from "having to resolve the transference" in every case. I described this work in my paper on "Psychotherapy of Nazi Victims." Empathy has as its shadow an encompassing acceptance. *"Tout accepter, tout pardonner"* the saying goes (to accept everything, to pardon everything). I can give an example of a Holocaust victim who felt very unhappy in his marriage. His wife had not experienced the Holocaust. The man suffered unbearable torture and deprivation in a concentration camp and was, in my opinion, entitled to much love and compassion. His wife did not want to take care of him, she wanted "a man" and not a needy child like her husband. Because of his deep seated needs and demands for unconditional love, this man spoilt relationships. As an analyst, I had the task of working on his shadow in order to help him lead a more normal life; my identification with the victim was a hindrance to this work on the shadow which I had to overcome. These problems are formulated in my paper "Victims and Victimizers," where I tried to show that we are at the same time both victim and victimizer and that identifying with one aspect of the archetype may constellate the other aspect.

As a beginning therapist I was very enthusiastic and only later on did I find that this enthusiasm had a healing effect. It is connected with spontaneity. How can we keep this in the course of many years of work? For me, to keep in shape means taking a break every so often, being in nature, and being involved in creative work other than therapy, such as writing and lecturing. It also means being open to new ideas, such as the holistic approach, the consciousness-raising movement, parapsychology, energy-work, etc.

In the course of the years I dealt with many so-called "early disturbances." Such cases require a lot of patience because the therapeutic process moves very slowly. I am often reminded of my own slow development and this gives me strength to accept patiently the slowness of the process.

I try to free myself from any preconceived ideas. I remember a woman coming to me after years of Freudian treatment with a conflict about whether to continue treatment or to start learning at a University. She could not, because of technical reasons, combine the two. I felt her deep frustration, having foregone learning because of the Holocaust and because of her immigration right after the war (1945). She was happy that I encouraged her to study and that treatment could be postponed. After a year of successful learning, she started therapy, continuing her studies on a smaller scale.

Very soon I found that tests can influence me and take away my spontaneity and empathy, especially in the early sessions. Therefore I don't read test results before I am impressed by the patient in a direct personal encounter. I often sent analysands, after a first session with me, for a chirological test, as in the case of a 65 year-old woman about whom I had doubts with regard to analytical treatment at such an age. My own evaluation and the one of the chirologist are published in an article by Hael Haft-Pomrock ("Psyche and Soma in Chirology: Personality Changes in Analysis as Reflected in the Hand," Spring, 197, p 186 ff).

I can do very unorthodox things when really feeling the intensive need of a patient. A woman who, at the beginning of treatment, was full of anxiety because of my forthcoming absence for many weeks, asked me to take her for a little walk to a place that she could see from her flat, in order to keep the contact with me while I was away. I did not make any interpretations at that time, but consented, being aware of the problems that could create for us later on. Apparently because of the genuineness of my consent, this turned out subsequently to be a very important step in her inner development.

I have often asked myself "how to do it" with cancer patients. I remember especially one patient whom I accompanied until his death at 35, where the unconscious did not take notice of his illness. Many changes in his personality occurred during the course of the work and he could live to enjoy the life remaining for him. Here I really felt what it means to let the unconscious lead the process. Another man who turned to me in anguish after a cancer operation (he had been in treatment with me some ten years before the operation), felt after a few sessions that he was strong enough to live his remaining years without support. I felt that this independence, in spite of his illness, was important for him and I could honour his wish to stop treatment.

I asked an analysand of some twenty years ago to write a few lines for this paper. Here is her answer:

How you did it—a subjective view from your analysand: I was consistently given the space in which to experience material that came up from drawings, dreams, active imagination and charged moments within the analysis itself—and to deal with it. Actually, having been an intellectual type and very weak in my feeling function, I was never encouraged to "understand." I was always supported to "feel." "Dealing with the material" was a kind of feeling the material down to the gut level and giving it reality—a concrete existence within myself. And so I learned to feel and accept my feelings.

The feeling of having space within the analysis was mentioned by another analysand who further remarked that the change in his personality happened gently, without any pressure. These reactions confirm my earlier statement that it is desirable not to have any preconceived ideas and let changes happen gradually. I try to give space for psychic development.

An important point to the question, "How do you do it?" is the additional question: "How do you do it on yourself?" In other words: in order to do it I have to work on myself. Mostly I do this by myself, but also by sharing a dream, a meditation, an active imagination or a problem with a colleague. For me doing therapy is more an art and a human endeavour than a science or theory.

APPENDIX

The following paper on empathy, translated by the author from the original Hebrew into English, was first presented at a meeting of the Department of Psychotherapy at Tel Aviv University in December 1975 and later published by the Israel Society of Psychosomatics in 1976. It is presented here as an example of the papers on therapy written by Dr. Dreifuss.

EMPATHY

In August 1975, I found in the daily newspaper *Ha aretz* a column called "Proposals for new Hebrew Expressions," written by Jonathan Ratosh, where he translates the word "empathy" into Hebrew *"kameir,"* from which the noun will be *"kemira."* In the Bible this word appears in some places. In Genesis 43:30, in the story of Joseph in Egypt, it is written: " ... for his heart yearned towards his brother." First Kings 3:26 says about the mother whose child King Solomon wanted to divide into two: " ... for her heart yearned upon her son ... " Hosea 11:8 renders God's words with regard to his people, " ... my heart is tuned within me, my compassions are kindled together."

Also from these places in the Bible we learn how intensively empathy is connected with emotions and feelings. This strengthens the idea of love and compassion belonging to empathy. The word empathy—in German, *"Einfuehlung,"* meaning to feel oneself into somebody or something—shows a process of feeling for somebody with the purpose of understanding. Sympathy seems to be more a process of feeling alone, feeling with somebody in his sorrow, with less accent on the understanding.

Empathy should be essential in every doctor-patient relationship. It demands also patience, as it is an enduring process. If there is too much empathy, too much accent on feeling and compassion, there is a danger that one may no more understand the patient. Therefore, one needs also abstraction or reflection, which brings forth a separation from the object, leading to *"Erkenntnis des Objekts,"* as they call it in German.

In other words, empathy as well as abstraction are needed in order to become conscious, because both of them together give the possibility of grasping the totality of the object. One could also identify abstraction with intellect and empathy with feeling, and both are needed for a more comprehensive understanding.

Jung dealt with the problem of empathy in his book, *PSYCHOLOGICAL TYPES*, which was published in 1920. At that time, typology was a centre of interest for research and Jung clarified the concepts of "abstraction" and "empathy" which Lipps had introduced into the field of aesthetics.

Jung's interest turned later more and more to the unconscious, i.e. to the archetypes, complexes and symbols. He saw in empathy a conscious therapeutic attitude, which was self-evident. In treatment, empathy is needed for the patient and for the contents of his unconscious.

Empathy into psychic processes is very important in order to understand the images of the unconscious and to feel them. For the purpose of attaining this, personal analysis is important and necessary. In personal analysis, a new centre of the personality is slowly vivified and brought to consciousness. In Jungian Psychology this new centre is called the Self. Then, the patient is experienced and understood not only from the head, the intellect, but also from the heart, feeling.

The patient and the contents of his unconscious can be grasped only by lowering the level of consciousness. We should be connected to them from the centre of our personality. It is well known that the analyst should be at the same time involved and not involved in the analytical process. Suspending intellectual judgement may often be necessary for a certain time when the analyst must be an accepting good mother, and only when solid contact is established may one come to interpretations. This, for instance, is necessary in cases of severe anxiety.

In his book, *ON THE PSYCHOLOGY OF THE TRANSFERENCE*, Jung describes different relationships between analyst and analysand. Not only is there a connection between the egos of the analyst and the analysand, but there is also a connection between the ego of the analyst and the unconscious of the analysand and of the ego of the analysand and the unconscious of the analyst. Last, but not least, there is a direct relationship between the unconscious of the two persons involved in the analytical process.

The degree to which the analyst is in good relationship with the centre of his personality (the Self in Jungian terminology), i.e., open to the unconscious, to that extent can he receive that of the patient. The following example will illustrate this point:

I had a patient with a very negative father-complex. Her father was a strict, remote, unrelated, authoritarian person. We had established a good contact. In one of the analytical hours, in the middle of the session, she suddenly said that she wanted to go home. Without reflection, I agreed and let her go with empathy. In the following hour, the patient told me that my having let her go without questioning was a big experience for her, a step on the way to free herself from the negative father image. One may call my reaction intuitive or empathetic, but it was definitely not cognitive.

The concept of the collective unconscious helps us to understand what may happen between two people beyond conscious relationship. Jung's idea of synchronicity may be appropriate here.

In his book, *SYNCHRONICITY: AN ACAUSAL CONNECTING PRINCIPLE,* he relates that already in 1920, investigating the phenomenon of the collective unconscious, he met with events which are connected in a meaningful way without any causal connection. For example: A patient told a dream about a scarab which was holy to the ancient Egyptians. Then Jung heard at his window a little noise and saw a bug like a scarab trying to come into the room, and all this in a time and place where the scarab did not normally exist. An outer event corresponded to an inner, psychic situation. This event caused Jung and his patient to have a feeling of "awe," a feeling of the "strange," the "hidden," the "non-understandable," and the "mysterious."

The whole field of telepathy, empathy and synchronicity can be explained with the concept of the archetypes which have a numinous effect, lowering the NIVEAU MENTAL, and thus providing the possibility of experiencing something beyond the ordinary, a feeling of unity which can not be understood rationally. Empathy is connected with an irrational element, but also with interest in one's fellow creatures.

But we also need empathy and love for ourselves. If we suffer from our weaknesses and learn to accept and understand ourselves, to have empathy with ourselves in the human condition, then we may also have empathy for the suffering patient. We may thus see love as the great mediator in a situation which can not otherwise be changed. (I am speaking here of the "normal" human condition, not neurotic suffering.) Psychic suffering is often connected with development. Suffering belongs to the human being just as much as happiness.

It is interesting to observe which patients bring forth empathy in us and which do not. This depends on us. We must try to become conscious of our projections. In practical work it may be important to talk with the marriage partner in order to check one's reactions. Too much persona of the doctor, i.e. playing out of the doctor role, may be damaging to empathy as well. But authority is also necessary.

Jung points out that within the analytical process of transformation, there is always a symbolic experience of death. The old personality, old attitudes, and infantile wishes, die and make room for a new personality. This death in the process of inner development is connected with rebirth, with becoming a different individual. Through this process, the archetype of death and rebirth is experienced which provides the basis of belief, thus overcoming the fear of death.

Experience of death and the encounter with illness and suffering, as well, are important steps on the path of our maturation as human beings. Empathy, compassion and love can help us to unite the opposites such as life and death, good and evil, opposites that cannot be united otherwise.

RESPONSE TO DREIFUSS BY McNAIR

My initial reading of Dr. Dreifuss' paper was a very positive one. I felt him to be reassuring, gentle, patient, and personal. I was touched by his openness and spontaneity. My subsequent readings of the paper were more revealing to me.

Dr. Dreifuss seemed able to maintain a balance within his issues, always including each point's opposite ("I do it," "I don't do it" . . .) I appreciated his objectifying his "analyst." I myself have rarely heard analysts do so, either as a reflex-transference or long-term evolution/developmental construction of it. Over-identification is the norm, in my experience.

Not unlike so many of my colleagues, I am an immigrant from another realm (engineering). Thus my development as a therapist has been shaped more by my interaction IN the work than by an ambition TO fulfill. I am constantly absorbed by the issues of phenomena and impact, more than, say, technique and outcome. Apparently for Dreifuss, the conscious human relationship IS the therapeutic relationship.

I found Dr. Dreifuss' reflection on Jung and the study of human nature truly validating for my own "use" of Jung, while he relies upon his own belly and heart for his "true" response. I was pleased to hear he sought out several supervisors simultaneously. Having done a similar thing myself, I, too, found it enlightening and liberating: there is no "one" way!

After fifteen years in the field, the issues and problems I find myself confronted with now are significantly different from those of five and ten years ago. I am deeper into the "territory" of the work. Thus, Dr. Dreifuss' comments on transference constellation is most relevant; learning from patients is crucial for him. Responding to intuitions and spontaneous associations is likewise valued highly and, above all, slowness. His compassion for impatience, method, and "naming" as being natural pitfalls of development is comforting. I could not sense how much, or to what degree, he advocates mutual involvement in positive/negative transference moments.

How one survives the impact of this profession socially, emotionally, and physically is as crucial in my development as the responsibility towards my client. The long-term effects of this work seems excruciating and, at times, unbearable. Therefore, taking breaks, as Dr. Dreifuss suggests, seems paramount, not just recreational. Cellular impact needs to be addressed more completely. The primitive affects take their toll, if not recycled properly. I would like to hear more of his effort in that direction.

In all, my phantasy of Dr. Dreifuss is that of a man who has witnessed, experienced and absorbed a great amount of psychological life and finds fulfillment in his slow, personalized approach. "How does he do it" is answered by thoughtful reflection and appreciation of experience's teaching, not by theory or dogma. Ambition "to become" is not announced, nor is any passionate struggle with the psyche necessarily addressed. Perhaps that is the reward for years spent. My personal concern was, before reading his paper: "How to survive its effects on me," not how to do it. It still is.

Questions:

1.What about sexuality?

2. What about age/era of life developmental patterns?

3. What about utilization of the therapeutic relationship for one's personal issues?

4. What about time off, time out?

5. What about a balanced life style?

6. What inherent compensations and healing has taken place for him after years of practice?

7. What has worsened as a result of this work?

8. How did he receive instructions for direction from the anima to pursue his path (form, signposts); i.e. how did it shape him?

RESPONSE TO DREIFUSS BY SPIEGELMAN

Like Dr. McNair, I found Dr. Dreifuss' approach warm, comforting, empathetic, as he emphasizes. He has learned from experience, trusted the process, continued to grow. He has interacted with a variety of patients and colleagues. He would be a person to whom one would refer a loved-one, a suffering person, a misunderstood individual, and trust that care would be present, that individuality would be respected. Furthermore, his remarks about listening to his body, experiencing the process as having two central aspects of relationship, to the Self in the other and in one's own being, are very compatible with my views.

Where, then is my doubt? It is in the dark side, the shadow. What about his own hostile reactions? His sexual reactions? What about all those things which are not, apparently, empathetic? He moves, he says, "left and right," as do I. Yet I find that many of the "left-handed" reactions are hostile, un-social, or otherwise taboo. Yet, in their depth, these usually connect with a larger Eros which seeks at wholeness and stops far short of doing any damage, longs for greater union and consciousness. Where is Dr. Dreifuss with this?

I remember, in our Zurich days, Dr. Dreifuss, when he was going to be away for a time, referred a patient to me. He was a black American who had been in Europe a long time, and had been seeing Dr. Dreifuss. When I saw this patient, he was seedy, whiny, and I was overcome with disgust at his self-neglect and self-indulgence. Here was a man who had completed university yet was living a totally useless life. My affect was so strong that I had to tell him what I felt. I am afraid that I even yelled at him. After several sessions, he came in shaved, shaped up, and telling me he had a job and was now on his way. The therapy ended. I do not know if that was an effective intervention, really, or not. Was the kindness of Dr. Dreifuss the right response to this man, at that time, and mine in error, or the reverse? Or were both right and wrong? Anyway, the opposites were constellated. What does Dr. Dreifuss think now?

REPLY TO SPIEGELMAN

I vaguely remember my hours with the black American Spiegelman mentions.

I think we were both right and wrong. Maybe I established a trust in him so he could change, and that enabled him to take Spiegelman's affect in a positive way. I don't know, of course, how my work would have continued and developed, had I not referred him. I am aware of the fact that I had and still have difficulties expressing my own hostile reactions. I know that awareness of the shadow is not always enough to get closer to the Self, but often a shadowy act is needed in reality.

Here is an example of my own hostile reaction: A very dependent, needy analysand reacted to my telling her that I wanted to end the hours on time, that I could not support her need to stay longer than the allotted time, by tears and aggression. Subsequently she became more conscious of her shadow.

With regard to myself, I got out of an excess of empathy, I set limits, I could be hostile. My shadow, taken as a natural, instinctive yet hostile reaction, helped the analysand to become aware of her lack of borders, of her limitless demands on others which were childish and spoiled many of her relationships. Not expressing my anger or hostile reaction makes me behave artificially, hurting the other more. I know all that—and still work on it. I know that disharmony belongs with harmony, but my natural tendency is to avoid disharmony. [Re. sexual reactions: see answers below.]

REPLY TO McNAIR

Like McNair, I am also an "immigrant" from another realm. When I was 20 years old and studying chemistry, I took a course in philosophy and once had a long personal talk with the professor, at the end of which he said that I should become a rabbi! He apparently felt my deep concern for the "cure of souls" many years before my becoming a psychotherapist.

I agree with McNair that the conscious human relationship is—for me—the therapeutic relationship. Yet I am aware of transference and countertransference. The "rabbi" in me is concerned with the cure of souls, a religious attitude outside the religious establishment. One shadow side of my "rabbi" is a tendency to preach.

I can very well understand McNair's concern with "how to survive." The answer to this question must be very personal. My life-long interest in Jewish texts and their psychological meaning has helped me in that. In recent years, I have been studying Kabbalah, but without any ambition of "knowing"—I just enjoy listening to the Kabbalist's way of trying to understand the mystery. It is most important for me and exciting to repeatedly find archetypal motifs in Jewish mysticism, e.g. to see that the "chakras" can also be found in Judaism. So, learning more about Judaism, delving into my Jewish spiritual roots, brings me archetypal experiences and to the realisation of how the Self expresses itself in all religions, in all human beings. This experience makes me more humble and tolerant.

Are there ways of doing psychotherapy with less personal involvement? Maybe, but not for me! Only by being completely there with the analysand can I do psychotherapy. Being there, for me, means to be empathetic and aware at the same time, in order to prevent identification and involvement. This attitude asks for a certain way of life. For me, to consciously sacrifice desires for many activities, is paramount in order to "do it" the way I want to.

Answers to the Eight Questions

1. **What about sexuality?** I have tried, several times, to answer this question. Apparently it hits a complex, even at the age of 64, as I write this! Pondering its meaning for me with regard to psychotherapy, I wonder about the enormous power sex has had on me and on mankind. The sexual energy that can rule us brings to light my mystical experiences and sex as a symbol of my creativity. Behind the pleasure principle lies the union with the soul, to become one with her. This is a meaning which is often unconscious. My experiences with women, my analysis, and my continuous path toward consciousness, my incest-dreams and so on, have formed my personal attitude to sex, which reflects itself in my psychotherapy. Because of the archetypal energy in sex, the human aspect of it is very often neglected. Then sex is lived from a purely egocentric point of view and soul connection with the partner is lacking.

The sexual demands of my female patients are often disturbing and I try to relate to them with tact, empathy and firmness. In addition to my professional responsibility, I know deep down that acting out in treatment is damaging to the souls of analysand and analyst. I try to be aware of my countertransference, asking myself what attracts me to the analysand, why do I want this person? What does this woman represent for me? What unconscious content wants to be taken into consideration, wants to be integrated? In which direction do I have to grow?

So the question is: Where am I unaware of the psychic situation of the analysand? What content do I disown? Women with well-developed intuition and thinking have helped me to integrate these functions. Neglecting my body at certain times may show itself by an attraction to a sporty type; a fascination for a young woman may show me that I am too fatherly or that the incest-symbol is constellated, meaning a new phase in individuation. But, possession by the anima can be so strong that becoming conscious of it is a slow and painful process.

I remember a dream of mine in which a woman analysand drove a car down hill while I was sitting next to her. The dream clearly brought to consciousness that I was losing control of the situation. By becoming conscious of my anima projection, connected with my creativity, I got "back to the wheel."

Talking about sex invariably brings love into discussion. Very little is written about love by psychotherapists—maybe because it is a "hot" theme? But, let me draw your attention to those moving passages in Jung's autobiography, where he acknowledges that he "falters before the task of finding the language which might adequately express the incalculable paradoxes of love." He further stresses that "I was again and again faced with the mystery of love, and have never been able to explain what it is."

Love is—for me—a state of being, of giving one's love. If I am in this state, I cannot fall in love, because I am already there. And from there, my empathy, my warm feelings, flow to the analysand. This love also helps me to sacrifice sexual demands which come up in me! Taking the different opposites of love—namely hate, power, fear—into consideration, helps me to clarify situations of love. The symbolic understanding of sex and love under the heading of union of opposites is most helpful to me. It helps to overcome the perils of difficult transference-countertransference situations. The union of opposites, the numinosity of the process and of life are experiences which are always "there," as well as love and sacrifice, for both analyst and patient. Analysis is one aspect of doing therapy, the other one is synthesis; and it is love that unites the opposites which cannot be united otherwise.

2. What about age/era of life development pattern? At the age of 64, when writing these lines, I am definitely different from, say, 25 years ago. Tens of years of experience bring about changes of attitude. I am more aware of different approaches in life situations. I am also more flexible. I am aware of social changes which influence me and my therapeutic work. I am less influenced now by the theoretical concept of the first and second half of life, but I feel that structuring is most important for many people. Personally, I sense that I have attained—more or less—what potentially was in me and I am thankful for this. Yet, I remain open to what life still brings. I am grateful for every day I can get up, be healthy, see patients or read and write or enjoy life, nature.

3. What about utilization of the therapeutic relationship for one's personal issues? I had to think a lot to find an answer to this question. Am I repressing something? When I broke an arm last year, an analysand who was an orthopaedist offered to examine me although I was in treatment with another doctor. I consented and got some valuable advice. Another analysand, a psycho-therapist and poet, read a paper of mine in English and offered to translate it in Hebrew for publication. A student analysand ran into financial difficulties, but could not accept my offer to continue treatment without pay. He offered to do some library work for me, which I accepted. I was aware of the possible disturbances in the analytical relationship and discussed it with these analysands. In all these cases, the process was not disturbed. Why? Maybe because with them there existed a human/therapeutic relationship which was not disturbed by a one time "utilization."

On another level, I "use" therapeutic relationships for my own inner development, a kind of continued test to check my own human reactions and shadow problems. In doing therapy, I am time and again confronted with my own complexes and with archetypal situations and this forces me to work on myself.

4. What about time off? For years my regular schedule was 30-35 hours per week (now much less!), taking time out for a long lunch break, starting in the office at 7 A.M. (I am not a night-worker). Some days I see patients at this hour, or I write and try to understand my dreams, meditate, do active imagination. I work a 50-minute hour, with no time out between the sessions, yet here and there an hour free. When the children were small, I took a day-and-a-half off per week, i.e. four full working days with patients. For some years now, I have been in a rhythm of three weeks work and one week off. Lecturing and teaching are additional, but preparation is included in time off. I also organize discussion groups and lectures with "The Analytical Psychology Club of Haifa," which I founded some 20 years ago, and now in the "Center." In the summer, I take four-five weeks off, sometimes two weeks in winter, during the semester break. Luckily, I have been very healthy and hardly lost a day's work because of illness.

5. **What about a balanced life style?** To be with the family was and is a balancing factor. Theatre and concerts, swimming and walking are a need not to be neglected. My social life is very small—I enjoy the company of just a few friends; I don't like parties! I haven't smoked for over 20 years and don't drink. Writing is an inner need which sometimes becomes a demon! Doing nothing, letting go, allowing time to flow without having to do anything, not even meditate, being lazy, all help me to balance somehow. I am by nature a doer, active; "not doing" and being passive had to be learned.

6. **What inherent compensations and healing has taken place for him after years of practice?** After years of practice, I feel that I am more at one with myself. I accept what I cannot change. The healing has been and is the connection to the beyond. Before my analysis, I was searching for meaning within the Jewish tradition. Now I have my personal way of relationship to the beyond, and as a consequence, more human feeling and love. The years of practice, success and failure, have taught me to be true to my own self and not to psychological theories. The main healing for me is modesty, humility in what I can achieve, and I hope for help from the beyond. I learned to let things happen, not to push, and time and again I am impressed by the changes that happen or don't happen!

7. **What has worsened as a result of this work?** Social contacts in their superficiality became more and more difficult. At times, I can accept them as balancing my therapeutic relationships; at other times I avoid them and become "anti-social." I can be impatient when feeling that I waste my time, when social contacts don't give me recreation.

8. **How did he receive instructions for direction from the anima to pursue his path (form, signposts)?** Talks with the anima in projection or as inner figures, goddesses, have shaped me. A certain naivete goes with my openness, the puer can overcome the senex and involve me in new ventures. Sharing with a friend helps! The anima in her motherly-caring aspect has accompanied. In my work as an analyst with Holocaust victims she leads me, but also confronts me with the question of meaning and lack of meaning. The anima also demands that I formulate what occupies me. With her I write these pages!

Therapy: How I Do It

by

DR. LITT. ARVIND VASAVADA

As a fresh graduate from the C.G. Jung Institute in Zurich, working in mental hospitals at Jaipur and Jodhpur, successes and failures with patients made me feel I was doing therapy. The results affected me. I was happy with successes, and unhappy with failures. Much later, when I was in Chicago and had learned from success and failure, I began to feel that therapy was happening. Success and failure did not affect me. It did not mean I was indifferent and insensitive to the clients, their feelings and their depressions. I was with them in their confusion, situations of stalemate, or breakthroughs. I was with them in the spontaneity of the situation. I was flowing with them. We both were facing the Unknown and the Unpredictable. I was content to be with whatever was happening. Most of the time, I had to let the clinent learn to stay with what Is and let them feel It as It is. It was clear for me now that I was not DOING therapy. I did nothing. Whatever was happening in a situation was happening as it had to.

The therapy situation, the sacred place, includes me and the client; and we are both in the process. We both are facing and experiencing the Unknown. Inability to find any direction when it happened became an humbling experience before the Unknown; an experience of my limitation before It; and acceptance of my nothingness, which at times was a religious experience. This is borne out very well by Dr. Meier's book, *ANCIENT INCUBATION AND MODERN PSYCHO-THERAPY* (1), and also by Jung. Reality of what they wrote and experienced became reality for me.

It seems to me, as Jung also often said, that we all are guided by fate, the Unknown. It takes us through the tortuous journey of our life to our Individuation —to Wholeness. We may refuse this guidance at our own cost. Truly, we cannot even refuse it for long. It is more powerful than our will.

The western science of psychotherapy, in terms of Freud in the beginning and Jung later, intrigued me while I was studying, earlier on, for my Master's degree. It fascinated me. Dreams and their interpretations clearly can bare many hidden processes of the mind. It was totally a new dimension to me. I saw how Freudian interpretation of dreams uncovered mental processes. During this period, I was closely following a case of a relation who had become paranoid schizophrenic. Whatever Freud wrote about such cases was confirmed by the life history of this person. He was dominated by his powerful mother and behaved like a child before her at the age of 30. Even though he was married, he had strong homosexual tendencies. How to help him? Books could not teach the psychoanalytic technique. It had to be learned by living experience. Here was a

35

meeting ground between East and West. Spiritual tradition has to be learned from a guru, a master. There was none to teach the Freudian technique.

Experience and work at a Spiritual Healing center in Central India made me wonder at some of the successes. I learned that faith could heal, but my curiosity to know how remained unsatisfied. I wanted to understand how the mind goes wrong, and with what technique it can be set right. I wished to understand both the processes experientially: the process of the disturbed mind, and the steps taken to help. The frustration with Spiritual Healing intensified my search to find the way. There was no possibility to go West to learn it. I had no means for it. I fell back on the study of the Yoga Sutras of Patanjali. Again the study of books seemed unhelpful. I saw the similarity between Freud's method of free association and meditation, but how to use meditation to understand the process of helping the disturbed mind to balance, was the question which had no answer. It also became clear that going back to the past and uncovering the repressions released tension and brought about balance temporarily. However, old habits—conditioning or the Samskaras—repeated themselves, and one fell back into the old habits. It was the problem of really deconditioning the mind totally from unhealthy patterns. The therapy of Freud and Adler helped bring patients to social adjustment—the so-called normality. That did not mean enough, however. I saw within me that though I was fairly well-adjusted in society, I was neither happy nor contented. I was still a disturbed person, "freaking out" here and there, often confused and in conflict, stuck in many situations of life. There was no spontaneity in life. Traditional and social morality is also a conditioning—conditioning by collective consciousness. I did not know myself clearly. I was not able to guide my life without conflict. The psychoanalytic why was not the answer. I needed to discover more, understand more of my own Self before I could see clearly the processes of mind within me and others. One recurrent saying of the Upanishads haunted me: "One who knows the Self, knows all: Unheard becomes heard, Unknown known."[2] The Yoga Sutras also said a similar thing in a different way.[3] The fully deconditioned mind sees everything clearly. Psychological healing was possible only by going through this process of Self knowledge. Who would teach me that?

In 1938, I had an opportunity to go to Europe and learn what I wanted. In 1939, I wrote to Dr. Freud that I desired to learn psychoanalysis. Many months after that, I received a letter from Anna Freud, saying that due to turmoil in Europe they had moved to London. Although Dr. Freud was too old to undertake training, she would be willing to train me. But this opportunity passed away, unavailed, because of World War II.

Some time after this, a friend and a long-term devotee of Shri Meher Baba arranged a meeting for me with the saint. I asked him if he would assist me in helping mentally disturbed persons. He spelled out on the alphabetical board (since he did not speak), "One should first know whether the person needed help. A help at the wrong time can be an interference with the natural process of healing already going on. One has to know the Self first in order to help others. I will help you." I was not told what to do. I had only the assurance of his help. I had to begin my work within on my own.

Whatever I had learned from books and felt correct within, I wrote out in a paper, "Yogic Basis of Psychoanalysis," and I presented it to the Indian Science Congress Session in 1940 in Benares. Despite writing this paper and intellectually understanding the link between yoga and psychoanalysis, I was struggling and fumbling. There was a deep void I felt within every now and then. Nothing came to fill it.

Years rolled on, and in about 1945-1946, I wrote to Dr. Jung about my desire to learn from him. He replied that he did not train anybody then as he was growing old, but recommended me to Dr. Meier. He wrote back, telling me that he could train me if I came over to Zurich. But where was the money for all this? And soon the Indian political situation was in transition by 1947.

By then, I was teaching philosophy and psychology in Kota. In social contact with friends and students, I expressed the desire to learn the ancient wisdom of Self-Realization, if there were someone to teach it. One day a student friend told me that he would arrange such a meeting with one who lived and knew this wisdom.

A few months after this, it happened one morning while I was getting ready to go to the college. The friend asked me to accompany him to his home to meet this person. The first question that I asked of this person was whether it was necessary for me to have a guru. This was because I had heard all sorts of stories about so-called gurus. He asked me a question, in return, "What do you do professionally?" I told him that I was a professor and taught philosophy and psychology to students. "So, those who want to learn philosophy and psychology have to come to you, is that not so?" he said. "Yes," I replied. "Then you have to come to me if you wish to learn the ancient wisdom."

Later, he came to my apartment in the evening and gave a discourse; and after a dialogue between us, he brought home to me experientially that senses, intellect, and such apparatuses available to man need the light of the Self to know things out there. They are blind without the light of the Self. The Self is the light. It was a mystical experience which remained with me for three days, during which I did not know what I taught and did. It convinced me that this person, though a householder, knew and lived what he taught. This contact remained until I went to Zurich. Many summers we lived together and I had the opportunity to see him in all the situations of life. He lived what he taught.

During this period, I came across *MODERN MAN IN SEARCH OF A SOUL* and another book of essays by Jung. I could see now that Jung was a very different kind of psychologist. He taught from a different level than that of Freud. He talked of Self-Realization, something never heard in the textbooks of Western psychology. His way seemed different from that of my guru. It appeared more like the Tantric way. The way to Self lay in understanding the relationship between man and woman. Each man has Anima within and woman her Animus, which he or she projects upon a person outside. Only by going through this experience does one come upon the Self. Anima or Animus are the guardians of the unconscious—the Self. In this manner, he was talking about Shiva and Shakti within us, and their eternal union within. I was reminded of the story of Shiva and Parvati from Shiva-Purana. Parvati, as Sati in her first birth, after marrying Shiva, burned herself into ashes with anger towards her father when he insulted her and her husband. The fire transformed her, and in her next birth, she as Parvati married Shiva. But this happened only after the death of Kama, the god of Desire—who was burned to death by the fire from the third eye of Shiva.

All this made me aware of my strong fascination for my wife. As friends studying together in Bombay, we became very close to each other. But the economical and social distance between us made her unattainable as a partner in life. This realization brought intense suffering. The pain of separation, having reached its intensity, transformed into a mystic experience of Oneness with the Universe. I felt as if the whole Universe, the trees and flowers in the garden (this happened in a garden on a full moon night) were in tears with me. The desire of attaining her dissolved. We remained friends from a long distance, until fate arranged the marriage. Yet this union in marriage never felt complete as I began to realize in the course of years.

My guru read all this in our relationship, my attachment to her which imprisoned us. He started working on it. The mystic joy of earlier and a few later meetings turned into pain and suffering. I had become aware of this imprisonment in attachment to my wife. I knew I had to face it and get free from it, but was never prepared to go this way. I felt my way was to completely dissolve myself in union with her and transcend the separation. Being with him during this period was a torture. I was feeling as I were being baked alive. My wife felt differently from me. She realized the value of what was happening in accepting the way of my guru. The process of dissolution remained incomplete.

I felt Jung's way of going along with the fascination—and accepting the naturalness of fascination—perhaps was leading to the same goal of Self-realization, Eternal Union. I had to go his way.

It was now 1952-1953. India was free from British rule. Scholarships to go abroad were available. Luckily, my professor, Dr. S. Radhakrishnan, was Vice-President of India then. I ran up to him in New Delhi and spoke to him to help me get a scholarship to study with Jung. He was kind enough to call the Education Secretary to give me a scholarship. Now I could make my pilgrimage. The fascination to learn Jung's way seemed even greater than fascination for my wife. How I could leave her back home, I wonder, even now!

Coming over to Zurich, I started to work with Dr. Meier and Dr. L. Frey, as it was impossible to work with either Dr. Jung or Mrs. Jung. I had the good fortune, however, of meeting Dr. Jung professionally and a few other times at critical periods of my analysis. I learned a great deal from what he had to say and his presence.

The analytical process, with dream interpretation, made me see the process I had gone through with my guru in India in a new way. I was learning a new language of identifying psychological processes. Ego, persona, shadow were distinguished as the vestures of personality. Indian psychology did not analyze the contents of Psyche that way. The analysis further emphasized attention to whatever was going on in daily life and dealt with that. This was again a difference from the guru's way. The main focus in the guru's way was toward learning to be a spectator of the psychic drama. According to the guru's way, ego-involvement, the conditioned ego, creates the problem. Learning to be a spectator helps free the ego from involvement with happenings. Ego involvement is attachment to objective situations. An object being a part of the process of Prakriti changes into its opposite and thus one involved goes through the see-saw of opposites—gets into imbalance like the swings of a pendulum. A pendulum allowed to go through its momentum balances itself naturally.

Here I saw the meeting ground between Indian Psychology and Jung. Jung also said that the psyche is in constant motion of change into opposites—the principle of Enantiodromia. Identification with any pole creates the conflict. Jung, through the analytical process, led man to see and experience these swings—the tension. The experience of close proximity of the poles brought tension to its extreme stretch. If one could stay with it, the third factor—the transcendent function—appeared. An insight was gained and a new outlook changed one's attitude toward the earlier situation.[4] Again, in this manner, Jung's way confirmed for me the understanding of traditional Indian wisdom that psychological problems cannot be solved on that level. Transcending that level, rising to the level of the spirit, the Light—the Self—dissolved the tension, because it begins to be seen from the standpoint of wholeness, the Self, where all is included in harmony. This understanding helped me to use either of the approaches, according to the situation and the need of the client. Going through the experience of the whole gamut of swings or learning to be a spectator of the drama both helped to decondition the mind—the ego. The moments of deconditioned mind are moments of Eternity—Pure Light. One then sees clearly in that moment.

Deepest involvement happens in relationship with the opposite sex. As I said earlier, I had understood Jung in this respect in my own fanciful way. Somehow Jung's way helped to dissolve the feeling of separation, or in other words, helped one to experience the union by accepting the projection and working it out. That is how I had understood it while I was in India. Experience of Anima projection in Zurich intensified the yearning for union. It did not dissolve the sense of separation. I learned the same, but in another way. One has to withdraw the projection—situations naturally happen when the image breaks and a sense of desolation comes about. Staying with this alone helps the withdrawal—and one then can find one's other half within. Jung was as much right in this area as my guru. The approaches, however, were different. I feel both the approaches are important. Different people need different medicine.

It became clear to me during my analysis that confrontation with the Anima or different images depended upon my attitude and the "hook" within me towards persons. Becoming aware of the inner images or the "hook," and working on it, changed the image. It also changed the relationship to that person. Something similar happened with the archetype of the Self. I was fascinated by experiencing alternatively the archetype of the Wise Old Man or the Divine Mother, and the Black Magician or the Witch. I became aware of my identification with the archetype of the Wise Old Man and my dependence upon the Divine Mother. It was an interesting discovery as to how dreams, rightly understood, can be helpful in the journey to Selfhood. Here was the meeting ground between the two wisdoms: individuation of Jung and the tradition of gurus. Archetypal images continue to appear in dreams or continue to be projected until one is totally aware, in other words, free from the "hooks" within—one becomes totally deconditioned. What is that experience of totally deconditioned mind or ego—the experience of Wholeness? It has to be one free from images, a kind of emptiness and thought-free space. The tradition of the gurus spoke about it.

Jung was silent on this point. From the very beginning, when I met Jung to pay my respect to him as my guru, and later a few times at critical stages of my analysis, I had felt Jung knew That which IS. I could experience profound depth within, as I did with my guru. Why was he silent about it? Why did his writings stop at the archetypal images of Self? One feels tremendous energy in experiencing such archetypes. What is behind the image? What is the source of this energy like? Once, when he came to greet Dr. Lilliane Frey on her birthday, I was with her. I got a few minutes with him then. I asked him what is behind the archetype of Self? He was silent. His silence intrigued me and remained with me for years in India. In the course of time, I got a satisfactory answer which I brought out in a paper published in the *JOURNAL OF ANALYTICAL PSYCHOLOGY*, London.[5]

I could feel Jung's situation. Though a scientist, he was called a mystic by the scientists. Jung, a psychologist, came upon the realm of the divine beyond psychology. He led some of those who came for counseling to experience the realm of the spirit—Self. Jung's way thus led to religious experience beyond dogma for anyone, whatever faith he belonged to. Men of established religions thought he was trespassing on their domain. But this is what a guru does. Perhaps Jung felt that men in the West were not yet ready for such direct experience and its pronouncement. The way for the Western mind lay through exploration of archetypes—a demonstrable experience only, at this point of time. Direct confrontation of the divine brings total annihilation of the conditioned ego or mind (Fana in Sufi terms) at first; it is then the door to grace (Baka in Sufi terms).

I happened to be in Zurich before Jung passed away. I met Mrs. Aniela Jaffe, who knew of my correspondence with Jung. She tole me, "Professor Vasavada, we will soon find the answer to your question to Jung." She was referring to *MEMORIES, DREAMS, REFLECTIONS*.[6] I was satisfied when later I read that book and came upon his words on page 353. It was more than clear how Jung experienced the divine. It is the realm beyond knowledge. It is the realm of Eros—its incalculable paradoxes, experiencing which one felt humble. Knowledge gives way to experiencing the divine in all its manifestations.

For this paper, I had to write all of this autobiographical stuff. Writing all this once again, I went through two traditional processes: the guru's and Jung's, and came to realize what I have been doing with myself and others. The way of the guru or of Jung happens to be taken as the need arises. It seems to be my fate to speak about Jung through Eastern eyes, and also to speak about Eastern tradition through Jung's eyes. I am here and there and no-where. The way of gurus gave the clarity of the goal to which we all are being naturally led. Jung called it the individuation process. There is not the slightest difference in this between the East and Jung. For both traditions, it is the highest value.[7] It is wholeness, holiness—it is neither my wholeness nor yours. It includes all. We are all contained in it. It is that state of being which is pure and unconditioned. It is throught-free open space. Mind or ego, on the way to deconditioning itself of samskaras, or false vestures, experiences this Light—the Self.[8]

Thus the processes of deconditioning can be many. The guru's way of learning to be a spectator—not caring about happenings personally, or Jung's way of going through current relationships, experiencing the swings of opposites and learning to be a spectator, brings one face to face with the transcendent function. Staying with whatever the situation is, objectively, in a relationship or the subjective situation of depression, stalemate, or confusion, or an archetypal situation in a dream—allowing its total impact on the organism, or what Dr. Gendlin would call focusing on it—is the way. Beyond the words or feelings that describe the situation is the Unknown. We have to experience its quality and let it speak. Both the analyst and the client have to wait and watch for what comes next from the Unconscious—the Unknown. There need not be an "Aha!" experience always. They are not frequent. If we do not expect and hope, we begin to see many different faces of the divine—the Unknown. Knowing this, we are content to be with what IS—the Indescribable and Unspeakable. We begin to accept the tortuous journey to individuation, which has its own natural rhythm. Spontaneity begins to come into life, off and on.

It seems clear to me that archetypes and archetypal situations cannot be understood. There is no end to their varied manifestations because the energy behind them is incalculable. All that one does is to experience them, feel their nuances of feeling, which may begin to hit the right spot within. Or it may not. The more puzzling the archetype, the nearer are we to the Unknown, because it is telling us something important—stop knowing. Enter into the Source and be It. All the archetypes have their origin in the same Source. The Source is important.

Therapy thus becomes, once again, undertaking a journey to Selfhood with each person who gives us this opportunity to explore the Unknown along with him. Because of what we have undergone earlier, it becomes easier to be patient, knowing the rhythm of the client. Whatever happens on the road is quite important, and yet not important, because the whole scene or outlook changes when THAT happens.

It is also easier to encounter projections of the Wise Old Man or Healer put upon us, because in depth we know that the Healer is doing its things both to us and the client. The client, in projecting the archetype of the Healer or Wise Old Man, is experiencing something within. He is becoming aware of that within him. Maybe, later on, he will see that it was always there. The problems of Transference and Counter-transference become minimal. From all these experiences, I feel the role of analyst or healer or guru can not be put on as a persona. If it is put on, one knows very well, from the beginning years of practice, that it is a big burden and a great hindrance in one's journey to Individuation, and that of the client, as well. Wholeness, holiness, can not be put on as a role, as a persona. It is always there, because individuation is natural, it is there right from the beginning. We become aware of it in due course. Light shines in the heart of every man and is guiding the path. The alchemical situation of analyst and client coming together begins to do its work of illuminating the dark corners within.

Jung's way is the way of Enlightenment. It is not a technique, it is a way of life. It cannot be taught, but can be lived. It cannot be narrowed to trained therapists only. Everyone needs Enlightenment, everyone feels the call of the Divine within, whatever his profession. Jung's way is not the way of specialization. It is an open road, each one with intense yearning to be his Self can follow and live it, doing whatever he is called to do in this world. This is the way of the gurus. The guru is available to anyone, whosoever comes: how long he comes and what he does with the wisdom received is not the concern of the guru. He is merely an instrument of the Divine. Whatever happens through him, happens.

I have thus had to follow two different paths and they became useful to help those who came to me. Following either one of the two, the journey ends and the doors of the Divine open and a new journey begins, of which no one can talk. It is unspeakable. If entering the door happens, it will radiate. That which IS is the highest value; all paths lead there and end there. That which IS is indifferent to paths because all belong there; they are included. In this manner, the label of a particular school is no longer divisive and distinguishing, but connotes a pilgrim following the same journey's end with others. He is a part of the community of seekers—a pilgrim.

REFERENCES

1. C.A. Meier. Northwestern University Press, 1967.

2. BRIHADARAYNAKA UPANISHAD. 2.r. and 3.8.

3. Patanjali. YOGA SUTRAS I. 48. THE TEXTBOOK OF YOGA PSYCHOLOGY, R. Misra, Julian Press, New York, 1963, p. 163.

4. "The transcendent function does not proceed without aim and purpose, but leads to the revelation of the essential man. It is in the first place a purely

natural process, which may in some cases pursue its course without the knowledge or assistance of the individual, and can sometimes forcibly accomplish itself in the face of opposition. The meaning and purpose of the process is realization, in all its aspects of the personality, originally hidden away in the embryonic germ plasm; the production and unfolding of the original potential wholeness." *COLL. WKS.* Vol 7, p. 186.

5. *THE ANALYTICAL PSYCHOLOGY OF C.G. JUNG AND EASTERN WISDOM,* 1967.

6. *MEMORIES, DREAMS, AND REFLECTIONS,* C.G. Jung, Pantheon Books, New York, 1973, p. 353.

7. " . . . so always the inner experience of individuation has been appreciated as the most valuable and important thing in life. It is the only thing that brings any lasting satisfaction to man. Power, glory, wealth are external and futile. The really important things are within. It is more important to me that I am happy than that I have the external reasons for happiness. Rich people should be happy, but often they are not, they are bored to death, therefore it is so much better for man to work to produce an inner condition that gives him an inner happiness. Experience shows that there are certain psychological conditions in which man gets eternal results. They have something of the quality of reaching beyond man. They have a divine quality and yield all that satisfaction which man-made things do not." *DREAM SEMINARS,* Volume 1, p. 210.

8. "The aim of individuation is nothing less than to divest the self of the false wrappings of the persona on one hand and the suggestive power of the primordial images on the other." *COLL. WKS.,* Vol. 7, p. 260. See also: "But the more we become consciouse of ourselves through self-knowledge, and act accordingly, the more the layers of the personal unconscious that is superimposed on the Collective Unconscious will be diminished. In this way there arises a consciousness which is no longer imprisoned in the petty, oversensitive personal world of the ego, but participates freely in the wider world of objective interests. The widened consciousness is no longer that touchy, egotistical bundle of personal wishes, fears, hopes and ambitions which always has to be compensated or corrected by unconscious counter-tendencies; instead it is a function of relationship to the world of objects, bringing the individual into absolute, binding, and indissoluble communion with the world at large." Ibid., p. 275.

COMMENTS BY SPIEGELMAN ON VASAVADA'S PAPER

In reading Dr. Vasavada's paper once more (I had read it earlier as one of his contributions to our joint book, *HINDUISM AND JUNGIAN PSYCHOLOGY),* I again felt the wonder and privilege that Jungian work had brought into my life. The tremendous variety of people—ethnically, religiously, individually—that I experienced in Zurich (Vasavada was there, then, too) and continued, as we see in our present volume. Jung would surely be happy to see the wide variety among those attracted to his work, subsequently to advance so many features of it on the way to their own wholeness.

Dr. Vasavada's story is especially poignant—one whose task was to explain Jung to the east and vice-versa, but from authentic inner eyes deeply immersed in both. He does more than that. Who can read of his early struggles to absorb the west, the conflict between his love for his wife and his loyalty and trust in his guru's direction, without feeling a pang of pain for our eastern brother, so like us and yet so different?

The reader may forgive that I pose no question here, but merely salute my friend and spiritual comrade, who shows what it truly means to live at two ends of the earth, physically and spiritually, and to unite them [The reader who wishes may find more of Vasavada, and also my questions and comments, in our joint book, *HINDUISM AND JUNGIAN PSYCHOLOGY*, Falcon Press, 1986.]

REJOINDER BY VASAVADA TO SPIEGELMAN

It is in no way comfortable to live when one is confronted by two cultures, one's own and the other adopted. The struggle to bring understanding between the two is truly an inner struggle. When you do not understand the language of your friend you feel isolated. The break in communication is felt like darkness within. Trying to bring understanding with the other is trying to deal with your discomfort of darkness. This has happened to me occasionally. It is again looming large on the horizon, since I came across James Hillman's *ANIMA*. I could follow him earlier. We had fruitful dialogue on his *RE-VISIONING PSYCHOLOGY* and *DREAM AND THE UNDERWORLD*. Now, reading *ANIMA*, nothing resonates within, it is all darkness within. It is completely different from how I think. Have I really understood Jung? I cannot ignore this darkness, which means I have to connect what he says with inner experience—a common source from which both kinds of thinking originate. It is not an easy task, because here you cannot do anything. It is a state of deadlock. What it is to wait in the darkness! There is no time sense here and yet one has to contend with someone within who is impatient! How long one has to wait for the darkness to clear up and the Light to shine!

Though it is darkness, Light informs that it is darkness.

COMMENT BY McNAIR ON VASAVADA'S PAPER

The notion of the "inability to find any direction" is a very familiar condition to my rational/scientific attitude. Likewise, "my nothingness."

Jung's notion of fate, that "tortuous journey of our life to our wholeness—we cannot . . . refuse it for long" is a most profound dimension of this work for me. I feel, at this time in my life (age 39), that "fate" is the prime mover, and to that I yield. Yet my destiny is confusing; what is the personal part, my role, place etc.? The feeling is that of being on a moving sidewalk; Alice is saying "you have to run fast to stay in the same place": or Winnicott's Intermediate zone: where is my teddy bear, my blanket? Could it be my increasing awareness of mortality and death via somatic symptoms, hence my own body?

I enjoyed hearing about the transitory nature of Freudian/Adlerian "social adjustment." These have been stops along the way for me, too. I was struck by the statement of Shri Meher Baba: "One should first know whether the person needed help." This brings up a significant issue to me, that of epistemology. How do I know? The more the patient "believes" I "know," the more ignorant I find myself feeling. Or, better yet, I find myself feeling—not able to know.

For me, a most lasting mental concept of this paper came when Dr. Vasavada compared Jung's psychology to Tantric Yoga. I had studied Tantric Yoga and yet it remained distinct and separate. The notion that the Anima/Animus are "guardians" of the unconscious was very enlightening. I have since spent much time mulling over this perception. This notion has been most pertinent when working with women patients. However, I find that with men, it seems that our animas need to find some mutually compatible interest to meet at all, else we are lost to some Alpha-Ape exercise!

Having started my academic career in math/science/engineering, the natural sciences are, for me, generous with metaphor and simile. Dr. Vasavada's image of a pendulum being allowed to balance itself is very apt and helpful. I also found reassurance in his comment that "there need not be an 'aha' experience. They are not frequent." Coming to an awareness of the realm of silence has been more subtle and soft for me. Hence, I find confusing the current interest in clinical mapping and parochial dogmas when, as Dr. Vasavada states: "It cannot be taught, but can be lived. It cannot be narrowed to train therapists only . . . it is a way of life."

This paper was very moving for me and after a needed reflection period of four weeks, I was finally able to take pen in hand. I very much appreciate his "perception through Eastern eyes." One question arises for me: Given the inherent masculine-feminine separation and subsequent conflict deeply imbedded in the Western Psyche, how does Dr. Vasavada perceive such a conflict now that he has witnessed it first hand and lived within its culture for some time? (Or, that one has to give of God for God, as Meister Eckhardt said.)

How I Do It

by

DR. MED. FRITZ BEYME, FMH

CAN IT BE PROVED?

Am I a charlatan? A mere quack making his living on a general prejudice? Or can it be proved that psychotherapy is efficacious? This question has been the thread of Ariadne in the labyrinth of my daily work. It embraces 8953 patients since my practice was opened in 1957.

The problem had been rubbed into me by H.J. Eysenck in a survey on nineteen studies "reported in the literature," covering almost eight thousand cases, and dealing with both analytic and eclectic types of treatment [33](p. 28). The conclusion that psychotherapy gave no better results that spontaneous recovery challenged me.

APPRENTICESHIP UNDER HOFFMANN-LaROCHE

I realized however—and not without bitterness—that I had in no way been prepared to tackle such a difficult problem. What I needed was a thorough apprenticeship in planning and statistical evaluation of clinical trials. So I decided to get the necessary know-how from a pharmaceutic firm. Fortunately the multinational giant Hoffmann-LaRoche let me try out the newly admitted anxiolytic "Librium" on patients suffering from anxiety and general nervousness.

No matter what may be the theoretical approach leading to a classification of neuroses, one always hears patients complain about a group of more or less closely correlated symptoms summarized in the non-psychiatric medical literature under the names of neurocirculatory asthenia, anxiety neurosis, effort syndrome, or neurasthenia.

What I needed next was a measuring instrument to quantify results with the tranquilizer. I chose an inventory devised by Wheeler, et. al. [70], in which a clear definition of the syndrome is given and a sample of 173 patients is compared with a control group. For every item like palpitation, fatigability, difficult breathing, nervousness, pain in chest, sighing, vertigo, etc., it was decided by questioning whether it was present or absent. If Librium was of any use, then the score of my patients should move away from the critical group towards that of Wheeler's control group. In 1961 my first paper was printed. Of 20 patients treated with Librium during four weeks, five responded very well, ten well and five poorly. Only one patient complained of side effects.[6]

Two years later an analogous paper on the results with Valium on 20 neurasthenic patients could be presented.[7] It did not satisfy me, however, because the question of a spontaneous recovery had not been considered. To resolve this problem you have to compare two groups, one of which receives the new medicine and other treated either with a placebo or a generally recognized pharmacon. I decided to use classical sodium bromide which was generally applied in eastern Europe according to a book on neurasthenia that had appeared in 1959.[46]

This time I used a crossing-over technique. Every patient received both medicines: either Valium during the first week and sodium-bromide during the second week or the other way round. The Valium-first group, with twelve persons and 224 combined symptoms at the start, decreased by 82 symptoms in the course of a week. When these patients switched over to sodium-bromide, the sum of their symptoms increased by 12. In the other group, symptoms decreased from 212 by only 33 points under sodium-bromide, but were further reduced by 44 points after a week of Valium.

At the time when Jung published his papers on the word association test, this would have been regarded as ample evidence for the superiority of Valium. But, during the first half of the century, theory of statistics had made tremendous progress and standards had been raised. It had to be determined whether the difference was significant and at what level of probability. Had the sample been chosen according to current standards? Was it big enough? Did the results correspond to a Gaussian distribution so that Student's t-test could be applied? As distribution of data appeared non-parametric, the chi-square test seemed indicated. But then data should be independent from each other, which was doubtful. Finally, Dr. N., the then expert of Hoffmann-LaRoche, advised me to apply five different methods. I must admit that I enjoyed this very much. Having taken part in the very first course on statistics for physicians offered by the University of Basle and having gone through endless homework for the sake of exercise, this was the first time I could do the real stuff, something really useful, something which brought me nearer to my original goal of learning how to tackle the results of psychotherapy. Let me add, for the sake of completeness, that all five methods showed the difference between Valium and sodium-bromide to be highly significant.

It was only after three more such clinical trials[10] [11] [14] that I dared approach psychotherapy. In the meantime I had learned to distinguish between hard and soft data. If a child wets the bed,[2] that is a hard fact. The same applies to migraine and nightmares. [24] If somebody states that tension headache can be improved, we have to consider this as a soft datum which cannot be proved. So I decided to investigate further my results with migraine[15] [17] [21] [23] which were very satisfactory so far and fully in accordance with those of H.G. Wolff,[72] the great master in this field.

Wolff (p. 465) had published results obtained from 64 patients treated according to his principles. Eighteen had practically lost their attacks and only seven had failed to improve. He compared his results with those of classical psychoanalysis obtained from eight such patients by "well-trained and able psychoanalysts (p. 463) at the New York Hospital after long periods of treatment.

Neither the intensity nor the frequency of the migraine headache in these patients was reduced dramatically. The possibility suggests itself that the psychoanalytic method of therapy is faulty for these patients . . . " (p. 463)

If Wolff has shown the superiority of his psychotherapy over psychoanalysis in relation to migraine just as I have proved Valium to be more efficacious than sodium-bromide in neurasthenia, we both have neglected one point of paramount importance: the possibility of spontaneous recovery giving even better results. There was no "control" compared with the two "experimental" groups (Eysenck, 33, p. 31). Neither had there been any control-group in Cremerius' recent book on the results obtained from 523 cases treated by psychotherapy at the medical outpatient-department of the University of Munich, which had come out in 1962, the very year when I embarked on my paper.[29]

So I realized that the introduction of a control-group demanded by Eysenck would be a major contribution. The ideal design, for the sake of science, would be an "Own-Control-Cross-Over" experiment. If this arrangement can be made at an outpatient department under the pretense of not having enough therapists for starting treatment immediately, such a procedure would be impossible in private practice. Patients would not hesitate to go to another therapist! My best bet was to take drop-outs for control. So the control-group consisted finally of ten patients who had left me after 1-5 sessions and whom I followed up by telephone up to three years. They were compared to an experimental group of fourteen patients treated according to the principles of H.G. Wolff. Improvement according to very precisely defined criteria was found in all fourteen patients and only in three persons of the control group. The difference between the two groups proved to be highly significant, the probability of mere chance being smaller than one in a thousand.

This paper was presented to G. Benedetti, professor at the University of Basle. He found it important enough to be published in PSYCHE, the leading German periodical in this field. Professor Mitscherlich from Heidelberg sent it back with two minor criticisms which we considered to be very appropriate. Having changed the manuscript in accordance with Mitscherlich's suggestions we were very surprised when he refused it once more—this time without furnishing any reason. We could only guess: it must have been the fact that "minor psychotherapy" had given better results than classical psychoanalysis, while migraine was considered to be one of the major indications for psychoanalysis at that time. Had Mitscherlich thought of the patients instead of defending the position of psychoanalysis he should have been pleased at the results, given that the incidence of migraine is so high that there would not be enough analysts in all the world to cope with this disease.

Being rebuffed by Mitscherlich, Benedetti published the paper in PRAXIS DER PSYCHOTHERAPIE[15] where he was one of the chief editors. Among the echoes there was a big surprise: a letter from Peru in which the chief editor of the REVISTA DE PSICOPATOLOGIA; PSICOLOGIA Y PSICOTERAPIA asked me for permission to print it.[16]

After this pilot study had yielded promising results, my next goal was to establish a base line for the spontaneous recovery rate from migraine. Wolff's statistics had not taken the dimension of time into consideration. They had only given information about the final outcome of treatment, no matter how long it had lasted within his limits of three months to five years.[72] (p. 465) My new paper[17] was based on an experimental group of 22 patients and a control-group of the same size. Half of the treated group had gone entirely without any migraine. But in the control there were also two happy individuals totally without any attack. No doubt that Wolff would have been forced to admit that "frequency of migraine headache in these patients was reduced dramatically."[72] (p. 463) So there had been spontaneous recovery.

Isn't a sample of only 38 cases too small to reach statistical significance? The four-fields test showed that the probability of the difference between the 50% recovery of the therapeutic group and only 10% spontaneous recovery of the control group being due to mere chance was lower than 2.5%.[37] When a patient asked me what he was to expect, I could from now on tell him, using statistical methods: "There is a 50% chance that you will have no more attacks after 15 months if you follow my treatment, and only 10% if you do not." If he wanted to know how sure he could be of this prediction, I had to rely on another set of parameters: confidence limits. With a certainty of 95%, the probability of his having no more migraine in the sixth trimester would lie between 20% and 70%. And if he went on asking whether a prolongation of treatment beyond these 15 months would improve his chances I could say: "Probably not, for the rate of recovery tends to decline in my experience after 18 months of treatment." This is important if you consider the financial side. Just think of the fact that analytical treatment usually reckons with three years or even more.

Of course my accuracy of prediction was more sophisticated than most patients cared to understand. The main thing for them was to make sure that their doctor knew what he was talking about. They could easily see that he was not trying to spread vague hopes. So they had a positive future perspective before them and tended to be more compliant than when they had reasons for doubt in my approach.

This time encouragement came from Germany. A. Jores, Professor of clinical medicine at the University of Hamburg, wrote in his book on patients with neurovegetative disturbances the following sentences: "There is no treatment that really helps in migraine except psychotherapy. This has been proven by Beyme."[42] (p. 105) In the seventies, psychosomatic medicine became a subject for the final examination of physicians. At that time, there existed no German text-book on this subject. So Jores undertook the task of editing one and asked me to write the chapter on migraine and other headaches.[21] One of the main features of this chapter is the table of differential diagnosis which produces several medicines for migraine prevention and attacks. I did this so I could be sure to be on firm scientific ground and to prevent critics from saying: "How can a mere psychiatrist decide whether the patient is not suffering from some other kind of headache? Does he really know what he is writing about?" If my diagnosis of migraine was not accepted by the reader, then all my deductions gained from data as hard as headache attacks were erected on uncertain ground. With this cooperation in conjunction with 32 well-established authors, I could now enjoy the pleasant feeling of having made my scientific reputation.

As long as people do not take an author seriously, he may produce any number of jewels: who will care about looking at them more closely? But now I had erected a widely accepted foundation in the field of treating migraine by advising people how to organise their daily work, how to manage their ambitions, how to cope with their aggressions or how to relax by means of autogenic training.

I could now embark on the subject of unconscious causes of migraine attacks. A Swiss proverb says that you should not shoot sparrows with cannons. Only after having exhausted the possibilities of minor psychotherapy, with simple advice dealing with conscious conflicts and voluntary changes of attitudes, producing order on the surface of the patient's life, did it then make sense to me to dig any deeper.

A lucky coincidence brought me a corresponding patient just at the time when I was ready to start such digging. His attacks had been reduced from once a week to one every month by autogenic training and helping him to behave more assertively so that he could live up to his real talents and reach the goals of adequate ambition. Now he came back to me because his attacks had increased again for no apparent reason. They mainly occurred during sleep, from which he was aroused by terrible pain. It seemed obvious to me that these attacks must have been released by dreams whose content should be similar to the typical situations of conscious life apt to release migraine according to H.G. Wolff. Only the patient was not aware of any dream!

A search in a brand new text-book on headache[56] taught me that Dexter and Weitzman[30] had recently shown nocturnal migraine to be associated with Rapid Eye Movements immediately preceding it, but that this had not been the case with nocturnal tension headache. Supposing that these REM patterns had been concomitant with dreams, they questioned their patients in this respect. In spite of their great interest in the subject, they had not been able to register one single dream. Their patients had encountered exactly the same difficulty in recall as my own. Therefore their inference of nocturnal migraine being released by dreams remained indirect, being based on EEG and Electromyographic patterns only.

We surmounted this obstacle by auto-suggestion. A series of formulas, devised together with the patient and repeated by him several times every day, brought results after a few weeks. First only a fragment remained in his memory: he knew that there had been some kind of dispute with his mother. But then more details could be remembered and we wound up with the extensive protocols of twenty dreams. One can imagine my joy at finding so many nuggets, thanks to a more powerful technique after a team of renowned gold-seekers had been searching in vain at the same claim. What I found confirmed

Dexter and Weitzman's hypothesis. All seven attacks of nocturnal migraine which occurred during this period of observation were preceded by a dream.

But what about the dream content? Thirteen out of the twenty registered dreams were not followed by attacks. As expected, Wolff's releasing factors of anger and resentment[72] (p. 410) could be found. But that was not the main point. What helped best to discriminate between dreams followed by migraine and those that were not, was Jung's hypothesis of dreams having a dramatic structure with exposition, development, culmination and lysis. "The fourth and last is the lysis," he wrote,[43] (p. 254) wherein "the solution or the result is obtained by the dream-work (there are certain dreams in which the fourth phase is missing, which can form a special problem . . .)" No fourth phase was found in six out of the seven dreams followed by migraine and only one out of the thirteen dreams with a solution preceded an attack. The four-fields test showed that the contingency between dreams without solution and nocturnal migraine was highly significant, the odds against mere chance being more than 999 in a thousand.

So it was the first time that a criterion from outside the psychological realm had been used to prove beyond a reasonable doubt that dreams without a lysis really represent a special group by themselves. It has always been Jung's major problem that analytical psychology lacked an archimedian point: "The tragedy is that psychology does not make use of consistent mathematics, but only of statistics related to subjective prejudices. It also lacks that immense advantage of an archimedian point, which a science like physics enjoys. The latter observes physical events from a psychological standpoint and can translate them into psychological contents. The psyche, on the other hand, only observes itself and can merely translate psychological contents into other psychological contents."[4] (p. 464)

Now a migraine attack represents a physical event that is strictly comparable to what physicists can observe. In somatic symptoms that can be objectified, we have found an archimedian point which allows us to support our psychological hypotheses by criteria lying outside the psychological field.

If a discovery is worth anything, you should be able to buy something with it. What could be done with finding nocturnal migraine to be associated with dreams without solution? Perhaps migraine could be avoided if dreams could be brought to a lysis?

When I had finished my studies at the Jung Institute, I was so persuaded of the autonomy of dreams that it seemed impossible to influence their content by a decision formed while awake. But in my early years of private practice a happy mishap taught me that this was not quite true. A client had exhausted my patience by presenting, day after day, the same dream in which a murderer brandishing a dagger pursued him until he awoke screaming and sweating. Of course I collected associations and of course I added amplifications and of course the interpretation amounted to the murderer being nothing else but his shadow, in this special sense his own repressed aggressions. It is not nice to observe how one's own therapeutic arsenal is used up without changing the stereotyped anxiety dream one iota. So one day I lost my patience, saying: "Why do you keep running away? Why don't you stand still for once?" Great was my surprise when, at the next consultation, he came triumphantly with the following news: "When the murderer turned up again, I remembered your telling me to stand still, which I did. Then the murderer also stopped. So I screamed for help, and several other men appeared. When the murderer saw them, he ran away himself, and we pursued him as far as the airport Dubendorf, where we encircled him and handed him over to the police." That was the end of the anxiety-patient's recurrent dream.

So I was not surprised when I found similar results in Garfield's book on creative dreaming.[36] Instead of lengthy explanations, I told the migraine-patient to buy the book and to proceed along its lines so as to behave more assertively in his dreams and to bring the drama to a solution. Being an intelligent man of considerable will-power, he succeeded, after some months, in entirely eliminating dreams without a solution. At the same time, nocturnal migraine disappeared and was absent for more than nine months, whereas diurnal attacks only occurred twice during the same period of observation.

This paper has been accepted by HEXAGON (Roche), a bi-monthly distributed free of charge to physicians in Western Europe, the Americas, Africa, the East and Australia. It appears in German, English, French, Portuguese and Spanish. "Treating nocturnal migraine by creative dreaming" (Garfield) appears in the first HEXAGON of 1986. While writing these lines I am already impatient about the echoes.[23]

One should not jump to the conclusion that I always treat recurrent anxiety dreams by losing my temper and telling the patient to pull himself together. In 1946, while working at the psychiatric clinic at the University of Leiden, I discovered that it was possible to use a day-dream technique which allowed the subject to live the whole drama through again and to experience similar affects, but this time under the protection of the therapist. I published my results in Dutch.[3] It is now widely applied in German-speaking countries and runs under the name of "Katathymes Bilderleben" (Leuner). While studying at the C.G. Jung Institute in Zurich in 1950/51 I tried to get lecturers and training analysts interested in the method but in vain: How could a mere student who had not even passed his propadeutic examination hope to be taken seriously by the establishment of that time? Leuner's first paper on what he called an "Experimental Procedure to Validate Symbol-Interpretation" came out in 1954. And in 1955 the technical term "Katathymes Bilderleben" appeared on the title of one of Leuner's publications for the first time. That was eight years after my Dutch pilot-study.

Even when Leuner himself came to Zurich in the fifties to present his method, the VIPs failed to grasp the importance of this new approach. It was, in fact, the director of the C.G. Jung Institute, Franz Riklin, who ridiculed Leuner, beginning his comment with the words: "If you understood anything about psychotherapy, you would know that . . . "

During the following years, Leuner's group gained adherents and his method momentum. In 1978, a first International Congress for Catathymic Imagery was organized. In Switzerland, a Society for Psychotherapy with the Day-Dream (Catathymic Imagery) was formed. It organizes seminars. In 1985, a textbook of 500 pages appeared,[49] from whose literature I could infer that some Jungian analysts have at long last integrated this powerful weapon in their therapy and their research.

As already intimated, I use catathymic imagery mainly for coping with recurrent anxiety dreams. In the first half of 1986, Folia Psychopractica Roche will publish my "Working up anxiety dreams by catathymic imagery" (Leuner). For Jungians, the main interest of the paper lies in its demonstrating how aggressive energy of the aggressor in the dream (the shadow) passes into the ego of the dreamer. What is more: It can be shown in consecutive spontaneous dreams that the ego's aggressive energy has been boosted. Instead of running away from a dangerous enemy, the dreamer now becomes able to attack the opponent, e.g. by throwing him over the parapet in the top apartment of a high-rise. The Dream Hostility Count (DHC) of Saul and Sheppard[59] provides a measurement of the gross amount of aggressive energy contained in each dream. It could be shown that this quantity had remained unchanged by the treatment.

This seems to confirm Jung's hypothesis, borrowed from physics, of the conservation of physical energy.[43] (p. 32-45) What had changed radically, however, was the direction of this energy. By the introduction of vectors, this process could be quantified for the first time. In dividing the egofugal hostility (throwing the robber over the parapet) by the egopetal hostility (the robber climbing up the high-rise), I could compute the Ego-Hostility Quotient (EHQ). It could be proved that the dreams that followed the treatment by catathymic imagery ranked higher in regard to their EHQ. Statistically, the difference was highly significant (p lower than .005).

This paper seems an ideal example to illustrate how difficult it can be to get something published in a scientific periodical if the author is not in close contact with some person pulling the ropes of power. I had offered the m.s. to *HEXAGON* during the seventies but got it back without any comment. About ten years later, Hoffmann LaRoche asked me whether I would take part in the clinical evaluation of Diclofensin, a new antidepressant. I answered: "Only under one condition! If you agree to publish my paper on catathymic imagery in your series Folia Psychopractica." The bargain was accepted. The editor was told to publish and he did not even care to look at the rough copy. All he did was to give me his technical conditions: 30 pages of 30 lines, each one being composed of 60 elements. When he received the m.s., he was very enthusiastic about it, and we had lunch together. My hope to have found a new medium for future papers has been deeply disappointed, however. When I received the final proofs,[24] I was told that Roche is giving up the Folia Psychopractica at the end of

1986—much to the displeasure of the editor, as a matter of fact.

Besides interesting Jungians and Leuner's adherents, it may also appeal to behavior-therapists, because their techniques of using an anxiety-hierarchy and treating by reciprocal inhibition is applied to the autonomous personalities of the dream in exactly the same way as they desensitize a phobic by imagery instead of life-situations. Working with imagery is the first phase of systematic desensitization.

BEHAVIOR THERAPY

During the first year after beginning my practice, I did not have enough patients to fill my schedule. We did not even earn enough to make both ends meet. So my wife took a job typing for $1.50 per hour while I made beds and took care of the household. Having a fresh diploma from the Institute, I wanted to have as many people as possible profit from my analytical training. But that was not remunerated accordingly by health insurance, to which 95% of my clients belonged. The session was counted as 20 minutes long in 1957—no matter how long it lasted. Having nothing else to do, I kept patients for an hour, charging for only twenty minutes. At the rate of one session a week, I could arrive at half the intensity of treatment done during my supervised training analyses at the C.G. Jung Institute. To my great surprise, at least three quarters of my clients proved to be unable to profit from Jungian analysis. Roughly speaking, one could reckon that all those below the 75th percentile in an intelligence test like Raven's Progressive Matrices[57] could not be treated by this method.

What was one to do with these patients? At that time, I read about Wolpe in one of Eysenck's books and got in touch with him while he was still in Johannesburg at the University of Witwaterstrand. He sent me his reprints, and I started working along his lines—mainly with patients suffering from phobias. In 1958, his *PSYCHOTHERAPY BY RECIPROCAL INHIBITION*[73] made him famous and he made his way up to the position of Professor of Psychiatry at Temple University in Philadelphia. In 1963, he founded the periodical, *BEHAVIOR RESEARCH AND THERAPY*, and in 1964, a paper of mine was printed in its second volume.[9] Not only did Wolpe accept a publication of mine, he went so far as to send me a patient: a lady from Lebanon whose phobia had been treated by a psychopharmacist at a posh private clinic on the lake of Geneva. Unsatisfied with the result, the husband took her to a psychiatrist at Manchester who recommended Wolpe: "You have to be treated by systematic desensitization and reciprocal inhibition. If you cannot stay at Philadelphia for half a year and are living in Geneva, the nearest man able to help you is Beyme in Basle." So she came the hundred miles from Geneva once a week and got rid of her phobia in the course of the predicted six months.

Slowly my success with phobias became known and even fellow-analysts sent me their patients for treatment by behavior therapy. So I soon had enough phobics to form groups and to communicate the theoretical knowledge they needed in a series of seven consecutive sessions. They learned how a conditioned reflex is formed and extinguished, how a stimulus hierarchy and a reaction hierarchy are built, how massed practice is used, what is meant by a "dominant" (Uchtomski),[63] by positive reinforcement, by negative reinforcement. They had to realize the importance of the time factor in anterograde and retrograde conditioning, to understand Hull's famous formula, $sEr = D \times sHr$ and the importance of motivation. At the end of each session they received a summary of the lesson which they could take home and consult while completing a multiple-choice questionnaire prepared for them by a psychologist. At the following session, the home-work was discussed in the group and difficulties elucidated. So patients had the possibility of digesting this complicated matter. About 75% proved to be able to cope. That is three times as many as had been found to be intelligent enough for Jungian analysis—a factor of great importance from the social point of view.

RELAXATION BY AUTOGENIC TRAINING (H. Schultz)

If Wolpe and his followers inhibited anxiety by Progressive Relaxation,[39 40 41] I did the same by autogenic training (Schultz). This method is widely used in German-speaking countries and has been popularized in North America by Luthe.[51] It is based on auto-suggestion and can be taught in classes of any size. Its creator, Professor Schultz, used to have several hundred physicians in the same course. If there exists an advantage of small groups over such huge classes, it remains to be proved. Seven sessions at two-week intervals are sufficient, and the patient does not need more than six daily repetitions, occupying him from three to four minutes each. Twenty minutes of daily exercise compares very favorably to the one or two hours which Jacobson asks for his patients with his progressive relaxation. So the number of drop-outs is much smaller with autogenic training than with Jacobson's method.

It was Jacobson, I believe, who proved that Neurasthenia was closely related to abnormal tension in skeletal muscles. Relaxation, therefore, by no matter which method, can bring improvement of neurasthenic symptoms such as breathing troubles, palpitation, chest pain, nervousness, dizziness, fatigue, limitation of activity, sleep disturbances, tension headache, etc.

Having used Schultz's method since 1945, I applied it widely in my practice and gradually specialists in internal medicine became aware of my results. They had observed similar successes with benzodiazepines, only to discover that symptoms came back in most cases when they discontinued the drug. In 1965, I had so many patients referred for autogenic therapy that I organized courses with groups. To my surprise, progress was better, on the average, than with individual treatment. Up to now, I have treated about two thousand patients by this method.

This does not mean that their personal problems were ignored. They were attacked in individual sessions. Autogenic training is no panacea. It is an auxiliary technique, allowing one to replace minor tranquilizers in the majority of cases and thus to avoid later dependency on these drugs. If the director of the Public Health Insurance reproached me for wasting public funds by seeing patients more frequently than the average of my psychiatric colleagues, he had to admit that I prescribed far less medicine than the average.

THE SACRED AVERAGE

As already mentioned, 95% of my patients were members of the Concordat of Swiss Health Insurance, which supervises the bills of every single physician and compares it to the arithmetical mean of the group of specialists to which he belongs. In 1957, we were only thirteen psychiatrists for a population of about a half-million inhabitants. Today we are 73 for the same number. When I started, doctors were paid by insurance and not by the individual patient. Accounts had to be presented for periods of 90 days. If, at the end of the year, the insurance found that I had transgressed the average beyond a margin of tolerance, it could demand a refund, after having consulted a Commission of Confidence composed of representatives of both physicians and insurance. At that time, the average number of consultations per patient and per 90 days was 3.5, and the average duration of each session was 25 minutes. If the reader remembers that I saw my analysands about 12 times each and if I add that about one third of my patients were treated analytically, he can draw the conclusion that I had gone vastly beyond the sacred bounds of tolerance. This got me into trouble with the representative of the concordat who warned me at the end of the second and the third years. Not having yielded to this demand, I had all my bills re-examined by the Commission of Confidence at the end of my fourth year of practice. It was only thanks to the fact that expenses caused by my prescriptions were considerably lower than average that I escaped a demand of refund from the Concordat. By economising on drugs, the therapist's extra expenses had been partially compensated.

Another reproach from the Concordat is typical for the short-sightedness of its then most powerful representative: I had ordered more X-ray examinations than the average. The reason was that I had found a considerable percentage of cases with neurasthenia and/or depression to be caused by focal diseases. To quote one typical example: a patient treated by a colleague for depression with large doses of the anti-depressant Tofranil was referred to me because his state of health worsened. When I asked him about somatic troubles, he complained about pain in his left calf. I palpated the place and found it warmer than the surrounding skin. Suspecting a deeply localized thrombophlebitis, I sent him to the corresponding professor. Also suspicious of a focal infection, I referred him to an otologist and a dentist. The dentist X-rayed the teeth and found three granulomata which were removed. The otologist ordered X-ray pictures for the sinuses, which were partly offuscated by a chronic infection. He found a chronic tonsillitis in addition to it. After all somatic conditions had been cured, the depression vanished like the Cheshire cat, leaving only a smile behind. Being related to a disease (depression) and not simply to dental treatment, the health insurance had to pay for all those X-ray pictures. But no other psychiatrist of Basle had ever plunged into the diagnosis and treatment of focal diseases. That was a field which the Swiss faculties of dental medicine had refused to consider seriously. All my knowledge on this subject has come from postgraduate courses organized by the German Study Group for Focal Research.

Thoroughly fed-up with being harassed by the insurance regulations, I decided to comply with their orders to the letter so as to avoid future trouble. This meant that analysis was out of the question for people who depended on insurance paying their fees. It was to be reserved for the happy few wealthy enough to pay for themselves. There exists a society for Jungian psychology in Basle, and I was the only Jungian analyst with a diploma, so one would expect private patients to come to me in flocks. In reality, they preferred to go to Zurich. The local society has sent me no more than two clients in all these 29 years. It was the Jung Institute of Zurich who helped me the most. But this could not change the fact that the bulk of my daily work consisted in "minor" psychotherapy. Analysis represented the dessert that crowned this simple daily fare, and not every day's meals were enabled by such refinement.

This had the great advantage of showing me that excellent results could be obtained without having to delve into the unconscious. First, exhaust the possibilities of minor psychotherapy before using depth-psychology, which Freud compared to major surgery! Advice: How to organize one's day, how to behave assertively, how to fix one's goals in respect to the level of aspiration, of expectation, of performance. Give advice about physical fitness[58] to combat hypokinetic disease[48] closely related to neurasthenia, and which physical exercises to practice daily in order to fight chest pain or tension headache. Simple advice appealing to consciousness and will-power combined with relaxation exercises brought highly satisfactory results in migraine, tension headache, irritable colon, and many other disturbances. This is perfectly within the reach of the family physician and does not require any advanced specialized training.

My next level of intervention was "middle psychotherapy," by which I mean hypnosis, hetero-suggestion, auto-suggestion, conditioned-reflex work as with a waking apparatus in cases of enuresis,[31] (p. 405), behavior therapy, creative dreaming in cases of nocturnal migraine[23] and non-analytical group therapy.

Brief and "middle psychotherapy" proved to be perfectly adequate for about 95% of my patients. Only in one out of twenty did I find analysis of the unconscious to be indicated. Nowadays, the cost of analysis can be assumed by health insurance. But this is optional and has to be granted by their "physician of confidence," who can refuse without any possibility of appeal. Even if he accepts, this is valid only for a short period of 10 to 20 sessions, whereupon a new well-founded demand has to be handed in and a new approval has to be waited for—the general idea being to discourage application of this method by getting both therapist and patient tired of being harassed by red tape.

This change of attitude on the part of the insurance trust has to do with a vast transformation of the Zeitgeist during the third quarter of our century.[35] Chemistry is now considered a doubtful asset. Psychology has become "in." Everybody is talking about complexes and unconscious roots of diseases. Whereas only three of us were approved analysts in 1957 and the other ten practicing psychiatrists still doubted whether depth-psychology would have any future, today's psychiatric establishment consists of trained analysts. At least 60 out of the 73 practicing psychiatrists whom we find in the Basle telephone-book of this year have received some kind of officially recognised analytical training. This change in the composition of the psychiatric corps, of course, moved the sacred average up considerably, and sessions of one hour can now be fully remunerated.

ACADEMIC CAREER

The sophisticated reader would not follow me, of course, if I tried to make him believe that all my research work has been done for the mere sake of scientific curiosity. I had been chosen for an academic career in 1946 when I presented my doctor's thesis on the anatomy of a rare disease of the brain,[1] which is now called morbus Fahr.[25] Ambition being one of my main motors, it flattered me that I received a grant from the Swiss-American Students' Exchange to move to a U.S. university for a year and do some research work on the treatment of amenorrhoic schizophrenics with sexual hormones. I had been intrigued by the sudden recovery of such a patient during my first year of internship at the psychiatric clinic of Soleures and decided to follow up along this line. In order to update my knowledge about tests, I went to the psychiatric clinic of Leiden, because the Dutch were more advanced in this respect than any Swiss psychiatric clinic. For the second phase of preparation, the biochemical part, I then worked under E. Abderhalden in Zurich as a research-fellow to learn how to determine his "defense-enzymes" in the blood, which should allow me to discover which hormonal glands were working sufficiently. Abderhalden told me that it should be a matter of life or death to me to learn as much biochemistry as possible before leaving for the American university. It seems that I took his advice too literally: after only four months of extremely hard work, I found myself coughing blood and nearly dying of tuberculosis in February of 1947.

Concomitantly with biochemical work, I had started my Jungian analysis. Jung himself refused to take me on account of his poor health and told me to consult Dr. C.A. Meier. When I moved to a sanatorium at Davos after four months of analysis, I continued to work on my dreams up there, as soon as a very slow recovery permitted. During my four years on the "Magic Mountain,"[52] I read all of Jung's books. As everybody knows, they contain an abundance of quotations in Latin and ancient Greek. Annoyed by being unable to translate the Greek quotations, I learned this language, hoping also to be able to go to the original texts one day and, perhaps, even to use them for research along Jung's lines. In this I was applying the "Reglas y consejos sobre investigacion scientifica" of the Nobel-prize winner S. Ramon y Cajal[55] which had guided me during my doctor's thesis and which resulted in a three-page flattering letter from Professor Hallervorden, the director of the Max Planck Institute for Brain Research. Ramon y Cajal strongly advises always to read the sources and never to content oneself with secondary literature. Surmising that conditioned reflex research, initiated by I.P. Pavlov,[54] another Nobel-Prize winner, would offer much in the field of psychotherapy, I also made use of my time in Davos to learn his difficult language. It was only twenty years later, when getting acquainted with behavior therapy, that I could make practical use of Russian. The concept of the "dominant," which adds an important dimension to the theories of learning, had been introduced by Uchtomski, and the book containing his research work on the dominanta was only available in Russian.[63] Contrary to Western usage, it is almost impossible to obtain any reprints from Russian scientists: Letters requesting such contacts remain unanswered. Nor are scientific texts easily available in Russia, as an employee of the chemical giant Geigy told me. It was from a book shop in Prague and not in Moscow that he had been able to get me Uchtomski's book.

While I was at Davos, the C.G. Jung Institute in Zurich was founded and C.A. Meier became its first director. So it was natural for me to matriculate myself there at the end of my time in Davos. After the propaedeutic examination, I looked around for an internship at a psychiatric clinic, in order to finish my training as a specialist. Nobody wanted me because of my "history" and the possibility of a relapse of lung TBC. Fortunately, Professor Staehelin of Basle was ready to run such a risk because he was one of the patrons of the Jung-Institute, having been a personal friend of Carl Gustav. His ultimate goal was to found a chair for Jungian psychology at the University of Basle, and make me a lecturer for this subject. He also saw to my getting an internship at the second clinic for internal medicine for one year—this training being indispensable for obtaining the diploma of a specialist in psychiatry. He even got me a grant from the National Fund to finance my further studies at the Institute necessary for the Diploma. Being on the editor's board of the Swiss Archives for Neurology and Psychiatry, he had my diploma thesis printed there.[4] "Our next step, now, is your 'Private Lecturer's Paper,' " he said, "and then you will be the first lecturer on Jungian psychology at our University."

When my Privat-Dozenten paper[12] was presented in 1962, Staehelin had completely forgotten his Jungian projects. "What a shame," he said. "There are three psychiatrists in the running to become lecturers at the same time. That is one too many. As you have gone into private practice, whereas the other two are still working at the clinic, you will understand that it is you who have to step back."

In the meantime I had become lecturer at the C.G. Jung Institute, covering such subjects as theory of neuroses, psychosomatic medicine, psychopathology, and behavior therapy. I did not lecture, however, if by this one understands reading a prepared manuscript to the audience. As a student I had the experience that I could not write fast enough to take down everything a lecturer said and that I was not experienced enough to distinguish between important and accessory information. So I decided to facilitate things for my students by letting them have mimeographed copies of my lecture and to spend the double hour at the institute on discussing difficult points which students found in the text they had received one week earlier. Thus they did not have to split their attention between listening and taking notes but could fully concentrate on the complicated subjects. It was a great satisfaction for me when, in the late 1970s, the New York group asked for some copies of my "Theory of Neuroses" which had been developed in twelve double hours in winter 1961/62.

I enjoyed lecturing very much because it forced me to think everything through once more, consulting the original papers, and because it gave me feed-back during the discussion. It was hard work, however. Every hour of lecturing demanded fifteen hours of preparation. As long as my practice was not flourishing, that was no problem. But when it became a full-time job, I had to "steal" time for the Institute, and my daily work often started at four a.m. Unable to keep this up, I asked James Hillman, the then Director of Studies, for a leave. It was granted without difficulty and tacitly extended. Until this day nobody ever asked me whether I could care to resume lecturing at the Institute. It seems that when you are "away from the window," as a German saying puts it, you are definitely out.

My ambition, however, did not allow me to retire on this statement. If Staehelin had forgotten about his Jungian plans, it might be that Kielholz, who had become professor of psychiatry in Staehelin's place, could be interested in obtaining a lectureship for me on a different basis. Kielholz has become famous for his research on depression in the meantime. In 1979 I found his books on depression even in the libraries of psychiatrists in Jordan. But in the 1960s that was not yet the case. What he needed badly at that time was a confirmation of his merely clinical findings by appropriate psychological tests, a subject hardly existent in Switzerland at that time.

Asked whether he would be interested in a lectureship for clinical psychology, he agreed. I then asked Eysenck whether he would be ready to admit me to the Maudsley Hospital for the necessary practical training. With Eysenck's positive reply I went to the director of pharmacological research at Roche, who decided that Roche was interested in Basle having the first chair for medical psychology in our country and that they would pay me for my transport and stay in London. So everything went smoothly as far as external factors were concerned. With the flying ticket and the hotel voucher already in my wallet, I was prevented from taking off by a premonitory dream:

I was following some kind of guide up to the top of Basle's water-tower. Above the brick-tower, which exists on the objective level, there was perched a huge steel-tower, the kind of construction used for television. My guide then started climbing up this tower on the sort of ladder one uses for climbing cranes. Near the very top, there was a kind of arm sticking out to the side and my guide went on to climb out horizontally towards the end of the arm which became frightfully thin towards its point. Curious about what was to come, I followed the guide until I felt the arm would no longer bear my weight. Suddenly, my guide jumped into the void and dissolved in air. Terrified, I decided not to trust him any longer and to climb back again. It took all my strength to reach the steel-tower and finally the brick-tower. I awoke sweating and with diarrhea. Even my temperature was slightly above normal.

Discovering that ambition might lead me into ruin, I cancelled everything. And that was the end of my academic career. I realized that my constitution was not strong enough for such a life. I must add that the chair for medical psychology was founded in spite of my resignation and that Professor Hobi, who has occupied it for many years, has contributed substantially to the solidity of Kielholz's research.

PSYCHOLOGICAL TESTS

If I abandoned the academic career of medical psychology, I certainly did not give up my interest in psychological testing. "The young research worker must get hold of the latest and most differentiated methods because they are least exhausted. The time spent on fruitless endeavours is not lost. If the method has a high differentiating power, then the discovered facts will gain great importance and reward our efforts with compound interest." This advice of Ramon y Cajal[55] (p. 65) has still proved so useful that my doctoral thesis of 1946 is still mentioned in a paper which appeared thirty years later.[25] I had been able to show by X-ray spectrography, a method that just came out, that the calcifications of the examined brain consisted of hydroxylapatite, a fact unknown until then and which went far beyond the then customary quantitative analysis to determine percentages of calcium, phosphorous, iron, etc., which, of course, had also to be done.

In my histopathological work, various sophisticated methods like Ramon y Cajal's neurologia coloring[1] (p. 18) helped me to see what was wrong. In the same way, I use the Progressive Matrices Test (Raven[57]) for quantifying intelligence, the Wechsler-Bellevue deterioration coefficient for measuring loss of intelligence,[67] the Wechsler Memory Test[69] for memory disturbances, the MMQ for neuroticism,[32] the Befindlichkeitsskala of the Munich Max Planck Institute for Psychiatry,[74] the Hamilton Scale[38] for depression, the Freiburg Personality Scale[34] for personality profiles, and Wittenborn's Psychiatric Rating Scales[71] for quantifying simultaneously on the three dimensions of paranoid schizophrenia, depression and anxiety. This is my present aresenal, the few tests remaining after having discarded well over a hundred different measuring instruments which I found inadequate for my purposes. The reader may look in vain for Jung's Word Association Test, for the famous Rorschach, for the nearly as famous MMPI. Not that I did not give the Minnesota Multiphasic Personality Inventory a fair chance. I even translated it into German and Roche was kind enough to print my translation on the back of the original cards. Unfortunately, Swiss patients lost patience with so long and tedious a sorting out of cards. They had come for treatment, they told me, and not for such silly stuff, which may be o.k. for Americans but which they flatly refused to comply with. Typical for the size of a company like Roche is the fact that the right hand often does not know what the left hand is doing. So Roche did not make any profit out of my negative experience. They did not even care to contact me in this respect. No, they came out with a programmed course of a German version of the MMPI in a joint venture with the editor Hans Huber[26] trying to get Swiss practitioners interested and proposing to evaluate the protocols for them on a computer basis, similar to what a medico-chemical laboratory does with blood or urine. Of course this was bound to be a financial flop.

Another test on which I "lost" an awful lot of time—about 500 hours, to be more explicit—was R.B. Cattell's IPAT 8-Parallel Form Anxiety Battery.[27] It had appealed to me because it was based on the unprejudiced and extremely sophisticated mathematical method of Multiple Factor Analysis.[62] Cattell allowed me to translate it on condition that I find an editor. I did so, cooperating with one of his pupils, J. Fahrenberg of Freiburg, but after much work, only a 5-page paper resulted. I did learn about tests though.

If the MMPI and Cattell's Anxiety Battery had turned out unsuitable for Swiss patients, the same was not true for all my translations. The Wechsler-Bellevue[67] intelligence battery, which I introduced at the psychiatric clinic of Basle, proved to be a hit. Few were the VIPs, however, who recognized its value. It was only four years later, when Huber, Bern, edited the "Hamburger Wechsler,"[68] which had been translated and revalidated in northern Germany, that the psychiatric establishment condescended to take this "American stuff" seriously. For practical purposes the main asset of this battery was the "Deterioration Quotient," which allowed the quantification of loss of intellectual functioning as a result of head-injury, thanks to the fact that it could be compared with "Average (Normal) Deterioration Quotients at Different Ages"[67] (p. 166). This quotient also permitted one to determine the amount of recovery one year after the trauma. This, of course, was of paramount importance for the assessment of annuities to be paid by insurance. Dr. H.R. Richter, one of the most prominent experts of the SUVA, the Swiss Insurance regarding accidents, soon found that I was the only one who could furnish precise and valid information. So he always sent me the cases for which he had to give an expert opinion. Being a neurosurgeon, he wrote the neurological part himself and left it to me to quantify mental deterioration.

HOW TO BECOME INDEPENDENTLY WEALTHY

When our second daughter was three years old, she developed the habit of singing at five o'clock in the morning, much to the displeasure of our neighbours! One of them so violently banged against our door that he broke his hand! We risked being evicted from our apartment. This would have meant having to find new premises for both living quarters and practice—a financial catastrophe! So we discovered that we had not paid enough attention to making money.

Having had excellent results with a "How-To-Book" on scientific research, I asked myself whether something comparable to Cajal's "Rules and Advices . . ." could not be found in this field. It was during that phase of our life that a patient brought me an issue of the *Saturday Evening Post* in whic Clement W. Stone was portrayed, a man who had made a personal fortune of $150 million in twenty years and who said that anybody would be able to do what he had done provided he used "The Success System That Never Fails."[61] First of all, I had to make a decision and to fix a time for its completion: What we needed were premises from which we could not be thrown out. So I decided to buy a house or apartment and to move within three years, i.e. by April 1, 1968. It was then that I experienced the tremendous power of a firm decision for the first time in my life. For on the prefixed date, we did move into a three-bedroom condominium and could expand in the five rooms of the practice. This gave me the opportunity of using one room for music therapy, which no psychiatrist in Basle had done thus far. It also gave me a room for group therapy, equally a novum in a free psychiatric practice. These two measures allowed me to "Do Twice as Much in Half the Time"[61] (p. 13).

This brought me to read books on management and operational research.[28] I used PERT (Program Evaluation and Research Technique), "Waiting Line Models," ogives for quantifying new patients seeking treatment. I also studied marketing manuals like that of Kotler.[47] Not entitled to advertise, I got specialists in gastrointestinal diseases interested in my therapeutic results by writing each one a letter at the end of treatment—a feedback badly neglected by most of my psychiatric colleagues. I got cardiologists to send me patients for autogenic-training groups. The outpatient department of the neurological clinic of the university sent me headache patients for group-treatment. So did the gynaecological outpatient department with frigid patients. Soon I had more groups than I could cope with unless I applied my mathematical tools in conjunction with operational research.

This supplied me with far more new patients than the average psychotherapist. Once a colleague interested in social psychiatry conducted a research by means of a questionnaire. It turned out that the average number of new patients was about seventy per year, whereas I had around 450 and the second-ranking colleague had around 250, but he also had a full-time psychologist with him.

So our financial goal was reached in due time and on the first of April 1968 we did move into a condominium. Now our daughters could not only sing early in the morning—for it was much better insulated than the rented apartment—they could listen to their stereo set at full volume without fear of being kicked out of the premises.

In September, the Soviet army invaded Czechoslovakia. This provided an incentive for us to make a new financial decision. It should be added that my family immigrated from Silesia towards the end of the last century. In the region of the rivers Oder and Neisse that form the frontier between Poland and communist Germany, Beymes owned vast farms and forests between the end of the 17th century and the second World War. Several members of the clan disappeared in Siberia or were made prisoners. Others were expropriated by the communists and some of them fled to Western Germany.[64] One 60 year-old lady crept into a wooden box and had herself smuggled into the German Federal Republic.

So my wife and I formed a plan to buy real estate in Canada—just in case! And in April 1975 I purchased a 500-acre farm in the Eastern Townships near Montreal. "To Succeed—Select Your Environment," as Stone puts it[61] (p. 115). "If You Don't Have the Money—Use OPM!" We didn't, so took the advice of Stone and Hill[62] (p. 140) and financed it mainly with Other People's Money which has been paid back in the meantime.

Not that this was easy: we nearly ran into trouble for earning too much! Everywhere health costs had risen enormously. What lay nearer to the VIPs of insurance than to cut the income of the M.D.'s? So an upper limit was fixed, beyond which the practitioner would have to have his bills examined by a commission! Having gone through all this once already, as the reader may remember, I was only too pleased when it turned out that my income was situated just underneath that value. It was a narrow escape!

So we tried to make money independently from health-insurance. I held courses on relaxation at a School for Adults. I designed a taped course with slides based on "How to Stop Smoking in Five Days,"[53] which had an immediate success rate of 80% and for which smokers paid the amount of 100 packages of cigarettes out of their own pockets. Financially this proved to be a flop. my colleagues could not be motivated to send their smokers. On the other hand, I was not allowed to advertise!

HOW I DO IT NOW

After twenty-nine years of work in his own practice, a psychiatrist is able to retire. I once closed down for nine weeks, three more than usual in summer, only to discover that the additional three weeks represented no marginal benefit. What I missed most was the feeling of being needed. I enormously enjoyed patients saying "How fortunate you're back again!" Not that hobbies are lacking. We could spend summers on our farm, which my wife likes very much, and take care of the woods, which are in bad shape. Our tenant, being a veterinary and part-time farmer, has no possibility of attending to it, and I just took a course on forests and their diseases at the University. We could spend winters in Amman where I was given permission to work with patients in order to learn the local Arabic dialect. I might devote more time to water-colour painting instead of attending courses only once a week. But nothing would give me the feeling of being needed as much as my present patients do. So I prefer to go on working half of the week with my patients and to reserve Saturday morning for science.

Let me describe a day like many others, yesterday fourth of February 1986: 8:30 a.m., the first patient arrives. He has been in my files for seven years and came originally because of anxiety reaction with fear of dying and pain in the chest. During the last two or three years he had been seeing me at a rate of one hour every other month. Recently, he had a relapse because of his mother getting leukemia. Though 37 years old, he is still very attached to his parents and extremely stressed by the thought that he might lose them soon. So he needs one hour a week again to discuss his troubles which he writes down on innumerable sheets of paper.

Second comes a new patient who was referred to me for autogenic training by Professor Battegay, head of the outpatient department. After these two hours, two more patients had been jotted down in my schedule, but they both cancelled for imperative reasons. So I work only two hours this morning instead of three. I record on my telephone tape the request to call again after 2:30 p.m. and I go shopping.

The afternoon begins with another new patient. He had heard about me from a former patient. He suffers from manic-depressive illness and his psychiatrist recently retired. He had heard about autogenic training and hoped it would help him to cope with over-eating and obesity. I give him Eysenck's MMQ to measure nervousness and the Depression Questionnaire of the Max Planck Institute of Munich[74] to quantify depression. While he is busy, I complete the file for my wife who will send him his first bill after three months. As soon as he has completed the tests we discuss his life-situation for a preliminary superficial orientation, whereupon he receives the program for the course and goes to listen to a relaxation-tape which is combined with the "Aire" from Bach's Orchestral Suite No. 3.[45]

While he is lying in the music room with his head-phones on, I welcome a third new patient with agoraphobia. She, too, had heard about me from another lady who got rid of her phobia thanks to behavior therapy. So she was by no means taken aback when, after the introductory tests and short history-taking, she finds herself between head-phones in the "group-room" absorbing the first lesson of my phobia-course which occupies her for one hour.

While she has her taped lesson, I see the fifth client of this day. He needs one full hour. He is a lecturer at the University and has been blocked in his career by intrigues. This made him slide into a depression.

During this hour the monitor on my desk shows me that a sixth patient has entered the door: a young lady lacking self-confidence while taking exams as a doctor's aid. She only comes to listen to a tape for PMA (Positive Mental Attitude) largely based on the book of Stone and Hill[62] (p. 18 and passim). In order not to leave my lecturer unoccupied during the four minutes which putting her headphones on and writing out a prescription require, I give him a problem about his career to ponder. On my return, he has not yet found a solution for it. So his time has not been lost. While in the corridor, I meet the patient with the relaxation tape. He just comes out of the music-room. He tells me exactly what he had felt: heaviness in the limbs, warmth in arms and abdomen. "Wonderful!"

When the session with the lecturer is nearly over, a seventh patient appears on my television screen. He goes to the waiting room while the lecturer makes a new appointment and leaves, without seeing the two other patients. Nor could he have been seen by them—a matter of discretion. The seventh patient of the day is a head-master whose mid-life crisis had been discussed during the five years since the beginning of therapy and whose recent depression has slightly improved under Masprotilin. Having adjusted the dosage we make another appointment two months hence.

While he is still talking with me in the consultation room, people from the autogenic training keep dropping in and sitting down in the group-room. It is their sixth meeting and I count six participants whereas there had been nine at the start three months ago. We begin punctually at 5:30 p.m. While we discuss their experiences since the last session a fortnight ago, a belated seventh patient enters. Only then do we proceed to the new exercise: the cooling of the forehead. This is not merely a subjective perception! It can be proved by a skin thermometer showing a reduction of temperature of about one degree Fahrenheit. Fortunately, people never go as far as to ask for this objective measure. Even the most critical skeptic among them is amply satisfied after measuring the increase of the temperature in his fingers during the second exercise. Once he has been shown his sensation of warmth to be more than fancy, even the obstinate doubter is satisfied. Biofeedback greatly facilitates group therapy, for the smile of superiority on the face of a doubting Thomas does not fail to exert a negative influence on the group spirit.

After one hour the session ends. While patients leave the premises, I jot down the conventional ciphers agreed upon with the health insurance. A gentleman's agreement fixes that I do not charge for more than six patients, no matter how big the group. This time, therefore, only one patient goes free of charge. In a group of fifteen, the one that starts on March 18, however, nine of them will come gratis. This is done in order to reduce the expenses of our "health service."

My working day ends at half past six, but only when there is a group. If not, I close the office at half past five so as to have more leisure time at home with my wife. We hardly ever go out in the evening. It happens that we have to struggle against sleep and cannot hold our attention alert at bridge or at the theater. This, of course, cuts us off from both social life and cultural activities. But as long as we keep up our practice, I cannot see any solution to this problem.

Only during vacations can we change our rhythm, as we found out during long stays in Canada. The question now is: how much longer shall we keep our practice? On this day we earned 1266 Swiss francs, about $625. More than half of it goes to taxes, and the rest to the fixed expenses of the practice. If we were residents of the Bahamas, income from rents and capital would leave us about the same amount of money in our hands. Therefore it cannot be for financial motives that we continue our work in Basle.

WHAT SHALL WE DO AFTER GIVING UP THE PRACTICE?

According to inside information from Swiss life insurance, a healthy man of 68 has a fifty-fifty chance of fifteen more years to live. If I continue to practice for another ten years, probability would give me nine more years to prepare for death. In the meantime, I hope that parapsychology will be advanced enough to give us an answer about the probability of there being a life after death.

But independently from science, I expect most from mysticism. It may be that Jakob Bohme, the Silesian mystic that lived from 1575 to 1624,[66] is a member of our family.[64] At that time family names were not completely fixed yet and both Beyme and Bohme were still used for the same clan.

Another fountain of mystic wisdom I hope to reach, once I know enough Arabic, is to get in touch with Sufis of our time. Not the kind you actually find in Basle now, but a group behind the periodical "At-tassauuf al 'islamij," which I discovered at the kiosk of Luxor railway station. If I write this here, it is in the hope that some insider might read it who is willing to guide me.

REFERENCES

Articles by Fritz Beyme:

1. Ueber das Gehirn einer familiar Oligophrenen mit symmetrischen Kalkablagerungen, besonders in den Stammganglien. *SCHWEIZER ARCHIV FUR NEUROLOGIE UND PSYCHIATRIE*, 56, 161-190; 57, 16-61, (1946/47).

2. Trockenkost bei der Behandlung der Enuresis nocturna.*Z.F. KINDER-PSYCHIATRIE*, 14, 16-19, (1947).

3. Over de toepassing van eidetisch verschijnselen (pseudohallucinaties) in de psychotherapie. *PSYCHIATRISCHE EN NEUROLOGISCHE BLADEN*, 4, 1-12, (1947).

4. Analyse eines schizophrenen Schwangerschaftswahns im Lichte der Forschungen von J.J. Bachofen, C.G. Jung und E. Neumann. *SCHWEIZER ARCHIV FUR NEUROLOGIE UND PSYCHIATRIE*, 80, 38-99, (1957).

5. Zum Andenken an C.G. Jung (1875-1961). *SCHWEIZER ARCHIV FUR NEUROLOGIE UND PSYCHIATRIE*, 90, 357-361, (1962).

6. Erfahrungen mit dem Psychosedativum "Librium" beim neurasthenischen Syndrom in der ambulanten Behandlung. *PSYCHIATRIA ET NEUROLOGIA*, 141, 280-286, (1961).

7. Erste Erfahrungen mit Valium "Roche" in der nervenarztlichen Privatpraxis. *PRAXIS*, 52, 734-739, (1963).

8. Vergleichende therapeutische Untersuchungen mit Valium (Roche) und Natriumbromid bei ambulanten Patienten mit neurasthenischem Syndrom. *PRAXIS*, 52, 1382-1387, (1963).

9. Hyperesthesia of taste and touch treated by reciprocal inhibition. *BEHAV. RES.THER.*, 2, 7-14, (1964).

10. Quantitative Auswertung der antidepressiven und anxiolytischen Wirkung der Kombinationsbehandlung mit Laroxyl und Valium anhand der Wittenborn Psychiatric Rating Scales bei 22 Depressiven. *SCHWEIZER ARCHIV FUR NEUROLOGIE UND PSYCHIATRIE,* 94, 429-440, (1964).

11. Verleichende therapeutische Untersuchungen mit Librium und Miltown bei ambulanten Patienten mit neurasthenischem Syndrom. *SCHWEIZ.MED. WSCHR.,* 94, 1147-1150, (1964).

12. Archetypischer Traum (Todeshochzeit) und psychosomatisches Symptom (weibliche Impotenz) Im Lichte der Forschungen von J.J. Bachofen, C.G. Jung und E. Neumann. *SCHWEIZER ARCHIV FUR NEUROLOGIE UND PSYCHIATRIE,* 92, 139-173; 93, 100-136; 94, 125-153, (1963/64).

13. El sueno de las bodas de muerte y la frigidez a la luz de las investigaciones de J.J. Bachofen, C.G. Jung y E. Neumann. Vortrag gehalten in Barcelona am 4. Internationalen Kongress fur Psychotherapie (1958).

14. Das neue Schlafmittel Mogadon und das Traumgeschehen. *PSYCHIAT. NEUROL.,* 149, 136-141, (1965).

15. Die Beurteilung des psychotherapeutischen Behandlungsergebnisses am Beispiel der Migraine. *PRAXIS DER PSYCHOTHERAPIE,* 10, 101-114, (1965).

16. El Juicio del resultado psicoterapeutico con el ejemplo de la migrana. *REVISTA DE PSICOPATOLOGIA, PSICOLOGIA MEDICA Y PSICOTERAPIA,* 5, 36-50, (1966), Lima, Peru.

17. Der Verlauf der Migran mit un ohne Psychotherapie. *PSYCHOTHER. PSYCHOSOM.,* 14, 90-117, (1966).

18. Vergleichende therapeutische Untersuchungen mit Valium und Butisol beim neurasthenischen Syndrom (Biometrische Auswertung der Versuche). *THERAPEUTISCHE UMSCHAU,* 23, 330-335, (1966).

19. Archetypal dreams and frigidity. *J. OF ANALYTICAL PSYCHOLOGY,* 12, 3-22, (1967).

20. Beyme, F. Fahrenberg, J.: Zur deutschen Bearbeitung des Anxiety-Tests von R.B. Catell. *DIAGNOSTICA,* 14, 39-44, (1968).

21. Die Psychosomatik der Kranken mit Migran und Kopfschmerz. in *JORES, A.: PRAKTISCHE PSYCHOSOMATIK. EIN LEHRBUCH FUR AERZTE UND STUDIERENDE DER MEDIZIN. UBERARABEITETE UND ERWEITERTE AUFLAGE.* Bern: Hans Huber, 1981, 213-226.

22. Psychotherapie bei Colon irritabile. *HEXAGON (ROCHE),* 11, 11-16, (1983).

23. Psychotherapie nachtlicher Migran unter Einsatz von kreativem Traumen nach Garfield. *HEXAGON (ROCHE)* Aprilnummer, (1986).

24. Verarbeiten von Angsttraumen im katathymen Bilderleben. *FOLIA PSYCHOPRACTICA ROCHE,* Nr. 26, (1986).

Other literature:

25. Barwich, D.: Symmetrische nevernkalkungen (Morbus Fahr) und ihr familiares Vorkommen. *NERVENARZT*, 47, 253-257, (1976).

26. Blaser, P., Gehring, Al.: *MMPI. EIN PROGRAMMIERTER KURS ZUR DEUTSCHSPRACHIGEN AUSGABE DES MMPI VON HATHAWAY UND McKINLEY*. Bern: Hans Huber, 1972.

27. Cattell, R.B., Scheier, I.H.: *THE MEANING AND MEASUREMENT OF NEUROTICISM AND ANXIETY*. New York: The Ronald Press Company, 1961.

28. Churchman, C.W., Akoff, R.L., Arnoff, E.L.: Operations Research. *EINE EINFUHRUNG IN DIE UNTERNEHMENSFORSCHUNG*, 4. Auflage. Wien: R. Oldenburg, 1968.

29. Cremerius, J.: *DIE BEURTEILUNG DES BEHANDLUNGSERFOLGES IN DER PSYCHOTHERAPIE. 523 ACHT-BIS ZEHNJAHRIGE KATAMNESEN PSYCHOTHERAPEUTISCHER BEHANDLUNGEN VON ORGANNEURO-TISCHEN UND PSYCHOSOMATISCHEN ERKRANKUNGEN*. Berlin: Springer, 1962

30. Dexter, J.D., Weitzman, E.D.: The relationship of nocturnal headaches to sleep stage patterns. *NEUROLOGY*, 20, 513-518, (1970).

31. Eysenck, H.J.: *BEHAVIOUR THERAPY AND THE NEUROSES. READINGS IN MODERN METHODS OF TREATMENT DERIVED FROM LEARNING THEORY*. Oxford: Pergamon Press, 1960.

32. Eysenck, H.J.: *MAUDSLEY MEDICAL QUESTIONNAIRE (MMQ)*, 2, Auflage, Gottingen: C.J. Hogrefe, 1964.

33. Eysenck, H.J.: *THE SCIENTIFIC STUDY OF PERSONALITY*. London: Routledge & Kegan Paul, 1952.

34. Fahrenberg, J., Selg, H.: *DAS FREIBURGER PERSONLICHKEITSINVENTAR, FPI, HANDANWEISUNG FUR DIE DURCHFUHRUNG UND AUSWERTUNG*. Gottingen: C.J. Hogrefe, 1970.

35. Ferguson, M.: *THE AQUARIAN CONSPIRACY. PERSONAL AND SOCIAL TRANSFORMATION IN THE 1980s*. London: Routledge & Kegan Paul, Granada, 1981.

36. Garfield, P.: *CREATIVE DREAMING*. New York: Simon & Schuster, 1974.

37. Geigy, J.R.: *DOCUMENTA GEIGY. WISSENSCHAFTLICHE TABELLEN*. 7. Auflage, Basel: J.R. Geigy A.G., Pharma, 1968.

38. Hamilton, M.: Development of a Rating Scale for Primary Depressive Illness. *BRIT. J. OF SOC. CLIN. PSYCHOL.* 1967/6, 278-296.

39. Jacobson, E.: *PROGRESSIVE RELAXATION*. 5th Impression, Chicago: University of Chicago Press, 1948.

40. Jacobson, E.: *YOU MUST RELAX. A PRACTICAL METHOD OF REDUCING*

THE STRAIN OF MODERN LIVING. 3rd Edition, New York: McGraw-Hill, 1948.

41. Jacobson, E.: *MODERN TREATMENT OF TENSE PATIENTS INCLUDING THE NEUROTIC AND DEPRESSED WITH CASE ILLUSTRATIONS, ETC.* 5th Impression, Chicago: University of Chicago Press, 1948.

42. Jores, Al: *DER KRANKE MIT PSYCHOVEGETATIVEN STORUNGEN. URSACHE, KLINIK, BEHANDLUNG.* Gottingen: Verlag fur medizinische Psychologie im Verlag Vandenhoek & Ruprecht, 1973.

43. Jung, C.G.: *UEBER PSYCHISCHE ENERGETIK UND DAS WESEN DER TRAUME.* 2. Auflage, Zurich: Rascher 1948.

44. Jung, C.G.: *DER GEIST DER PSYCHOLOGIE.* Zurich: Rascher, 1950.

45. Kleinsorge, H., Klumbies, G.: *TECHNIK DER RELAXATION, SELBSTENT-SPANNUNG.* Jena: Gustav. Fischer, 1961.

46. Klimkova-Deutschova, E., Macek, Z.: *NEURASTHENIE UND PSEUDO-NEURASTHENIE.* Berlin: VEB Verlag Volk und Gesundheit, 1959.

47. Kotler, P.: *MARKETING MANAGEMENT, ANALYSIS, PLANNING AND CONTROL.* Eaglewood Cliffs, New Jersey: Prentice-Hall, 1967.

48. Kraus, H., Raab, W.: *HYPOKINETIC DISEASE, DISEASES PRODUCED BY LACK OF EXERCISE.* Springfield, Illinois: Charles C. Thomas, 1961.

49. Leuner, H.: *LEHRBUCH DES KATATHYMEN BILDERLEBENS.* Bern: Hans Huber, 1985.

50. Lienert, G.A.: *TESTAUFBAU UND TESTANALYSE.* Weinheim: Julius Beltz, 1961.

51. Luthe, W.: *AUTOGENIC THERAPY* (6 Volumes). New York: Grune & Stratton, 1969.

52. Mann, T.: *DER ZAUBERBERG.* (2 Volumes). Stockholm; Bermann-Fischer, 1943.

53. McFarland, J.W., Folkenberg, E.J.: *WIE SIE IN FUNF TAGEN DAS RAUCHEN AUFGEBEN.* Genf: Ramon F. Keller, 1966.

54. Pavlov, I.P.: *VORLESUNGEN UBER DIE ARBEIT DER GROSSHIRNHEMIS-PHAREN.* Berlin: Academie-Verlag, 1953.

55. Ramon y Cajal, S.: *REGELN UND RATSCHLAGE ZUR WISSENSCHAFTLI-CHEN FORSCHUNG.* 3. Auflage, Munchen: Ernst Reinhardt, 1939.

56. Raskin, N.H., Appenzeller, O.: *KOPFSCHMERZ.* Stuttgart: Fischler, 1982.

57. Raven, J.C.: *GUIDE TO USING PROGRESSIVE MATRICES* (1938). London: H.K. Lewis & Co., 1954.

58. Royal Canadian Air Force: *5BX PLAN FOR PHYSICAL FITNESS.* Ottawa: Crown Copyrights, 1970.

59. Saul, L., Sheppard, E.: An attempt to quantify emotional forces using

manifest dreams: a preliminary study. *J. Am. Psychoanaly. Assoc.*, 4, 486-502 (1956).

60. Schultz, I.H.: *UEBUNGSHEFT FUR DAS AUTOGENE TRAINING, KONZEN-TRATIVE SELBSTENSPANNUNG.* 19 Auflage, beirbeitet von Prof. Dr. D. Langen, Stuttgart: Thieme, 1980.

61. Stone, W.D.: *THE SUCCESS SYSTEM THAT NEVER FAILS.* Englewood Cliffs, New Jersey: Prentice Hall, 1965.

62. Thurstone, L.L.: *MULTIPLE-FACTOR ANALYSIS, A DEVELOPMENT AND EXPANSION OF THE VECTORS OF THE MIND.* Chicago: The University of Chicago Press, 1950.

63. Uchtomskii, A.A.: *DOMINANTA.* Moskow: Izdateljstvo. "Nauka," 1966.

64. v. Uslar-Gleichen, H.: *BEYME-BUCH.* Bremen: Selbstverlag, 1971.

65. van der Waerden, B.L., Nievergelt, E.: *TAFELN ZUM VERGLEICH ZWEIER STICHPROBEN MITTELS X-TEST UND ZEICHENTEST.* Berlin: Springer 1956.

66. Waldemar, C.: *JACOB BOHME. DER SCHLESISCHE MYSTIKER.* Munchen: Goldmann, 1959.

67. Wechsler, D.: *THE MEASUREMENT OF ADULT INTELLIGENCE.* Baltimore: The Williams & Wilkins Company, 1952.

68. Wechsler, D.: *DIE MESSUNG DER INTELLIGENZ ERWACHSENER.* Bern: Hans Huber, 1956.

69. Wechsler, D.: *A STANDARDIZED MEMORY SCALE FOR CLINICAL USE.* New York: The Psychological Corporation, 1945.

70. Wheeler, E., White, P., Reed, E., Cohen, M.: Neurocirculatory asthenia (anxiety neurosis, effort syndrome, neurasthenia). A twenty year follow-up study of 173 patients. J.A.M.A. 142, 878-889, (1950).

71. Wittenborn, J.: *WITTENBORN PSYCHIATRIC RATING SCALES.* New York: Oxford University Press, 1963.

72. Wolff, H.G.: *HEADACHE AND OTHER PAIN.* 2nd Edition, New York: Oxford University Press, 1963.

73. Wolpe, J.: *PSYCHOTHERAPY BY RECIPROCAL INHIBITION.* Stanford, California: Stanford University Press, 1958.

74. v. Zerssen, D., Koeller, D., Rey, El: Die Febindlichkeits-Skala ein einfaches Instrument zur Objektivierung von Befindlichkeitsstorungen, inbesondere im Rahmen von Langsschnitt-Untersuchungen. *ARZNEIM.FORSCH.* 20, 915-918, (1970).

SPIEGELMAN'S COMMENT ON BEYME'S CONTRIBUTION

This, to me, is an astonishing paper, as I will explain in a moment. I knew Dr. Beyme, albeit casually, in our overlapping days at the Jung Institute in 1956-57, and had been impressed with his background, his languages, his four-year stay for tuberculosis at the "Magic Mountain." I was in no way prepared, however, for this account of his subsequent career, which revolved around experimental and research design, modern statistics, behavior modification, conditioning, and a familiarity with the work of Eysenck, Wolpe, Hull, Pavlov, to say nothing of psychological tests like the MMPI, Wechsler, etc. I had been endlessly indoctrinated to such a view of psychology in my graduate school days and fled to Switzerland in order to be trained in a psychology with "soul"! Not only has a Swiss counter-part, trained first in Jung's work, had to learn all the "American" methods, he has ended up suffering the fate of many American therapists, required to perform brief psychotherapy, both because of the needs of patients and the demands of insurance companies! The opposites touch, it turns out, not only East and West, but also Switzerland and America!

I am particularly appreciative that Dr. Beyme presents us with a typical work-day, which has much more resemblance to the physician's office or the behavioral psychologist's practice than to that of an analyst. He ruefully notes that less than five percent of patients undergo analysis at all, yet he still seems true to his earlier commitment (witness: his dream precluding the ascent to an ambitious further marriage with behavioral psychology).

From his experience, as well as that of the general trend in the United States, one can see a gradual development of the field of psychotherapy into several sub-branches: (1) Brief psychotherapy (or "minor" as he puts it), with crisis-management or the use of drugs for symptom-removal; (2) Behavioral therapy, such as systematic de-sensitization, hypnosis, etc. for "re-learning"; (3) Analysis, with emphasis on "working through the childhood psyche," as Jung put it; (4) Analysis, seen as both a consciousness-raiser and a path of spiritual development. The first two methods or attitudes would include by far the greater number of patients (and insurance-paid!), the latter two more rare, and more in the way of "development" or "growth" than "healing" or "teaching." What does Dr. Beyme think of that?

Finally, I note Dr. Beyme's still alive interest in the spiritual path, and I do hope that his awaited Sufi-master will happen to see his lines in this book and guide him afresh in our common search. I would also like to meet such a one myself, so that he might join my "psycho-ecumenical" group!

BEYME'S REPLY TO SPIEGELMAN
Dear Spiegelman,

You cannot imagine the pleasure your kind letter "elicited." That is why I cannot wait before "reacting." Behavioristic jargon, isn't it?

What strikes me most in your comment is the idea of "coincidentia oppositorum": taking the iner world as seriously as the outer makes the technique of reciprocal inhibition or desensitization applicable to the "microcosm." And here I use a term of my famous relative Jakob Bohme.

What do you think of the ego-hostility quotient? I avoided the term "vector," in order not to scare readers with a pique against mathematics. I am using this invention of mine in a paper where I can prove within the microcosm of one single patient that dreams without lysis precede nocturnal migraine attacks more often than those with a solution. Their ego-hostility-quotient is significantly lower! Furthermore dreams followed by migraine have a significantly smaller EHQ than dreams without subsequent migraine. Here you have the archimedian point postulated by Jung. Migraine is clearly a point outside the psychological microcosm. It is at the same time a junction point where macrocosm and microcosm meet.

SPIEGELMAN'S SECOND REPLY TO BEYME

Yes, I think that the area of psychosomatics is a particularly good one to look for the archimedian point and that you have definitely made advances, particularly in the discovery of the lack of lysis in migraine dreams. Whether this is "proof" of the archimedian point is doubtful to me. That lofty place in natural science is usually attained by "readings on a dial" and expressed with formulas and equations with predictive properties. In our field, the "readings on the dial" are rare but do occur, as for instance, in Dement's "Rapid Eye Movements" and were even investigated by Jung at the beginning of the century in the Galvanic Skin Response. Yet it is difficult to significantly link these readings with subjective events, even though it has been shown that REM's are associated with dreaming. Secondly, our formulas or equations usually turn out to be far less general than we would like, e.g. Hull's famous formulas for habit-strength. But you are definitely on to something useful and I look forward to further papers. For me, the hoped-for "coincidentia" lies in pure mathematics in such fields as topological geometry, something that I hope to work on when I, too, can retire! In any case, that our opposite paths link up at this late date suggests, to me at least, that the psyche is also trying to link up psyche and behavior!

McNAIR'S COMMENTS ON BEYME'S PAPER

This paper offers such a great contrast when placed amongst the others I have read. Had I read it by itself, I would have imagined that experimental application of Jung's psychology was not that uncommon. But alas . . .

Having saved this paper for last (at 26 pages!), I had no way of knowing that it would be reflecting the image of my initial interest in psychology as an undergraduate in social psychology and in clinical psychology in graduate school. I had been yet another immigrant from engineering, so Beyme's attitude and application is something I feel at home with. However my path has taken me from extraverted thinking (experimental) to more introverted feeling and intuition. I am much more irrational, therefore, and subjective. So it is exceptional to me how Beyme has been able to stay with his initial attitude all these years. What fortitude and durability! 900 patients!

I found it helpful to imagine this professional approach in contrast to my own. It tended to make me momentarily more rational, more reflective upon "hard data," norms, actuarials in my own experience, as well as more objective, involved with details. In other words, I became aware of just how far I have shifted toward an intuitive, feeling, introverted, subjective perspective since entering the realm of individual therapeutic psychology.

I did appreciate the differentiation of Jung's psychology from the others, and their usefulness relative to a client's needs or "IQ." I enjoyed watching the different variables arise to create boundaries. Even the notion of the Doctor as "medicine." As Jung offered a prototype for psychic analogs to physical data, I appreciated Beyme's application of this attitude to migraine headaches (I kept getting the feeling that Roche was his "migraine"!).

I found it interesting to hypothesize dream imagery from waking life's norms—and find it to be true. Although the tedium of observational details has often gotten the better of me, I have a lot of respect for those who can maintain it over time. It yields invaluable images.

One thing that doing long-term psychotherapy does not yield is a "large" population. Beyme made me think of how often I have a phantasy of how long something will take: one year, two, three, etc. I do not often say it out loud. The more experience I gain, the more I am sensitive to that image however. I am not always sure how and why it will take that long. Nevertheless, patients often do ask, "How long will this take?" I usually explore their feeling phantasy or intuition rather than my own. Hmm. That he can operationally outline his course of treatment is so different than what I can do with my process.

The "uroboric" effect of being drawn back to working with clients because of the feeling value seems to be a common theme for us. I heard my own condition echoed about Mother Nature (the farm) being the great replenishment over the whole sublimated cultural form.

"Misery loves company" . . . It was good to hear "war stories" about the National Health Service!

To have maintained such a fidelity to Aphrodite in her statistical gown, and venture into the Labyrinth of experimental R and D for now thirty years is remarkable to me. Of interest to me would be Beyme's reflections upon the "efficacy" of his "life's question" now—at 68—and, in particular, vis a vis his "Ariadne's Thread." Did Theseus actually arise here? Beyme's theme of "battling" images attracted my attention, i.e., arsenal, weapons, attacks. I have to imagine it was a consciously chosen metaphor with which to lead into his paper (not a bad one-liner!).

The notion of a riddle, puzzle, or experiment all appeal to my intuition's appetite. What would Beyme conclude, after years of this sulphuric tenacity, for experimentalism and his role as a catalyst for Jung's psychology in his realm? I am not sure how the archetypal/transpersonal enters in here. One can imagine that with each obstruction and failure Beyme met, he was driven toward a deeper realm, (with Pirithus and Erebus?) If this be the case, how does it enter into the therapeutic event?

In regard to Beyme's capacity to endure, Heidegger's notion of "Austrag" or perdurance comes to mind. Beyme's durability seems somehow sustained by some intensity that "never lets up." Thus one can survive living on the edge of difference. Jung seemed to have had plenty of it too.

It was fascinating to hear about a typical day in such detail—the (his) body must truly be the Archimedean point. To be physically able to go in and out of so many imaginal compartments and not loose this fixed point feels like a meditation event! After years of the struggle does he see the possibility of Jung's psychology entering more fully into the collective's image of experimentalism? If so, how, I wonder?

By the way, what does become of transference and/or mutual process?

It feels heroic to me to carry the notion of the unconscious and Jung's psychology forward at a time of great reluctance and a National Health Service as an adversary. Like Jacob wrestling with the Angel, what did the nature of the opposition turn out to be? Does this destiny seem to offer fulfillment now as a life's struggle?

BEYME'S REPLY TO McNAIR
Dear Dr. McNair,

Thank you for taking so much trouble in discussing my paper. Striking—the fact that our ways led in opposite directions to the point where we were to meet. Intuition being my dominant function, I had to develop discursive thinking and, more important still, feeling. Here I was very much aided by my wife.

You probably just made a typing error when you wrote: "900 patients!" It is ten times as many: 9036 up to December 22, 1986. And they continue to drop in at a rate of two or three newcomers every week. Please do not attribute it to megalomania if I insist on this detail. Paul Watzlawick shows that with increasing size, you reach a critical level where mere quantitative change dips over into a set of new qualities.

My practice no longer has the character of the consulting office of an analytical psychologist. It resembles much more the out-patient department of a psychiatric clinic. I usually see around 200 different patients in about 2,000 consultations every year. Some only turn up once a year, and others find a phone call every twelve months sufficient: a new prescription for an epileptic or a chronic schizophrenic. On the other hand, I have to spend two hours every week with a depressive lady who seems to need me, just for repeating her ever-identical complaints over and over again.

When you write that Jung offered a prototype for psychic analogues to physical illness, I presume that you mean the four dreams of the 17 year-old girl: Her imminent death from physical illness Jung deduced from "animal life destroying itself" (Wirklichkeit der Seele, p. 101). Not having been able to find anything similar in Jungian literature, I decided to seek out examples in my own clientele.

Your interpretation of Roche being my headache appeals to me as being very witty. Most of my papers have been brought into print by Roche. Even the name "Roche" appeals to me, rock-climbing having been one of my favorite sports. But mountains have lost their Kirke-like fascination after I dreamed that my anima gave me a black pearl. Which brings to your question about transference. I wrote that I found myself coughing blood and nearly dying of TB. Hard work was not the whole story: I had unsuccessfully courted a fellow student. When, at long last, I was accepted after four years of thwarted efforts, it was only to be dropped again a week later like a glowing coal: the lucky captain of a merchantman in the harbour of Brest married her and took her home with him to America . . .

A sudden cramp in my oesophagus and a weight on my chest announced: something had gone wrong! That was months before she broke the news to me. It was only a year later that the TB manifested itself. My training analysis with Professor C.A. Meier had begun a half-year before I was transported to Davos in the mountains and continued after my return three years later. One night, after several anima-dreams in which unknown feminine persons had appeared, the girl in question turned up and presented me with a black pearl. Professor Meier suggested it might be the symbol of a psychic wound turning into a scar. Its physical homologue would be the calcifications in my lungs which show until the very end of one's life where there has been an inflammation that successfully heals up.

After this account, you will have no difficulty with my model of projection: something like a shower of little arrows that resemble what the Lilliputians shot at Gulliver. Occasionally I even happen to actually feel this process. I learnt to protect myself against it to a certain degree thanks to a young lady in whose presence my pulse used to rise from the usual 80-88 up to 144 per minute. "What if I started writing down every word she said; would I thus free myself from this nefarious influence?" Jung wrote about this: "A certain influence upon the physician is inevitable and also a certain disturbance or damage to his nervous health." From Freud we know that we should never take notes in the presence of the analysand, nor did my training analysts. However, writing in this context was to provide me with a protective "spell" against these projectiles. To my great satisfaction it functioned marvellously: my pulse no longer went up . . . I know, one should not keep out of the entanglement of transference, if one believes Jung; "Freud's technique tries to get the greatest possible distance from the process, which is humanly understandable but damages the therapeutic effect to a considerable degree." Let me heretically stress that in Jung's entire oeuvre I have not found a single proof for this bold proposition. Until further evidence to the contrary I therefore stick to my own line of conduct.

This image of projection also helps me to speculate about psychometry, i.e. extrasensory perception of information hidden in an object like a ring or handkerchief of some owner. On this ground, I clear the table after each patient in order to keep the next one from becoming entangled with what his predecessor had left behind. This helps me "to go in and out of so many imaginal compartments" during the ordinary working day with so many different patients. In order not to carry these contents home, I even developed the habit of going for a swim after the morning's consultation before sitting down for any meal. Crazy as all this may seem, we should not forget that we hardly know what "stuff dreams are made of" and better be careful before running into damage.

Another transpersonal experience: a strange apperception of darkness invading the office, which gave me sufficient time to intervene, when a patient was trying to shoot me. Mr. S. had come for a psychiatric examination, ordered by the Department of Justice. We seemed to be on friendly terms until I started to record the "family history," for which I had to sit in front of a type-writer, with my face to the wall. Suddenly, the light went out! This made me look around, just in time to see that the patient was unlocking a pistol. I spare you the details of the fight and will just add that in reality the electric bulb never had gone out. Was it Hades who warned me that I was on the brink of death? Professor Staehelin asserted that it was extremely rare for a psychiatrist to be killed. But that did not prevent Professor Beck's brains from being blasted out in Basle University Hospital a few years later. I have had other life-threatening and synchronistic experiences as well.

One of my central personal problems has been with aggression. In fact, I repressed enormous amounts of it, presenting a very pacific persona most of the time. As a boy, I had always fought it out, so as to know my exact place within the "pecking-order." After having been cruelly tortured during the whole of three weeks in a scouting camp, I decided to learn Judo. I managed so well that I ultimately went to the Olympiade at Tokyo! I insist on all this because Judo, the "soft way," also represents a philosophy, "Do" being the same word as "tao" and "soft" alluding to Nr. 43 from the Tao-te-King: "The softest stuff of the world goes through the hardest."

When I only just received the yellow belt, I had occasion to defend myself against three ruffians—successfully. From that day one, I could safely run away and avoid confrontation. I knew from experience in real life that I could fight it out, if I only wanted! This brings me to your Theseus and Pirithous. Theseus did not fight it out. He had set out to pursue the one that had stolen his cattle, but when the strong men met, they did not fight. They hugged each other, making friends, without knowing who of the two was the stronger. In spite of all this wrestling, I always felt very inhibited when I had to stand for my own rights. You cannot use Judo on a landlady who charges you too much or on a traveller who smokes in your non-smoking compartment. I always give in on the ground of a Swiss proverb: "The clever man gives in and the ass stands its ground."

Let me take up just one more question: Do I see the possibility of Jung's psychology entering more fully into the collective's image of experimentalism? My next paper will be strictly along the lines Eysenck recommends: "You state a definite hypothesis, make certain deductions from this hypothesis and then proceed to carry out experiments to prove or disprove your theory. That is the scientific method, and that is precisely what is missing in all the work we have been summarizing so far." (*SENSE AND NONSENSE IN PSYCHOLOGY*, 1957, p. 170.)

Let me close with two lines from Nr. 22 of the Tao-Te-King: They say about the "wise": "He does not uncover himself . . . He does not justify himself . . . He does not brag." But that is just what I missed most at the Institute in Zurich. Our teachers never uncovered themselves. They hardly ever told anything about their therapeutic successes or failures. Nor did we ever hear anything about their personal development—the mysterious "individuation." When I once asked Mrs. Jolande Jacobi whether she knew any living person that was "individuated," she became extremely evasive. When I insisted with "sulfuric tenacity," as you call it, she finally said: "Well, perhaps Mrs. Jung." So it seems necessary for the benefit of some young student who, like me, "wants to know it," to expose himself—albeit at the possible price of ridicule.

How I Do It

by

DR. MED. ADOLF GUGGENBUHL-CRAIG

It seems to me that I was born a Jungian psychologist. I probably always tried to understand the human soul through Jungian images—but it took me a long time to become aware of this; my family and my social background did not favour Jung at all.

My father was a great admirer of Freud; he was fascinated by his work on dreams. He saw in him a kind of prophet of the Old Testament—fanatical, stimulating—whose message, however, had to be understood with certain reservations.

When I was fourteen years old, my father's sister—who had been analysed by Freud—gave me his *INTERPRETATION OF DREAMS* to read. I tried to understand my dreams—with upsetting results. I seemed to be more pathological than I realized.

Jung was not considered at all highly by my family. My mother's brother even warned me against him. "Jung is a false prophet; he flatters rich ladies, plays up to the Germans, makes anti-semitic remarks, and strives to be a friend of the high and mighty," he said.

In 1942, I began studying theology. I wanted to become a Protestant minister, but psychology interested me nevertheless. I participated in seminars given by the Christian clergyman and Freudian, Oskar Pfister. During my theological studies I did not lose my Christian faith, but became less and less convinced that I was destined to preach and convert other people. I considered studying psychology and began to read the books of the classical depth psychologists: Freud, Adler, Reich, etc. and, finally, Jung. I did not fully understand him but felt very attracted to his idea that we are not only "individuals" but are connected to a collective unconscious which has a certain structure. This idea seemed to me very convincing. I experienced myself not only as an individual soul, but as part of a larger psychological unit. My being Swiss, for instance, meant much more to me than just being the final product of external cultural and social factors.

I met Jung himself for the first time at a lecture on astrology. I did not understand him. After the lecture, one lady after another stood up and showed, by citing examples, how very clever Jung was. This was known as a "discussion"—it rather put me off.

But what profession should I choose? I worked for a while in my father's publishing firm, then as an auxiliary social worker. I studied history and philosophy, but nothing satisfied me. Then I thought: people as confused and complicated as I am have to learn a simple, straightforward profession, something enabling them to earn a living—so I decided to study medicine with visions of becoming a psychiatrist later.

During my medical studies I once attended a lecture at the Jung Club and said to myself afterwards, "This esoteric wisdom and guru-admiration is not for me."

A few days after my final medical examinations (I had married in the meantime and had a son), I emigrated to the U.S.A. The hierarchical structure of the hospitals in Switzerland disgusted me so much that I decided to do my rotating internship in Rhode Island hospital and then worked as a psychiatric resident in Omaha, Nebraska. The training was purely Freudian, but I always made clear to my colleagues that I was a Jungian psychologist, and that for me the human soul is an objective reality, not an epiphenomenon.

After four years, I continued my psychiatric training in Switzerland and started a Jungian analysis. The first question I asked my analyst was: "Can I be a Christian and a Jungian analyst at the same time?" He replied, "Certainly, if you are first a Jungian and then a Christian." I said it would be the other way round with me, but would begin analysis anyway.

During my training at the Burghölzli, I met Jung several times, mostly in seminars. I was very impressed by what he said, but not so impressed by Jung himself and even less so by the people around him. It seemed to me that most of these people admired Jung uncritically. He was surrounded by admirers but seemed to have hardly any real friends. I realized, however, that his way of approaching the psyche suited me most—even though I had been influenced for a while by the Zurich Existentialist Medard Boss.

After many hours of supervised work—which I did rather unwillingly, objecting to the magical and prophetic tendencies in the field—I opened a psychiatric practice in Zurich. I considered myself a Jungian Psychiatrist. I felt very respectful towards psychological phenomena, very reluctant to "rape" the souls of patients by the use of fast or glib interpretations. I became more and more involved with my Jungian colleagues, became a founding member of the Swiss Society for Analytical Psychology. All this seemed rather ironical to me since I never really felt "in" with the Jungians! I had no personal admiration for Jung, and Jungian psychology never became a religion for me.

In my practice, I was careful never to do too much training analysis—never more than 15 to 20% of my hours. I also saw to it that I did not limit myself to Analysis, but also practiced general psychiatry itself, including evaluation work for the court, psychotherapy with juvenile delinquents and so on. But my psychiatric work is Jungian. In evaluating the legal responsibility of a murderer for instance, I use his dreams more than psychological tests or facts from his upbringing. I have to adjust my language to that used in court, of course, but I adapt only externally.

I never consider a patient "not fit for Jungian psychotherapy," but it can happen that I find I have not the ability to reach someone's soul.

Where do I stand now, after 29 years of private practice? I consider myself a classical, conservative Jungian Therapist, theoretically and practically. It is not easy to remain a Jungian over decades. Jung gave us a psychology free from causality, confronting us with images of the mysteries of the psyche and its pathology. Not all psychologists can stand the feeling of uncertainty which this constellates in us; even for Jung this was difficult. We long for causal explanations, want to be understood as scientists, and are relieved when a new wave appears which promises us relief—developmental psychology, child trauma, harmful "mammas and pappas," body work, or whatever it may be. Most outside influences on Jungian psychology—Kleinian, Kohutian, etc.—seem to me to be a betrayal of the way Jung showed us to confront the wonderful and frightening world of the psyche.

Another way out of our uncertainty, out of the anxiety and fear of the psyche, is to become "pseudo-religious," to consider dreams as prophetic messages from the unconscious, telling us exactly what to do. "The unconscious is always right" is a phrase which upsets me when I hear it. For me the unconscious never was and never can be a substitute for God. I am not a preacher, and I know as little or as much about what the meaning of life is as my patients do.

I feel very powerless as a Jungian psychotherapist and analyst. All I can do is to assist the patient to look at his own soul and its pathology: to be aware of its potentiality and to see more desirable aims in life than merely contented survival—namely individuation, which always includes religion as well as politics. To become aware of one's collective unconscious means to become aware too of one's obligation towards family, community, nation, state, etc.

But what do I do in therapy? Very little. Firstly, I do not promise a cure. I listen to patients, usually trying to get a rough idea who he or she is by getting an outer and inner history. Not only, for example, when did he or she have their first sexual intercourse, but when did he or she have their first overwhelming sexual fantasy. The cultural, social, ethnological and religious background interests me deeply—"So, his grandparents were Catholic, Romanisch-speaking farmers from Disentis" and such matters. I try to use images from their background; for instance, if the patient comes from a working-class background and is interested in soccer, I use a football player as an archetypal hero.

I interpret dreams, fantasies, events, but mainly with images, not with concepts. I amplify more than I interpret. I try not to give advice—although patients are eager for it. I also try not to take patients' stories literally, not to believe or disbelieve what they are telling me, but to say "How your mother really is or was we don't really know. But let us look at the person you describe as your mother; she is certainly very important for you—whoever she really is or was."

The relationship to patients is important, but I see it in the frame of mutual transference, not as a personal friendship. In my case, hardly ever has an analytical relationship developed into a friendship. I can think of only two or three cases, round about the time my father died. My friends are not my analysands or patients, and analysands are not my friends.

Mutual sexual fantasies between my patients and myself I consider very important. I discuss them frequently, hopefully not for my own gratification, but to help the patient to become aware, to know how he or she affects other people. Strangely enough, I identify very often with many of my patients. I "enter" into their lives which become more and more fascinating. Their lives begin to look like a Shakespearian tragedy, a novel by Kafka, or a comedy by Moliere.

Only when patients insist, and even then reluctantly, do I consider astrology. I consider it too much an escape from our "not knowing what it's all about" situation. I use typology sparingly, too—almost ironically, as: "One could call this extraversion." Typology simplifies too much, but it does make it easier, at times, to orient oneself within the complicated psyche.

I experience my job as a very lonely one. I deal with people eight hours a day, but with people who do not and should not care about me. I am merely a figure, a catalyser to be used and then, as it were, discarded. Of course I live from my patients materially and psychologically. They give me the chance to observe life—make me a "voyeur"! Through them I participate in business, politics, science, human tragedies and comedies. I live vicariously through my patients.

I often feel very tired. Tired of seeing patients, angry and discouraged and overwhelmed by a hopelessness. At such times, I wish I had chosen a "decent" profession—something useful like a road engineer or a builder of bridges. Or I feel frustrated materially when I see that most of my former school mates earn twice as much as I do—being neither more intelligent nor giving more libido to their work.

I am not a missionary. Few of my patients become Jungians. This often gives me an inferiority complex. Then I tell myself my duty is to the patient's soul and not to Jungian psychology. I do my best to help the patients to find their soul, and I do not know any psychology which is better equipped to do this than that of Jung.

After all these years, I am still a staunch and passionate Jungian psychiatrist—and still no admirer of Jung himself.

COMMENT ON GUGGENBUHL'S CONTRIBUTION BY SPIEGELMAN

I am touched by Guggenbuhl's presentation, strangely moved by his honesty and integrity. I feel my attitude is similar to his in many ways (e.g. I see myself as a "classical" Jungian, doubt whether Klein and Kohut offer much to the Jungian attitude, focus upon mutual transference and share sexual fantasies), yet quite different (I admire Jung greatly, am an active therapist). Yet these similarities and differences are but the superficial rumblings of a deeper commitment that I believe we both share (as do others in this book) in the fundamental integrity of the patient and the psyche.

I am reminded of how I met Adolf in the first place in Zurich, around 1956 or 1957. I had heard that he was being recognized as an Analyst without graduating from the Jung Institute. Angered that physicians apparently did not respect my esteemed school, I objected. I felt that neither personal analysis nor my own clinical psychological training were sufficient for recognition as an Analyst; therefore medicine, even psychiatry, was not sufficient either. I even objected that physicians did not have to take the Institute examination in psychopathology! My inferiority complex and resentment in relation to physicians stood in the way, but when I met him I came away with a far different viewpoint. Here was a bright, honest, well-trained person who was strongly individual, not at all inflated, had a tremendous eye for the shadow, and was just as committed as I was. It turned out that his not formally graduating from the Institute resulted in his giving a lot of his energy to that fine place later on, including becoming the chairman of its governing body, the Curatorium! Indeed, Adolf has given enormously to the entire field, both administratively (serving as President of the International Association of Analytical Psychology), and literally (writing several excellent books, among which his *POWER IN THE HELPING PROFESSIONS* is considered a classic in non-Jungian circles also). So much for superficial judgements. I have always been an admirer of his perception, his fairness, his diplomatic capacity to reconcile differences despite his bluntness and coming to the point.

I find myself drawn to ask only one question: How does he understand his peculiar experience of being so deeply drawn to what Jung had to say about the psyche and not liking the man himself? What does it mean, to a man who is so skilled in shadow-knowledge, that this discrepancy exists? Did he, like his father and uncle, see Jung's shadow all too clearly, or is it that Guggenbuhl just sees the true depth of Jung and is put off by that same shadow?

I have to conclude with a personal statement: Adolf, I loved what you wrote. My wife, Ryma, did too. It is a source of great pleasure to me to count you as a colleague and friend, and I, like you, regret that distance precludes more contact. You once wrote, in your inimitable way, something like: "Why is one burdened with people one does not like who live close, when those one does like live far away?" I wonder if it is that same discrepancy of existence, that split (like Jung and his shadow) with which we deal all those hours of the day, which contributes to making us tired.

REPLY TO SPIEGELMAN BY GUGGENBUHL

The question Spiegelman asks is: How do I understand my peculiar experience of being so drawn to what Jung had to say about the psyche and not liking the man himself? I would like to answer this by asking a counter-question: Does one have to like the man Picasso if one likes his paintings? Or the reverse: One of my best friends has a very negative attitude toward the Christian religion, but I like him very much all the same.

That I did not like Jung is certainly my personal problem. I strongly like or dislike people. Explanations of my feeling, however, often turn into rationalisations. Here may be one of the rationalisations for my personal negative feelings towards Jung himself: I felt that he was so fascinated by the psyche as a phenomenon, he wrestled so much with angels and demons, that there was not much space left for personal relationship, outside of the framework of master and student, teacher and admirer. This put me off.

McNAIR'S COMMENTS ON GUGGENBUHL

My own initial tack into clinical psychology was on the winds of existential philosophy, thus I enjoyed reading this paper immensely. I can only applaud Guggenbuhl's capacity to maintain the objectivity, the inevitable distance and isolation we as human beings must live in, without resorting to emotional/magical "resolutions." This has the feeling of an anti-hero to me: negation, inadequacy, helplessness, powerlessness, inferiority—all very affirming and seemingly Christian first, then Jungian, as he said.

Whether it was the result of his work with Boss or a personal position, Guggenbuhl's attitude sometimes carries the weighted tone of existentialism and the vacuous feeling of the voyeur. I know for myself that existentialism became a relevant philosophy during a period of my life when imposition and negation were the dominant attributes of my life's context (in my 20s). It has retained a constant value. My feeling associations to this were Rilke and Camus. Is there a direct relationship between "born to be a Jungian Analyst" and "comdemned to be free" (Sartre)?

There did feel to be a strong feeling pulse of Eros moving through the comment about friendship with clients at the time of his father's death. The time surrounding my own mother's death was equally difficult to contain.

Insular is a quality of introversion that I have come to acknowledge within my own nature; I also associate it with the Swiss. The feeling of distance it can create on a phenomenological level can feel like a vacuum to others. Yet if "no" gives "yes" its meaning, then being does arise out of nothingness. From my personal experience, I know Guggenbuhl to be a warm and generous human being who touched my life deeply at a desperate moment of anguish. I prefer to believe that I preserved his soulful impact as an echo within me, and not that I "discarded" him!

Guggenbuhl's remarks bring up some shadow reactions for me personally. The different transference problems and "projective identifications" which inevitably, over time, lead to some depth of kinship and intimate relatedness are all under the jurisdiction of an "ending" which I am reminded of constantly by the "end" of a session. Nonetheless, I do, on occasion, find myself ruminating about "I wonder what has become of so-and-so? It must be 10-15 years now." It feels as though a good amount of my soul and Eros went into that "work" and relationship. I know I have come to rely upon Mother Nature to replenish my vitality for what has turned out to be a vocation with considerable emotional and physical requirements. Guggenbuhl feels secure in not placing that burden upon his clients. So where does it end up? My questions for Guggenbuhl would be these:

1. To me, the notion of the "witness" brings with it a different spirit than that

of the "voyeur." Is this a matter of "choice"?

2. The attitude of "willing sacrifice" comes to mind when he mentions all the things the work isn't. How is your Eros able to re-generate itself? What physical symptoms are the analog of your approach?

3. It feels important that your dislike of Jung is expressed so emphatically—I just don't understand the substance of it. Would you elaborate?

4a. Did Adler's psychology have any particular lasting value?

4b. How is the existential attitude not a form of "solution"?

REPLY BY GUGGENBUHL TO McNAIR

Joe McNair asks so many interesting questions that I think it best that I limit myself and concentrate on the ones which seem to me to be the most important.

How is Eros able to regenerate itself?

I am inclined to say that it is a matter of grace—sometimes Eros seems to fade away and sometimes he reappears. His appearance is very much connected with my relationship to my family and friends. What you call "regeneration" probably happens there. With patients and analysands, I very often have the impression that I have to give my blood, that I lose blood and often become weak and helpless. Some kind of blood transfusion flows from me to the patient. I don't expect to get any blood back. I know that transference can not feed me, can not really give me Eros, because it is not meant for me. However, patients often give me very stimulating insights, new perspectives on the world of the psyche. Dreams of patients, their tales and life-stories, bring me in contact with the psyche once more, in a non-personal, transcendental way.

I don't know if there are any physical symptoms necessarily analogous to my approach—maybe the cardiomuscular system has to suffer, the heart, the veins, the arteries—the organs in which the blood circulates. I had two coronary infarctions and a bypass operation, and I am not sure if these were the result of overambition and too much aggression, by which psychosomatic medicine often "explains" afflictions.

I am glad that you mention the witness as something different from the voyeur. Would the voyeur be the shadow of the witness? If so, then there are two different attitudes which cannot be separated, they belong together.

And now the delicate question about my so-called dislike of Jung as a human being. I always had the impression that Jung had more admirers around him than friends. He appeared to me to be a master among disciples. People imitated him, spoke like him and acted like him. So, when I saw Jung, I felt a strong pressure to become an admirer. I felt the only way to approach him was by admiration. But I can only like somebody, feel comfortable in someone's company, when I am an equal, a comrade or a friend. All of this might have to do with my own psychology; the archetype of the master and disciple, of Guru and admirer, extinguishes in me the Eros of relationship. So, I disliked Jung in the sense that I resisted the pressure to admire him and yet had the impression that admiration was what he wanted.

Probably, I am not able to like a genius. I can take over his ideas, be stimulated, even admire them, but I can not relate with genuine feelings. I think it is one of the tragedies of a genius, that he is usually only admired and not loved. In that way, he is very much alone. Admiration is far removed from relationship to Eros. We stand in awe and fear before God, but we relate lovingly to our fellow human beings. Admiration seems to be a hybrid of these two attitudes which I can not manage.

The question about Adler I have to leave open; the answer would be too long. But how about the existential attitude as a form of solution? Soren Kierkegaard claims that existence is fear, loneliness and tragedy, and experiencing these, we might—as a solution—become Christians.

I do not like the word solution used in context with psychology or psychotherapy. To look for solutions might lead us astray—like a jack-o-lantern, an "ignis fatuus" might lead us astray. But I am not a disciple of Kierkegaard, either. I enjoy life, and enjoy my work, and I hope that this joy infects patients—sometimes.

What the Hell Am I Doing While Sitting With Analysands in My Office?

by

DR. PHIL. MARIO JACOBY

I am grateful to Marvin Spiegelman, the editor of this book, for providing me with an opportunity to ponder over the above question. As I have just reached my 60th anniversary and have been struggling for way over twenty years with the ups-and-downs of our strange profession, this opportunity comes at a good time in my life. I am also pleased that this paper does not have to take on a "scientific" air. The expectation to talk about my own views and experiences in a personal way suits me very much. For once, I don't have to mention what Jung, Freud, Neumann, Fordham, Winnicott, Kohut and others said and to prove by footnotes that I have not falsified their original statements by mingling them with my own thoughts and fantasies. Yet I also have to mention here that the ideas and propositions of these great psychologists were most influential on the MIXTUM COMPOSITUM of my own ways of being with patients.

In order to give an adequate picture of my present professional attitude I first have to talk about some experiences which were crucial for the way it developed. It was at the age of about 18 that I first heard about Sigmund Freud and his mysterious but apparently questionable findings. As I had become curious, I could not wait to read his *INTRODUCTORY LECTURES ON PSYCHO-ANALYSIS*; this proved to be an immense discovery with great impact on me. Here was somebody who had the courage to uncover in a convincing way the "truth" lying behind the conventional bourgeois spirit which, I felt, had been so suffocating to me.

Having grown up since my fifth year under the care of some relatives in a small provincial Swiss town, Freud was an incredible eye-opener, giving me the permission "to see." It was thus a great relief to see through the hypocrisies of the rigid sexual morality one had to conform to, which was, at the time, also backed up by the churches. Freud meant for me the real and genuine ethical attitude, having the value of truth at its pinnacle, against all the lies and repressions on which the general outlook of my surroundings was based. His uncoverings were at the same time a great support in my own attempts to get to know some hidden parts in myself.

I also vaguely knew that a famous psychiatrist with the name of Jung was living in Zurich, not too far from our town. He was supposed to have known Freud, but to have quarreled with him and also to have written on psychoanalytic matters, though in a much different way. Yet all I heard about his present situation from my Jewish relatives and from others was that this Jung had sympathized with the Nazis and consequently had an anti-semitic prejudice. Of course, these people had never read a line of Jung, but, during the war, all that counted was the attitude somebody had towards Nazi Germany and its horrible anti-semitism. Thus my aversion against having anything to do with Nazism prevented me from getting to Jung's ideas at that time.

In spite of my continuing fascination with all the enlightenment brought about by Freud's penetrating analysis, I increasingly felt that there were many more sides to life which I needed to explore. I was drawn at the same time to the world of music, poetry, literature, the visual arts and the theatre and found Freud's explanations of them flat. What was I to make of my experiences of passionate love; of the immense sadness, the "Weltschmerz," that crept in while listening to Schubert's wonderful "Winterreise"; of Goethe's poetic formulations about the mysteries of the human soul and its dark craving to find the right path towards the light; of Hesse and Thomas Mann; of J.S. Bach's "St. Mathew Passion," which had an overwhelming impact and left me with the conviction of having found my own bridge to the transcendent world? All these experiences were too rich and "numinous" (a word which I did not know at that time), to be coldly dissected and reduced to its primal cause, being "nothing but" the sublimation of some sort of drive-conflict. I instinctively refused to try to fit them into the frame of Freudian "truth," even if it meant being in a state of resistance. Consequently, I put psychoanalysis in one drawer of my psyche, thus allowing for life—with its inevitable vicissitudes and various intensities—to flow into some of the other parts and to take its own course. As soon as I ran into emotional difficulties and psychological problems in myself or in my friends, though, I tried to open that drawer to have access to a more or less amateurish way of psychoanalytic interpretation.

About eight years later, while in London studying to become a concert violinist, I came across a book of Jung (THE RELATIONS BETWEEN THE EGO AND THE UNCONSCIOUS), which impressed me and helped to revise my prejudice to a certain extent. But the real breakthrough to Jungian Psychology came only at the age of 30, after I had begun my own analysis. At this point, I want to mention that I did not enter analysis because I wanted to train as an analyst, or because I wanted a living experience of Jung's psychology. Neither was it my conscious intention to seek analysis in order to get to know myself better and to embark on a journey towards individuation. I simply went into analysis because I badly needed it in its pure therapeutical sense. The rest followed by itself once the process had begun to unfold. Today I still like to maintain that such a plunge into our field out of urgent psychological necessity may be a valuable beginning for a future analyst. If we do not know, by experience, how the pain stemming from various neurotic wounds really feels, how can we have empathy with the specific sufferings of our patients?

I also did not choose my analyst on account of her Jungian orientation but because of her specific personality. The fact that she happened to be a Jungian only gradually became very important. Various outer and inner circumstances had brought me to the baroque glamour of Jolande Jacobi's consulting room. Among the many things I learned in the course of our analytic encounter, there was something very crucial for my further understanding of analysis—something which occurred in spite of her very directive style and her attempts to manage the life of her analysands. I mean the following: It did not take me very long to get a rather clear perception of Jolande as a real person, of her particular originality but also of her shadow and her limitations. Actually such an awareness was not too difficult because she was open and spontaneous and did not hide her reactions. But being aware of this reality did not seem to influence my most vivid fantasies and dreams which came up in connection to her and which took on, at times, quite archetypal dimensions. I knew about her human weaknesses and felt critical of them, yet, somewhere in my fantasies she was at the same time an omnipotent goddess protecting me in all my life circumstances, and in certain dreams she was even able to perform supernatural miracles. These experiences showed me what the phenomenon of transference is about—and this in contrast to a real human relationship based on mutuality. Our psyche makes use of a real person for the sake of its unconscious purposes—be it, hopefully, for the sake of its individuation urge or, at its worst, to create psychotic delusions. Transference feelings and fantasies may take their course sometimes regardless of adequate reality testing by the ego.

Today, thinking back on my relationship to Jolande Jacobi (which lasted until her death in 1973, long after the analysis had been terminated), my memories bring up much less of the critical attitude I held against her intrusive style of analysis. Instead, there arise feelings of deep affection for her, as the colourful person she was.

Not long after starting the analysis I began to live through some years of complete fusion with Jung's miraculous world of Dreams, Gnosticism, Alchemy, Myth, and Mysticism. Jung's ideas provided answers to my most urgent questions and incorporated those sides of me which had not found their place in the Freudian world. I eagerly tried to absorb the whole bulk of Jungian findings. But, as I saw later, such an endeavor also has its drawbacks. Being pumped up by so much knowledge about the background of mankind's conscious strivings and about the mysteries of the living unconscious, can lead to a kind of inflation and to a missionary zeal to preach about those crucial insights to people, whether they want to hear them or not. What happened in my case was that Jung really provided the soul-nourishment I seemed to have needed. But his extensive body of research provided, at the same time, many ideas which—to be honest—had little to do with my own genuine concerns and were beyond the scope of my own experience. Thus, instead of absorption and integration of knowledge leading to a true "Aha-experience," it led to an inflation. (I do not think I am the only one to whom this happened. It can quite frequently be observed among Jungians.) That I really was in an inflation became apparent by the fact that I could not bear to hear the slightest relativization of a Jungian idea. I also looked down on the "superficial rationalism" of the teachers at the University, who did not seem to know anything about the depth of the unconscious. This, of course, made my obligatory studies at the university quite unbearable. The reverse side of this inflation was that, in bouts of depression, I suddenly had to doubt the whole endeavor and consider Jungianism a grandiose illusion. Soon afterwards, however, inflation took the upper hand again and the back-and-forth continued.

On the whole such an inflationary contempt of everything non-Jungian was rather encouraged by the atmosphere of the Institute at that time. The analysts giving courses and seminars were still Jung's direct disciples and the place was— understandably so—impregnated by a "Jungian spirit," as mediated directly by Jung's admirers. Jung himself, who was still alive then, seemed to be a wise, old "Mana-personality" living in a mysterious tower somewhere in the woods, in an imaginary world far away from the chores of our everyday banalities. But he seemed to give generously of his wisdom to some of our teachers at the Institute, who were the only ones who had the privilege of receiving direct messages from him.

Yet there came the day when Jung himself in flesh and blood appeared at the Institute. When he felt physically well enough, he wanted some discussion afternoons with candidates to be arranged. The man was way over eighty at the time but impressively alive, witty, human, natural and sober. He seemed to dislike slightly all the adoration going on around him, but, maybe in some corner of his soul, he also needed and enjoyed it. Although he gave the impression of being physically rather frail and had to talk in a faint voice, he still emanated great psychic strength from an inner depth. In the midst of all my own feelings of admiration for his extraordinary presence, I caught myself thinking: What a relief that I do not have to work analytically with this man. As my thoughts continued, I wondered whether his personality was not too overwhelming to allow enough space for his analysands and disciples to find their own true inner voice.

Today I feel that these years of full immersion in this Jungian world were essential for my personal and professional development. Not only did I learn through my own experience what inflation, idealization and merging with a Guru-figure feels like, but I also absorbed much of what is considered a "Jungian way of being," living in touch with the unconscious and being ready to read its signals.

The necessary and, as I see it, healthy disappointments began gradually while seeing my first patients. I slowly became aware that my fascination with Jung's ideas prevented me in many instances from being there enough for my patients, in the very place that they needed me to be. I expected them to relate to the unconscious, to take their dreams seriously, to do some inner work and to accept Jungian interpretations—otherwise I felt disappointed and doubted my capacity as an analyst to convey the essence of the whole endeavor. Thus I sometimes lacked empathy for their own immediate concerns and had an attitude of "knowing better." Though I know that such an attitude is a distortion of Jung's ideas on psychotherapy—as far as they are published—I also don't think I am the only one who fell into this missionary trap at times.

Interestingly enough, this period of gradual deflation was accompanied by a series of pertinent dreams. The figure of Jung himself had sometimes appeared earlier in my dreams, often at crucial moments. Now, however, I had peculiarly frequent dreams of Jung in which he did or said something unusually strange, not understandable, and sometimes incoherent. This was difficult to interpret. I thought, pondering about the dreams, that Jung may have uttered a kind of Zen Koan and that it was up to me to find the hidden wisdom. Eventually my analyst at the time (Dr. H.K. Fierz, who was known to have usually a pronounced understanding for everything paradoxical) dared to say: "It seems that your inner Jung has become quite senile." I had to admit to myself that this was in fact the case, and that my Jung image needed renewal.

After having graduated from the Institute, I began to work psychotherapeutically with heavily damaged people in psychiatric hospitals. I soon realized that I was barely equipped to work effectively with this kind of patient and that I had to learn much more about psychotherapy. This was not restricted to the patients of the clinic alone; in my growing practice I also felt the need to get better skills and a greater precision in my understanding of what was going on in my analysands. Thus I tried to absorb much of the literature on psychotherapy which was available in the late 60s. I recall Frieda Fromm-Reichmann's *INTENSIVE PSYCHOTHERAPY* and books of Searles and Balint, just to mention a few. My earlier interest in Freudian psychoanalysis was reawakened. In contrast to most of my colleagues at that time—who thought that the Fordham school in London was regressing back to the Freudian system which Jung had long ago overcome, and that the London group could therefore not be called "Jungian" in its true sense, and that it was therefore not worth bothering about—I read the London Journal and publications of the London School of Analytical Psychology with great interest. I found Fordham and some of his followers very stimulating and had many personal discussions with them. For a time I also had quite an extensive correspondence with Michael Fordham on matters of difference in analytical approach.

What I had found most valuable was that the London School had developed skills to reach the child within the adult patient by using transference/countertransference interpretations in a most refined way. Fordham's contribution to and ideas on child development, a field of great importance which had not been covered by Jung himself, seemed impressive and significant to me. Because of their somewhat "heretical" nature, they also had the effect of shaking up and liberating an attitude which tended to lead to indiscriminate worship of the unconscious. At the same time I also had to admit to myself that I found his publications rather dry and not appealing enough to my artistic temperament. I could also never bring myself to be keen on Melanie Klein's "breast-penis mythology," which had been incorporated, to some extent, into Fordham's work. Klein was just never convincing enough for me. In contrast, I felt a great affinity to Winnicott's approach, to his way of connecting sensitively to the mother/child dyad as it constellates itself in the analytic situation.

The struggle for me was now to reconcile the Jungian approach I had been trained in with the insights I had newly acquired. It was clear to me that I did not want to "throw out the baby with the bathwater." Some specifically Jungian dimensions were crucial to me and had become deep convictions. I am thinking here above all about the implications of Jung's psychology of religion with its stress on the personal experience of the "numinous." However, it was precisely in this domain where the dangers of Jung's psychology also became most apparent. I realized that for certain people Jung's formulations evoke superstitious beliefs, magical thinking, uncritical idealization and even deification of the unconscious. Some are unable to experience the contents of the unconscious truly symbolically, in an "as-if" fashion. They have to concretize them instead as fixed things or definite inner persons. Needless to mention here all the many people who have no access whatsoever to the unconscious, who can make neither head nor tail of something which is not tangibly "real." But all these observations did not mean a devaluation of Jung's genius and discoveries, for they themselves remained beyond question for me. The fact that they gave rise to so much superstition and concretistic magical thinking bothered me, however, and forced me to try and find some possible explanation.

It was mainly Winnicott's descriptions of the "transitional" objects and the "intermediary space" which made me realize that the capacity for symbolic experience is based on complex maturational processes. If these processes get severed in early infancy, for whatever reason, a living relationship to the symbolic dimensions will be more or less impaired. I saw that it is therefore unrealistic to expect every patient to benefit from Jungian dream interpretation. Many Jungians, including myself, repeatedly become discouraged if patients just do not have "the right attitude towards the unconscious"—as the saying goes. But there is no use in becoming pedagogic or irate about it, for that just shows the analyst's helplessness. Those patients need to be met wherever THEY are. They need the space and often the right kind of "holding" in the hope that some maturation may take place. It usually takes time, together with some unobtrusive encouragement, before they are able to "use" the analyst according to their psychic needs. It is the analyst's task to answer these needs sensitively, understanding them via his empathy and his countertransference reactions.

In general I very much dislike extreme positions, because they are always one-sided and therefore never do justice to a comprehensive grasp of the psyche and its complexities. I rather prefer to build bridges and tend to stress more the common ground of different approaches than their sharp differences. There are many varying viewpoints, each has its merits, and each may bring other aspects of psychic experience into focus.

I feel it important to be flexible enough and, over the years, have tried to assimilate from different psychotherapeutic approaches what was congenial to my way of being and doing analysis and left out what did not agree with me.

Essential throughout this time has been for me to maintain the depth of Jung's approach and the inner experiences it can further. For certain patients a more "classical Jungian analysis" has definitely been fruitful, and in this respect I received decisive assistance from M.L. von Franz during several years of regular control work.

As I look back now it seems clear that I was in a phase where some experimenting, with careful observation of the effect this had on my patients, was necessary—trying all the time and to the best of my knowledge, not to do any harm. During this time I dreamt that Jung was a little boy, and that I had been invited to visit him. We had a very good time together, playing all the games we imaginatively invented. This dream had an encouraging effect: apparently the image of my "senile" inner Jung had been renewed after several years. Pondering on this dream, I had to think of a passage where Jung writes:

> My aim is to bring about a psychic state in which my patient begins to experiment with his own nature—a state of fluidity, change and growth where nothing is eternally fixed and hopelessly petrified.
> (Collected Works, Vol. 16, Par. 99)

Winnicott's *PLAYING AND REALITY* fitted in here as well. I also had begun to read the works of Kohut and was very much in favour of his idea that playfulness must be the basic attitude of creative science, in contrast to the attitude of dogmatic religion. This again is not far from Jung's statement that scientific truth is a hypothesis which might be adequate for the moment but which is not an article of faith to be preserved for all time. Having a playful attitude towards images, ideas and concepts may avoid the pitfall of interpreting the patient's conflicts and experiences within a fixed system of theoretical beliefs. Concepts are needed, of course, as a basis for explaining empirical data (i.e. interpretation). But whether those concepts have a more Jungian, Freudian, Winnicottian, Kohutian or whatever flavour can be left to whatever will be constellated and is fitting a given analytic situation.

Kohut became important enough for me to spend much time and energy on his work, in order to grasp what he really wants to convey. In spite of his rather stiff writing style, I could not help feeling a certain kinship to his views. He speaks to the feeling realm of analytical practice and about many subtleties in the transference. This is in contrast to Jung, who arrives at his insights mainly through his experience with and amplification of the wealth of images from the unconscious. As I am most probably a "feeling type," my intense "auseinandersetzung" and experimenting with Kohut's approach was very helpful in refining my own analytic tools. It also resulted in my recently publishing a book on Individuation and Narcissism which I hope will be translated into English some day.

Some aspects of my approach in practicing analysis have been published in several books and articles. They show my struggle to integrate certain aspects of psychoanalytic views into my way of working as a Jungian analyst. I have done this over some years here in Zurich all by myself. Interestingly enough, some Jungians in the United States have done quite the same thing, in their own way, during that time. It seems to have been in the air. Today, attempts to integrate psychoanalytical approaches (not to mention Gestalt, bodywork, psychodrama, Transpersonal techniques, etc.) into the openness of Jungian psychology seems to have become quite a trend—for better and also for worse.

But let me return to the question of "What the hell am I doing while sitting with patients?" In order to give an answer to this question, I first have to be aware of the fact that there are always discrepancies between what one thinks one is doing and what one actually does. (There might even be illusions which fill this gap.) If, on top of that, one tries to write about analysis, one is again a step removed from the real experience of the analytic encounter, because one has, by necessity, to be selective. It is therefore nothing but honest to warn readers that they cannot get the full and true picture of how an analyst really works in his practice from his publications.

Having said that, there is only one thing I can say for sure: Practising analysis for way over twenty years has never become just a routine for me. Routine would be something deadly, boring, uncreative and probably also ineffective. Of course I get bored at times, but if so, I try to see this boredom in context. By this I mean that I attempt to see most experiences during the sessions as connected to the common therapeutic field which is created by and contains the patient and myself. In other words, I reflect on what this boredom may tell me about our relationship at the moment—already then my feelings of boredom have been overcome to a certain degree. It is not boring to try and get a handle on issues like: Why am I out of tune with this patient? Does he feel empty? What is his resistance about? What is his fear of involving me? etc. By putting my accent on the field of interactions, I do not, of course, want to say that everything has to be interpreted rigidly in this light. On the contrary, much differentiation is needed here, because I am likely to bring moods, complexes or preoccupations, consciously or unconsciously, into the session, which may be purely my own and having nothing to do with the patient. One cannot always be fully receptive and ready to enter the patient's inner world. Thus the question always needs careful consideration, whether and when countertransference feelings belong to the common field, thus having a "syntonic" value (Fordham), or, whether and when they stem from one's own complexes and or one's own subjective state. The sensitivity and alertness needed for grasping what is going on may not only yield subtle insights, it also prevents deadly routine.

To focus primarily on the interactions and their meaning in the common therapeutic field is, to my mind, in agreement with the discoveries of Jung. He really was the first to talk about analysis as an alchemical vessel and also wrote that:

> By no device can the treatment be anything but the product of mutual influence, in which the whole being of the doctor as well as that of his patient plays a part.
>
> (Coll. Wks. Vol. 16, Par. 163)

But the "classical Jungian analyst" and, probably Jung himself, does not seem to make much differentiated use of this crucial insight in daily practice. For me, however, the question of how to use the mutuality of transference/countertransference interactions analytically in a therapeutically productive way has become a key issue. Once I have become aware of my own inner countertransference reactions, the question as to what to do with these hunches comes up. Are they hints about what is going on in the patient, what is going on in myself, or both? Shall I bring them into our dialogue and, if yes, in what way? Or, is it the wrong time, and then would it be counterproductive? In order to determine what to do with one's hunches, a refined empathy is of help in anticipating how a patient may receive an interpretation. Obviously one is bound to make mistakes— sometimes for better and sometimes for worse. I usually try to make some notes in the evening about the content and atmosphere of each session during the day. I mainly try to retrace and to retain the moments and under what circumstances I felt tactless, intrusive, beside the point, moralistic, lacking in empathy, or just using empty routine interventions, etc. I think that, as analysts, we need to face the blunders we commit but with enough tolerance towards the fact that we cannot be "ideal" analysts. Such an ideal in its inhuman grandiosity would anyhow be counterproductive. Jungians are indeed familiar enough with the warning of not identifying with the archetype of the Divine Healer. But, on the other hand, this warning should also not be an excuse for too much leniency towards oneself and for a careless attitude towards one's patients. I feel that I can deal realistically with my own "mistakes" if I try to see them in the context of the dynamics constellated between the patient and myself during the session. In other words, if I can ask myself what had prompted me, in that particular situation, to put forward a questionable or indiscriminate intervention, I may become aware of a complex-influence which was working either in me, in the patient, or between us, an awareness which is ultimately of benefit to both of us.

In this connection, I would also like to say a few words about handling dreams. To my mind, even when pursuing the method of interpretation on a subjective level, it is of therapeutic value to consider the possibility that unknown inner dream figures may also have their influence on the here-and-now of the analytic situation. Of course, it would be naive, clumsy and probably (but not necessarily!) wrong if I were to interpret, let us say, an unknown, persecuting male figure in the dream of a woman to represent me, the analyst, in person. If I were to tell the patient that she must feel persecuted by me, she might rightly say that this is not the case and could, in time, even feel irritated by my obvious egocentricity in always relating her unknown dream figures to myself. Since the dream says nothing about me, the analyst, being the persecutor, I would not give such an interpretation. But, I may sense during the session that she is withdrawing into herself, some feeling connection between us might be interrupted. This may be a sign that unconsciously she needs to defend herself against certain thoughts which want to intrude (represented by the persecuting dream figure) and, let us say, disturb the image she holds of herself. If this image were to crumble, she would fear the loss of self-esteem and of the esteem she gets from her surroundings and, thus, also from me. Her defence against that animus figure unconsciously draws her libido away and prevents her from being fully in touch with me during the session. She may, more or less consciously, even be afraid that the persecuting animus might attack me directly by saying inappropriate things which, in her mind, would be disastrous. It could therefore be therapeutically helpful if I said to her: "It seems to me that you have withdrawn right now into yourself—could this have something to do with your dream?" In this way, her problem of getting invaded by thoughts or impulses she should not have, let alone express to others, could be dealt with in the here-and-now of the analytic situation. It could enable her to find out that it would not be such a catastrophe if, against her conscious will, that inner man would launch some attacks directly at me. I could survive it and we might then get to know just what this animus has to say. (It goes without saying that the same insight may, of course, also be obtained through active imagination, with the proviso that people have developed firm enough ego-boundaries and are gifted with this method.)

Of course I do not set my mind on forcing every dream into the context of the analytic encounter because this does not always make sense. What I really try to do is to further the connection between the dreamer and his dream, by getting him back into the very experience he had when dreaming it. Staying as close as possible to the dream experience may bring up more feelings and fantasies; sometimes sudden ideas about what the dream may be about, in terms of the waking ego, occur spontaneously. I do not use much mythological amplification, although this may happen to me spontaneously in certain situations. (It would lead too far afield here to ask myself whether these situations have special characteristics, but such an inquiry could be worthwhile.) On the whole, I think that for Jung himself research and the extensive use of amplification material was most important because it proved to him the existence of the collective unconscious and its archetypal structure and principles. In analytical practice, however, the use of mythological amplifications often serves as an intellectual defence against experiencing personally the emotional grip a dream may have. It sometimes leads away from the immediacy of the experience. This is a particular danger in the analysis of training candidates who "know" so much.

On the whole, my interest remains primarily with the question of how to meaningfully use the interrelations in the psychotherapeutic field constellated between the analysand and myself. In this connection, the London school has developed sophisticated ways of transference interpretation, which takes the analyst's countertransference into account. There is a lot to be learned from this procedure, yet for my tastes it is too extremely geared solely to the issues of transference. Robert Langs' ideas on "framing," which are presently advocated by some Jungians, would probably, if set into practice, have a stifling effect on my way of being. But one probably has to see the attraction of Langs approach as an extreme antidote against the tendency of some of us Jungians to take

Jung's ideas of mutuality and spontaneous responses naively as justification for changing analytic sessions into cosy tea-hours, or for giving the analyst the opportunity to unburden himself of his own problems at the expense of the patient.

Although my style of working analytically has changed considerably over the years, I still feel myself to be a Jungian analyst. Reading Samuels' book on *JUNG AND THE POST-JUNGIANS* shows the many different ways there are of working as a Jungian. It belongs to the essence of analytical psychology, founded by Jung, that the highest respect and support is given to the process of individuation, which can look different in each individual. I believe we will all agree that, in the last analysis, we ourselves, in our total personality, are the instruments of therapeutic activity. Whatever methods, techniques or non-techniques we apply, they must, to the best of our knowledge, be genuinely our own in order to be effective in the best possible way. And this, I believe, belongs to the spirit of Jungian psychology.

COMMENT BY SPIEGELMAN ON JACOBY'S PAPER

Dear Mario,

I am taking a cue from our mutual friend, Sonja Marjasch, and addressing my comments on your paper in the form of a "letter." First of all, as I read your excellent paper and the remarks about Dr. Jolande Jacobi, I am reminded of our days in Zurich, and your joyful, optimistic personality—at least at that time. I am touched by your "great" dreams of her and your appreciation of her when most people—including me, I deeply regret to say—were critical of this "extravert."

It seems clear to me that you followed your own nature, even then, and you have been rewarded by achieving a personal synthesis of extraversion (e.g. Freud, Kohut, etc., Jacobi) and introversion (Jung, Zurich). I also can now understand you better, as well as your attraction to the "London School." Your emphasis on the mutuality of the transference, it seems to me, is just such a resolution of these opposites, as it has been for me, as well.

QUESTION: Can one not just tell the patient, for example, that one is "bored," adding that the cause may lie in either participant, or the "third," the relationship itself? This is phenomenologically more accurate than interpretation, actually. The archetype effects both parties, of course, and this can be made conscious, for example, by inviting the patient's response or interpretation as well.

QUESTION: What about the non-child-centered material (numinous, religious and other collective contents) that comes up? Do you leave "personal" psychology then?

Finally, I want to thank you, Mario, for, among other things, referring to me my first control case in Zurich. Remember? It was also my first attempt to do analysis in German and only the kindness and forbearance of this University student in Germanistics made me feel other than a total fool! It saved me from the inflation you talk about but your confidence in me helped a lot.

Yours,
Marvin

COMMENT ON JACOBY BY McNAIR

I appreciated hearing Mario tell his "once upon a time" story. It continues to impress me how yet another individual finds his way to Jung's psychology while otherwise going in another direction—invariably, after age 30. It also appears to be true that each person moves deeper into Jung's realm rather than incorporating it into their previous vocation (myself included!).

I particularly like Mario's critique of Jungian "inflation." I have struggled with that often enough. The scope, depth, and range of Jung continues to impress me. I find myself amazed, then inflated, ultimately having to distill the value of something Jung presents to a level germane to my own life. Yet, humanities have suffered such occlusion in our culture that it does seem to require an adeptness to bring them into the midst of such concrete reductionism.

Mario's discussion of his frustrations with his patients' inadvertance to his wish or expectations sounds familiar. It is always surprising to me when an analysand is not interested in the "Jungian" direction, yet I cannot ignore a countertransference possibility here; to call it "resistance" is too self-serving.

What Mario does make me reflect upon is just how much, after almost 15 years, I have learned and/or do know about myself, human nature, or our culture that was not presented or promoted while I was growing up. It has taken a long time to absorb the impact of this realm of psychology and to gently integrate it. For myself as well, Winnicott and Kohut have contributed an additional perspective to the therapist's value as a human relationship.

I remember once, in Zurich, Mario telling us that he would write down his blunders, stupid remarks, arrogancies, etc. at the end of the day. This notion stayed with me and I began to do it myself. I have found it very helpful for relativizing my tendency to be absorbed by my main function.

For a "feeling type," Mario's paper is a lavish bouquet of thoughts! I found myself "thinking" in endless associative fashion to the points and people he said he was so glad he did not have to refer to! I discovered a dilemma in reading Mario's paper. I had unconsciously assigned him as a feeling-sensation type (from my experience with him) and here he is as thinking-intuition...confusion!

My image had no body or substance without him being present. I found myself feeling bitchy about the lack of substance in the paper. Aha! So I managed to focus my imagination on my "memory" of Mario—only then did my feelings return and thus plenty of substance. Mario generates a very warm, attentive atmosphere of interest and concern.

It's true I have come to enjoy a connection with "feeling type" people which helps keep my feeling awareness more in front of me. It is—like Mario cautions the reader—that a paper is not like the real thing. The map is not the territory.

REPLY BY JACOBY TO SPIEGELMAN AND McNAIR

Thank you, Marvin, for your complimentary and understanding response to my paper. Your idea of asking colleagues to reflect on their practice has proven to be very fertile; this capacity is one that you already demonstrated during our student days. You reminded me of the control case I referred to you then. Of course I remember; he was a good friend of mine. I witnessed how much the analysis with you meant to him, how he grew able to trust you and thus also his own inner resources. Witnessing his process, however, supported my too idealistic belief in the healing effects of Jungian analysis at that time.

As for your questions: there is indeed never a general answer to questions of psychotherapeutic procedure, and I think we all share the specifically Jungian attitude of openness to the unique situation. I had the following thoughts, however, as to whether and how to share the analyst's feelings—of let's say, boredom—with the patient. In my experience, boredom is often a sign that connection to the living "soul-substance" is missing. This may be due to temporary or chronic defenses such as cutting off, repression, etc. in the patient or also in the analyst. Yet it is precisely the analyst's aim to facilitate this vital connection whenever possible, and the way in which he proceeds to achieve this is part and parcel of his "art." As I tend to see boredom as a symptom, I rather hesitate to address it directly, but try to focus on the underlying experiences, conflicts or fears. Besides, the word "boring" easily activates complexes connected to rejection-fears and loss of self-esteem, and we know how complexes tend to distort the meaning of whatever is said. Since many patients suffer from the conviction that whatever comes out of them is just valueless anyway, in analysis their worst fear is to be boring to the analyst and thus lose his interest and love. Under the spell of a complex, they are made to feel unlovable and worthless.

It is exactly this fear which the analyst may pick up with his own feelings of boredom, which may be a "syntonic" countertransference reaction. In such cases, I would be rather hesitant to say directly to the patient: "I feel bored"—even when adding, "let's see what it means for both of us." On such occasions, I have sometimes said the following: "I may be wrong, but somewhere I get the feeling that you might be afraid right now of being boring to me." With such a formulation, I may avoid pushing the analysand right into the complex. Instead, I try to empathize with the experience of his ego which may allow him to connect to his fears and to express them. We thus may become allies in trying to understand and deal with the complex and its implications. In case my interpretative guess is incorrect or the analysand is not conscious of his fears or not ready to admit them, I never insist. In general, I feel it is important to see whether my communications will be understood by the patient the way they are meant, or whether and in what way they get distorted, misunderstood of idealized. If I feel that I can be direct with the patient about sensitive areas, the way you suggest, Marvin, I take it as a sign of his growing inner stability and of my trust that it will not shatter his sense of self-esteem in a disastrous way.

Now to your second question concerning the numinous, religious or other collective contents that come up: I hardly ever leave "personal" psychology, since collective material manifests in the person of my patient. (I sometimes have to withstand my temptation to get into discussions of general collective problems or religious questions, since I am eagerly interested in them. If it happens anyway, I am tolerant with myself and hope that it may also have meaning for the patient.) For me, it is of utmost importance how the person relates to his/her archetypal material and how it affects the inner state. I feel that the authenticity of the person's inner experiences has to be supported against two frequently emerging opposite dangers: On the one hand some patients tend to get inflated or use collective material (also active imagination) as a defense against painful personal issues; others may be haunted by destructive self-doubt and cannot believe that they are entitled to receive helpful inner images of a collective value. Therefore, I focus in the analysis at least as much on the relationship between the ego and the unconscious as on the contents themselves. I think this is basically in accordance with Jung—at least some of his writing.

My concern of supporting the authenticity of the patient's experiences touches on a tremendously complex problem. How am I to know what is an authentic experience for a person and what not? Do I know this even for myself? If I feel that an experience is illusionary or defensive, it may stem from the fact that the patient's way of experiencing is different from mine, or I lack the right antenna. Yet my uneasiness may also be an awareness of inauthenticity or unconscious doubts in the patient as well. How I deal with this is a matter of "art" or trial and error, part and parcel of our profession. In any case, I am in no way determined to see everything in a "childhood-centered" way. I try to be sensitive enough to the specific ways a patient may be able to make use of what the analytic situation offers.

I appreciate Joe McNair's comment, adding the dimension of Jung's typology to my issue. I still consider myself as functioning mainly with feeling/intuition. My writing expresses, above all, reflections on my feelings. To what extent is thinking involved in this kind of reflection? Is it not rather an expression of what Willeford called the rational pole of feeling (*Journal of Analytical Psychology*, Vol. 20, 1975, p. 18ff)? I have to confess however that the questions of typology are not of foremost interest to me—which in turn may be an expression of my typology!

My Three Offices

by

DR. PHIL. SONJA MARJASCH

Autumn 1985

Dear Marvin,

Thank you for asking me, "How come you are working today as you do?" I think that this is a very pertinent and challenging question.

I was 38 years old when, in 1958, I started to practice psychotherapy after training four years at the C.G. Jung Institute in Zurich. My first office was downtown five minutes away from the famous Bahnhofstrasse. I passed by the house recently and saw that it has now been taken over by banking and investment corporations. At that time the owner was a Jewish eye-doctor and I could share his waiting-room which had easy chairs covered with red velvet and a large mirror in a gilt frame. My office was small but it had a balcony from which I could catch a glimpse of the lake. This was very important to me. At the entrance I had a brass plate like the doctor and the lawyer who had his office on the same floor. My stationery was designed and hand-set by a well-known printer. I wore fashionable clothes and went to the hairdresser at least once a week. Thanks to recommendations from my training analyst, Professor C.A. Meier, and from colleagues and friends, my practice soon flourished; then more men than women came to see me. I had rather high fees and for a time earned more than I spent, which is unusual for me. From the outside everything went very well, yet I cannot remember a period in my life in which I was more afraid and lonely. In my analytical work I relied mostly on what I had learned and had little confidence in my own resources.

The first crack in this professional facade was in retrospect rather funny. An analysand told me a dream which to my delight had a dramatic structure and lent itself easily to associations and amplifications. After that hour I was relly pleased because my dream interpretation corresponded to the examples in textbooks. At the next session the analysand told me how important the last hour had been for him and I nodded approval. But then he said that he had been deeply struck by a remark of mine, which had had nothing to do with the dream interpretation. It was something that I said offhand and could not even remember. This was unsettling. What I had believed to be helpful because it was in tune with psychological theory had not made any impact: instead, a spontaneous remark had gone to the core. Seen in retrospect this clash between my theoretical expectations and the reality of the analytical process was bound to happen. It released my sense of humour and freed me of an overwhelming sense of responsibility. In the long run the discrepancy between theory and

101

practice made me aware of the limitations of psychological understanding. It also prompted me to explore fragmentary modes of expression both in the arts and in analysis.

Another seemingly trivial event had made me stumble as if my foot had caught in a hole. I had listened to a dream about two birds fighting and spontaneously exclaimed: "But where are YOU?" I missed the dream-ego which so far I had taken for granted. This made me look closer at the presence or absence of the dreamer in the dream and at the relations between the waking-ego and the dream-ego. It led me later to examine various forms of self-reflection, i.e. narcissism, introspection and introversion. I was intrigued by some Platonic interpretations and positive evaluations of the Narcissus-myth and wondered whether that back-flow of libido could, in certain respects, be compared to introversion. I pondered about this before I got hold of the detailed studies made by Heinz Kohut. Right now I am speculating about the function of introspection and about the difference between introspection and introversion seen in historical perspective and their interplay in analysis.

The first crack in the professional facade never closed and not long afterwards it was shattered by the suicide of a young analysand. He had made several attempts and been hospitalized before he came to me. We worked well together until his mother called asking to see me. I had been warned of her disturbing influence and would only talk to her in the presence of her son. This he refused and as he was going home over the week-end I asked him to tell his mother that we would postpone the meeting. In the same hour he told me a dream in which he was walking up in the sun to a hut in the mountains. Suddenly a cloud cast a huge black shadow over the meadow and the hut. He added no further comment, and at that time I was not familiar with this weather phenomenon. When I waited for him to come to the next session, I got a call that he had killed himself. He was a good swimmer and yet he had been found drowned in the lake. After twenty years the shock of this suicide is still fresh in my memory. Many years later his brother started to work with me and after a long period working together he, with great care and delicacy, found a way to relate to his mother, shortly before her death. Guilt feelings still accompany me but they proved to be fruitful in two respects. They have focussed my attention to the problematics of the double-bind and I have made several attempts since to describe them. The particular double-bind I had found myself in here was that both seeing the mother and not seeing the mother seemed wrong. It was only when I read Winnicott's description of the good-enough mother that the trap opened and I realized that from the very beginning I had been competing with the mother of the analysand, trying to be a better mother than she. Since that time I am also very concerned about any weather information in dreams or fantasies. Many years later I made the experience of cloud shadows, not in the mountains but on the Shetland Islands and there I saw the dramatic change from a sunny landscape into a dark, forbidding one happening within seconds. I now understand the weather in dreams as expressing the mood of the dreamer and would take such a cloud-shadow as a warning. This information about inner weather is often overlooked. Next summer I shall probably give a seminar on "Psychic Weather."

Another decisive event concerned at first only me but later had a great impact on my psychological work. A hereditary illness became manifest leading to an atrophy of certain leg muscles. I was encouraged to train my body as much as possible and I spent the greater part of a fine summer in and around the swimming-pool. It was then I realized how imprisoned I had felt in my downtown office and how much the emphasis on intellectual work had unbalanced me. It was a tremendous joy to be almost every day in the open air, in and out of the water. At that time, I was asked at very short notice, as a stand-in for a colleague, to give a talk on the animus. In this paper I made the point that the animus can be met not only in dreams and projections but also in the body and I described various forms of its appearance and possibilities of training. I fantasized how wonderful it would be to combine verbal therapy with massage and some other body training. This was in the early 60s and I had no inkling that my fantasies were part of a current trend. Today, many people do analysis simultaneously with body therapy in various forms and I find it an excellent combination. What I object to are violent means to break up resistances. I have always been strongly interested in defense mechanisms, in their advantages and draw-backs and how they could be improved. I think highly of Far Eastern martial arts and have since done T'ai Chi with a teacher of Chinese extraction, which helped me to regain my balance at a difficult time.

The enjoyment of outdoor life led me in the middle sixties to look for new lodgings with more space and light and I decided to live and work at the same place. So far my living quarters had been in that old part of Zurich which, to its inhabitants, is fondly called "Little Village." Now I moved into a spacious 4-room apartment where Zurich borders on Zollikon and which has a very mixed population. There are stately homes with large parks next to old, narrow houses with small shops and upstairs-rooms rented out to students and foreign labourers. The new apartment had a splendid view of the lake and a large balcony, which with the years turned into a veritable garden. The back rooms looked into a very quiet park. The front rooms served as office and living room and one of the back rooms as waiting-room. Soon my first cat, a red-and-white tomcat called Mauck, moved in and since then animals are my constant companions, also at work. I owe much to snow-white Zottel and he is fondly remembered by many analysands. On my travels to India I met the ginger cat Youyou in Kalimpong, and later Suka when she was still a puppy in Delhi. Both came home with me. They had been severely wounded and healed well. Youyou had such a radiance that his limp went almost unnoticed; Suka can outrun almost any other dog. My whole attitude to the analytical work became less intellectual. It now felt to me as if my first downtown office had been a mere branch of a paternal enterprise, still linked to the office of my father, who had been a Freudian analyst, and to that of my Jungian training analyst as well. Now

I had an office of my own.

I started to photograph again and do my own darkroom processing. For several years this was very important to me. I literally developed my own point of view and my own image of the world. It was very exciting to see the picture appear in chemical solution and I also learned how important it is to fix it at the right moment. Today, this darkroom has become a part of my analytical approach but it is now internalized. It is as if I have a rather sensitive film in me, registering the emotions of an analytical hour in the form of images. Depending on the situation, I withdraw during an hour within myself and try to process this image, i.e., verbalize it to share it then with the analysand. I often experience that these images have the effect of dissolving a block because they offer a variation of the problem he or she is struggling with.

In the first years of my second office I also started more consciously to find my own way of conveying psychological isights. Working in adult education I gave psychological courses in villages where I had to speak in dialect. Under these circumstances I could not use any concepts but had to find ways and means to explain dreams or partner problems in common speech. This led me to tell a story instead of using a technical term. My father and my maternal grandmother had both been excellent storytellers and they left me a sparkling treasure-house full of all sorts of tales. I hope that I made, and still make, good use of them. In analysis I now more often tell a tale to illuminate a certain problem than try to analyse it. Telling tales relates me to oral tradition and also serves as a link to an old love of mine, namely folk art.

With the years I had brought home all sorts of toys, mostly animals, from my travels to remote parts of the world, and I felt that they should be played with in order to stay alive. I therefore put them with some bowls of sand into the waiting room. Soon people started to play with them. I did not comment upon this unless an analysand drew my attention to what he had made. Playing in the waiting-room was to some analysands a help to step out of chronological time, to stop hurrying from one appointment to the next and enter what I call "poetic time." When this happened the waiting room turned for them into a "transitional space" or "third area" as Winnicott has named it. I became more and more aware of how fruitless interpreting any kind of psychological information is when an analysand has not experienced this transitional space between him and his mother in early infancy. If he has never enjoyed it or if it has become a dim memory, it takes long careful and patient work to evoke it. Without it the level of tension and anxiety is often too high, the analysand tends to block or over-adapt and he reduces vague psychic contents quickly to well-known classified facts with the help of intellectual interpretations. I remember a young woman who used to take a bowl of sand from the waiting-room into the office and while we were talking she made intricate patterns with some coloured beads. Re-creating her playground helped her to talk more fluently and freely. Seeing her nimble fingers at work reminded me of knitting, and childhood memories of summer evenings when the women sat in front of their houses and chatted, peeling apples or snapping beans surged up in my mind. Those were good times when speaking and acting were not separated. Gestures giving body to the words help to let the emotional undercurrents flow into everyday life.

Together with the sand-play my interest in patterns and patterning re-emerged. As such, it is of long standing. When I recently put in order some papers my mother had left, I found a booklet in which, at the age of ten, I had drawn all sorts of patterns to decorate household goods and dresses with. In my student days I was introduced to poetry, paintings, and philosophical speculation. My thesis for the Jung Institute was on a 17th-century "Consideration" of a quincunxial pattern or network from an artificial, a natural and a mystical point of view. My delight in patterns merged with my fascination in colour and deepened my understanding of folk-, archaic and tribal art. The increased sensibility to colourful patterning had direct consequences in the analytical work. It helped me to become more aware of correspondences not only within dreams or between dreams and everyday life, but also in everyday life as such, which is often considered trivial or prosaic. Patterns can be observed from a distance or experienced in making. Or they can be embodied by dancing. There are poetic worlds in which colours and patterns, moods, actions and relationships are wonderfully combined and intertwined. This happens for example in "The Tales of the Seven Princesses" by the Persian poet Nizami, where each story unfolds under the influence of one planet and is permeated by one colour in all possible shades. Each mood has its particular landscape as in the Indian paintings of certain rasas. In my psychological work I tried to become more aware of such "psychic landscapes," the weather experience being part of them. I once described a "landscape of violence" in a travel report, blending my own experiences at the Haymarket in Leningrad with memories of the life of Dostoyevsky and his description of that place in *Crime and Punishment*. "Psychic landscape" is a topic that is still in my mind and part of "work in progress."

In 1981 there occurred a further change in my life situation to which various events contributed. My mother had left me part of an old cottage ten miles out of town. When I was abroad the adjacent part suddenly went up for sale and was bought by a painter friend of mine, and at the same time the owner of the Zurich apartment decided to renovate the whole block. I went with the current and moved out of Zurich into the old house where I was greeted by the purring of the old tomcat Jucki. It was overbrimming with junk and beautiful things. By sorting them out and gradually redoing the house according to my own needs and taste, I cleared space for my third office, in which I practice now. The more accessible entrance is through the barn. The waiting-room on the ground floor has a big tiled stove and leads into a spacious study with a long row of windows looking into an orchard that is slowly turning into a wilderness. It has wooden walls and a low wooden ceiling. The furniture is very mixed and so are the objects but each piece has its personal history making it precious to me. On the window sills are flower-pots and water-jugs and "Victor," a decoy from Vermont is watching the few passers-by. From the avocado plant grown into a veritable tree hangs a snake-skin. On the shelves books mingle with things brought home from many trips. The pictures made by painters, children and unknown tribal artists all "talk" a very rich colourful language. The red covered couch has many embroidered cushions and so have the chairs. On the little table in front of them are flowers and a bowl of fruit. After the hour the analysand leaves through the kitchen and lands on a narrow lane on the opposite side of the barn. Thus at least one analytical tradition which my father taught me as a child, namely that the privacy of the analysand has to be strictly observed is still maintained.

Much more than an apartment, such an old house is in continual motion, some tearing down and re-building is happening all the time. I often use Calder's mobile as an example for the soul: You touch one part and it sets the whole in motion, with strong vibrations where you least expect it. It is the same with the house. Last winter when it was still bitterly cold and everything was frozen a veritable spring gushed out of the dirt floor of the barn and a rivulet cascaded into the cellar. The main water pipe leading to the house had been eaten by rust and had burst. It dated from the turn of the century and had to be totally replaced. Not only a new pipe was needed but several alterations of its way into the house had to be made. All this was rather upsetting and expensive and made me realize that water pipes do not last forever. I took it also symbolically as a hint that the same is true on a psychic level. One cannot rely on traditions forever. After a few generations the pipes leading to the source of life, and with them, the psychological theories and therapeutic techniques, have to be revised and partly renewed. Yet I also believe in continuity in the midst of change, and this continuity expresses itself in the way in which each analyst remains true to himself although his style may vary greatly over the years.

Life in the cottage is different from life in town. I spent much of my childhood in grandmother's village, and childhood experiences such as the change of the seasons are re-lived. Since a few days ago it is autumn, full of gold and blue mist. The apples ripen and from time to time one falls into the grass with a thud. I like this sound and it sets my mind going: The more I can wait in analysis for an insight to ripen, the less interpretation is needed. A ripe apple falling from the tree reminds me of a dream explaining itself, provided it is given enough space and attention. A change in dream recollections that I have observed happening over the years has impressed me very much. At the time of my downtown office the dream memories of my analysands were mostly visual, seldom auditory, but nowadays sensations of taste, smell and touch are also rendered. I think this is partly due to an increased emphasis on body-soul-connections as experienced, e.g., in different forms of body therapy.

This regained sensuous quality of the dreams helps to counterbalance the increase of iconographic knowledge and provides the dreamer with additional soul-nourishment. I now try to interfere as little as possible. Yet this is easier said than done. I am still too much inclined to push the river. I guess I am a Jungian because nowhere else would I have had space enough to follow its meandering.

Dear Marvin, I am now at the end of my recollections: As my thoughts turn back once more to my professional beginnings, immediately our endless talks and Ryma's excellent black coffee and sandwiches come to mind. I do not think that one can survive well in this work without good friends. I was, and I am, lucky to have them. As I write these lines dance music from a local fair drifts in through the window; it is an Indian summer night with a full red moon. I have warm feelings for that round of friends from the early days and close this letter with good wishes.

Sonja

COMMENT BY SPIEGELMAN
Dear Sonja,

I was delighted that your contribution to our Jungian analysts book took the form of a letter to me. You did not know that I had planned there to be a bit of "dialogue" in the book, in the form of questions and comments from an advanced candidate, Joe McNair, as well as myself, to the analysts. Your letter-style anticipated that dialogue.

First of all, "My Three Offices" is a gem. I am reminded of your Diploma thesis for the Jung Institute on Sir Thomas Browne, which the Curatorium called, "a jewel," a study comparable in subtlety, detail, sensitivity and originality, but this one has the added virtue of being quite personal as well. I remember your fourth-floor attic apartment in the old city very well, and your first office, too. What fun it was to be students, then, and discuss into the night, enjoy wine and cheese, and that famous goose dinner! Anyway, Ryma remembers it all, too. She liked your paper very much, as did my daughter, Tamar.

Professionally, I connect very well with your experience of having to "abandon" theory in the face of practice. I, too, had to change my style drastically from the way I was taught, although the basic theoretical constructions remained. For me, the old scientific standpoint still holds: in the face of discrepancy between theory and praxis, modify theory! But we are very much agreed on the need of the analyst to listen deeply to the inner images (I add, impulses and body reactions) that the therapy work engenders. I am also inclined to share these images and reactions with the patient.

Like you, I responded to the body aspect of the work, even to spending lots of years in Reichian therapy and even trying to do some for a few years, abandoning it as not suiting my temperament. Were we creatures of the time (the sixties) as you suggest? Or was this a necessary addition to the Jungian emphasis upon idea and image, word and communication? I think it is necessary, and I much appreciate your "sensation" way of attending. Whether I like it or not, however, I seem to be much more active: I need to share, reach out, give reactions, but I do not understand if this difference is also a temperamental one, or a product of the extraverted demands in our American society.

Your contribution is a true expression of individuality in every way and I am sure that both candidates and analysts will appreciate what you offer. That you, as a Swiss and a Zurich graduate, also call on the likes of Kohut and Winnicott will be pleasing to our English and American colleagues. The "transitional space" of which you speak is particularly difficult to engender in the fast pace of city living and comes, I find, only after much work on both the analytical relationship and the psyche.

Which brings me to the only question (other than the desire to hear your lectures on the "psychic landscape") that your work evokes. How do you approach the interactional, transference aspects of the work? I notice your fine receptivity, attention to the "third area" of Winnicott, and I conclude that your "holding" aspects and essentially non-interpretative attitude is the general one you follow. Do you still view the transference in Jung's fashion, as the interplay of the two psyches at an archetypal level, or in some other way? And, what sorts of things do you communicate verbally to the patient? Dream interpretations? Questions and comments? My impression of you, of course, is one of waiting, listening, communicating images and feelings, and it sounds healing and process-oriented as in nature, or with your beloved animals.

In any case, thank you for your lovely offering and I hope that candidates and colleagues will enjoy it as much as I have.

With fond memories and hopes for future talks, too, all my good wishes to you also.

                                                                    Marvin

REPLY BY MARJASCH TO SPIEGELMAN
Dear Marvin,

You asked me about transference. I am concerned not to spoil spontaneity by reflection and prefer expressing emotions to intellectual concepts. In the session, I hardly use technical terms. Together with the analysand, I try to become aware of the emotional flow between us, as well as its blockings. This implies verbalization of upsurging memories and images, changes of mood and bodily sensations. To the latter belongs a certain drowsiness which befalls me when our talk becomes dissociated from the emotional undercurrents. When this happens I draw attention to it and we look into what might have been neglected or repressed. I consider the psychological work as an exchange on the subject-subject level, open to both the inner and outer world. Weather permitting, the windows of my "office" are open and my animals walk freely in and out. Trivial happenings on the outside world can, on occasion, become meaningful within a certain inner context or be so incongruous that they release tension into laughter. As I work without conceptual gloves, I risk getting infected by the problems of the analysand, but when it happens it serves me as valuable information of what is going on in him and also helps me in my own work with myself.

COMMENT BY McNAIR
Sonja has such an intimate relationship to the soul-life of objects, like no one I have ever known. Organic life thrives from her attention, inert life is enlivened

by her wonder at mystery. I have had the pleasure to have spent time with Sonja while in Zurich the past three summers. My first memory of her is of a woman coming into the large lecture hall and having us form a circle. (I must include that last year they managed to bolt all the chairs into rows; no more circles!) She then proceeded to lay out her notes on a box-like stand; these were surrounded by photos of her cats. Fair enough. Half-way through her talk on "Dream Space," she pauses to move her photos—or should I say—the cats got up and changed position! I never thought to ask.

I had never seen such an integration of intuition and sensation, her imagination's sense of detail; "psychic weather" seemed an apt topic. Yet her understanding and integration of Winnicott's work was refreshing for me. I had studied his work while working with children. Then I found the same phenomenon in adults—those who had had no "teddy bear" had a different course through therapy.

To me, Sonja is truly adept in the "intermediate space" or "poetic space." Her notion of a photograph developing as an image of the therapy is a keen one.

What I enjoyed most about her paper is her capacity to "create" transitional space, her imagery and story-telling certainly helps that. She is a very animated personality. She feels at home in the "flux" of it all—for she has her "things." She gave us a seminar in the "talk of things" last year and my world is very much more alive than before, more "space." As the women "sitting and chatting," speaking and acting, are not separated, it reveals what Peregrinatio has to offer.

Sonja seems to have shifted from "Father" and interpretation (Bahnhofstrasse) to Mother—rural/folk-tale process; this is a very strong tension within my own life. I have dropped a lot of the clinical hardware I accumulated in academic psychology and subsequent training. Initially I adapted the Jungian concepts to the existing apparatus but as my deeper feelings and body's symptoms become more prominent, I seek more comfort in nature. Nature feels soothing; Sonja's house/barn is a total environment. Just leaving Zurich by train for her house I felt the city-thinking/acting fall away. This naturalistic atmosphere is, for me, more a true reflection of the organic human condition than the ever-increasing big city life that is quickly consuming Los Angeles. In ten years, I have watched vast horse ranches and orange groves be converted into condominiums and commercial property. I feel compelled to move rather than adapt.

What Sonja seems to have accomplished is to have eclipsed words for essence. If the "art" of the work is to consciously return to that childhood realm of the "transitional space" where the worlds of criteria and pleroma co-mingle, then this appears to be Sonja's and Victor's habitat. Well done! The redemption of the Soul in Matter. If, as Jung stresses, the deep, inherent conflict in Western society results in our charge to be conscious such that separation is not a viable option, then, to me, the notion of the Sapientia Dei is an evident direction, as it is in Sonja's work.

Sonja, your career's path is not unlike the dilemma so many men are finding themselves in—to a point. Most cannot permit themselves, or are unable, to find their way back to nature as you have done.

Questions: Would you consider it more likely that a woman could make that move? Some notion of "instinctual rapport"? As in Merlin's withdrawal to the woods, or Lao Tzu's? Or, perhaps, a capacity of the sensation type? It seems to be the quintessential move towards balance.

MARJASCH'S RESPONSE TO McNAIR

Thank you very much for your understanding and appreciation of my paper. I felt moved and a bit embarrassed when I read it. I must add as a postscript that, as I told you, my psychological approach is rather disputed amongst my Zurich colleagues. Some people like what I do and others not at all. I remember well how, years ago, an exasperated Jim Hillman called me a "ground hog" and right he was. I don't make those who prefer eagles to ground hogs happy and I really feel it is important to say so to balance out your approval.

Archetypal Medicine, or Analytical Psychology Made Flesh

by

DR. MED. ALFRED J. ZIEGLER
(Translated from the German by Ruth E. Horine)

INTRODUCTION: The Spirit of Mercurius

Although C.G. Jung was a doctor of the soul, so-called, we would be missing the point if we were to describe him as having been soulful, or a good soul, or as someone who was endowed with depth of soul and peace of mind. Jung was no shepherd of souls. His true hallmark was "spirit." It would therefore be more appropriate to call him "spirited," witty, cultured and the like.

To find out what this spirit was all about we best turn to Jung himself, his works: *THE SPIRIT OF MERCURY*, to which he gave a motto taken from a sentence in the "First Letter to the Corinthians": *SPIRITUS ENIM OMNIA SCRUTATUR, ETIAM PROFUNDA DEI*. In other words, spirit does not allow for anything to remain uninvestigated, not even the depths of God. Moreover, he held that this spirit was to be qualified as *SUBLIMIS*, something spontaneous, volatile, and active, a quickening substance which is airy in nature. Transcending sense perception, it was considered capable of generating images, and in these terms it was the complete opposite of matter.

These commonly accepted characterizations of spirit, were, however, not enough for Jung. On the contrary, as he developed the concept of spirit in his treatises, it lost in clarity, especially when the alchemistic Mercurius became its RIGHTFUL representative, a Mercurius who is phenomenologically related to the Greek Hermes. In this context spirit becomes the "varius ille Mercurius" for him, something fickle and deceptive. It sparkles with contradictions and even substance, matter is not a hostile element for this Mercurius, i.e., he is even capable of turning into matter. Apparently, his place is not just in heaven but also on the dung heap. Mercury, a glittering light and dark substance, which carries his name and may be solid as well as liquid and gaseous, is one of his most pertinent symbols, it appears.

As a matter of fact, in describing Jung as a man of spirit we also gain in understanding as regards his origins and early activities. He was the son of a clergyman and a mother who had a penchant for occult matters. It becomes more understandable why he turned to psychiatry, or illnesses of the mind, immediately after completing his medical studies and why he wrote a doctoral thesis entitled *ON THE PSYCHOLOGY AND PATHOLOGY OF SO-CALLED OCCULT PHENOMENA*. We can see why he travelled to Paris for further training with Charcot and the Salpetriere to witness cures of hysterical patients and that he was with Eugen Bleuler at the Burgholzli Clinic in Zurich at a time when everyone was eagerly researching into schizophrenia. The fact that Jung was interested in mysticism early on and that the alchemists soon became an authority for him is perfectly in line with his spiritual inclinations. The same applies to his efforts to come to grips with the natural philosophers of Romanticism and with the Unconscious, theology, orientalism, cultural anthropology, poetry, and so forth.

In terms of spirit—the mind—we are also better able to understand Jung's own mental health crises at a time when his "house was full of ghosts," as well as the style and contents of his 250-odd publications. Many of these were wholly written in the spirit of Mercurius and at times his writing is ambiguous and equivocal to the point of being unintelligible.

While the spirit of Mercurius was clearly subtle AND material for Jung, he was primarily concerned with another polarity, namely light and dark, something associated with seeing and looking-at, with light and shadow and therfore with consciousness and unconsciousness, with the Conscious and the Unconscious, in other words, something "half real" as it were. This may be, as it turns out, the main reason why Analytical Psychology remained more "psychology" than anything else and why so little of it found its way into medicine over the years; why, for example, no systematic attempts were made to develop a psychosomatic medicine according to Jung, except for what I myself have called "Archetypal Medicine." This particular spirit of Mercurius is not capable of meeting all the requirements of medical reality.

Until midlife, or thereabouts, my attention was also claimed primarily by the luminous image of Mercury. It only began to change after a period of rather melancholic despondency. My house did not, however, fill with ghosts as in the case of Jung. Instead it was invaded by a spirit of weariness, meaninglessness and apathy. As a result, my own Analytical Psychology began to change, although this process had actually begun a number of years earlier. The Jungian "topoi" of the archetypes, psychic energy, the Self and individuation, the meaning of animus and anima, and so forth, altered but without leading to fundamental modifications.

More than anything else, Analytical Psychology became more closely associated with medicine. In tune with my own basic existential condition, the mercurial spirit lost some of its purely visual quality and became a matter of "import," thus becoming heavier. It became increasingly conceivable that this spirit might also be pertinent to the science of curing bodies with its unmistakable object, the soma. While the Spirit Mercurius had also been the inspiration of my own diagnostic and therapeutic activity, its subtle and material qualities acquired increasing significance for me in addition to its light and dark components. Mercury was no longer a substance that merely changed from brightness to darkness. In addition to its volatile manifestations it revealed itself more than anything in its full metallic inorganicity.

It seemed to me that only now Mercurius had become a genuine analogy to the Greek Hermes, who was said to be the son of the resplendent Zeus and an immortal but shy nymph who dwelt in a cave. I am referring to the Hermes who, in addition to knowing his way around the Underworld and having the attribute of wings that enabled him to overcome gravity, also carried a caduceus. This showed that he was a deity who had much in common with the healer god Asklepios and last but not least, he even shared the latter's affinity to earthbound Gaia.

WEIGHTING PATHOLOGY

Clinical pictures of diseases, the imagery of pathology, had always fascinated me beyond measure. No doubt, I was more taken by illness than by health, just as Jung, who, however, was more attracted by the entire spectrum of psychopathological manifestations, by the delusions and hallucinations of schizophrenics, the often scurrilous behavior of psychotics in general, the singularities of neurotics, the eccentricities in religious life and other things of the same sort. Like Jung, my attention was always drawn to the scandalous aspects of human existence. However, I was more fascinated by body pathology, and with it by something considerably more static and heavier. In contrast to the rather ephemeral object of Jung's study, my interests focussed more on the material dimension, which tends to determine our existence with a dogged kind of fatality. The gravitational movement of the mercurial spirit was even more appropriate considering my personal bias.

For me, as for Jung in the case of psychopathology, there was never any doubt that these images revealed basic forms of human existence, which are normally meant to be lived, or have been lived through certain fundamental modes of behavior and our attunement to the world, in other words, in archetypal life patterns. Myths and legends, superstitions, religious customs, pre-scientific medicine, the occult philosophies and primitive rituals bear ample witness to this idea.

By way of example, it becomes possible to recognize human stubbornness in rheumatic stiffness, a fragility and a tendency to corruption in fractures, a probably malignant hatred in cancer, the strength behind desperate resistance in inflammations, or the problem of weightiness in obesity. Our body pathologies seem to be a dwelling place, as it were, for the rigidified forms of universal themes. This idea is time-honored, to wit: the archetypal images we find in the field of artistic and philosophical endeavor. The many pictures representing the blind, the lame and the dumb, the crippled and the leprous, the plagued and the miscreants are bound to have much profound meaning.

Automatically, the role played by Animus and Anima in Analytical Psychology—which Jung held to represent the male aspect in the life of women and the female aspect in the life of men respectively—began to lose some of its overriding importance. For the purpose of my approach, they continue to have special significance for an understanding of the physical symptoms of sexual changes, in gynecology and andrology. In this manner, the Animus-Anima concept may have lost some of its magnetic seriousness because all too frequently it makes for reductive explanations.

Moreover, pathogenesis, that is, the origination and development of diseases, also became more clearly understandable. Falling ill ceased to be "just" the "emission" of a psychodynamic process, such as, for example, an Animus or Anima problem. A given sickness no longer developed per chance, as it were, as though any other illness might have done in its place. As regards its form, localization and process, physical illness lost its role as a mere "hypophenomenon" of so-called psychic life. The clinical picture became a straightforward metamorphosis of the archetypal human patterns of life, mentioned earlier. Admittedly, the lack of facts and figures, the absence of well-defined boundaries in the archetypal world turned out to be somewhat annoying. In comparison with an illness that can be "de-fined" scientifically, the image of a disease in which we discern the somatization of an entire life pattern is something rather vague. For the purpose of "grasping" the illness, i.e. getting a grip on it, we may be at a disadvantage. But when it comes to possibilities for empathy, including material empathy, there may be some advantages.

There is no doubt that Jung, too, had some interest in body pathology and that he had some thoughts about its archetypal background but he was neither passionately or systematically concerned with it. He did emphasize the material dimension of the "primordial images" on many occasions and he did designate them as the "organs" of human life. Furthermore, he called attention to the idea that they are innate and therefore dependent on endocrine predispositions. However, at times all this tended to sound like lip-service. His spirit seemed to shrink from too much proximity to matter.

In brief, particularly after the turn of life, the phenomena described by Jung as archetypal revealed themselves to me as something to be pondered and weighed and therefore as something "ag-gravating." The same applied to Analytical Psychology as a whole. The Spirit Mercurius, which inspires both diagnosis and therapy, came to be lodged so firmly in matter, in heaviness, that the organs, in point, began to appear more important in terms of dying than in terms of living and the substantiality of Hermes increasingly appeared as his obvious manifestation.

ON PSYCHOSOMATIC ENERGETICS

A general theory of libido, which came close to becoming a theory of life energy for him, was formulated by C.G. Jung quite early on. The premise for his ideas on the energy household was, in fact, the theory of thermodynamics and its laws. Accordingly, he held that energy was subject to the principle of constancy, which meant that in a closed system it was bound to remain constant.

It would be reasonable to assume that Jung applied this principle to the human being as a whole. But this is true in theory only. For the psychologist and psychiatrist he was, it applied, in fact, chiefly to the psyche, as is evidenced by the oft repeated statement that he viewed "the psyche as a relatively closed energetic system." With this affirmation, Jung lost another opportunity to express himself in systematic medical terms.

The same goes for the way he applies the principle of energic equivalence, according to which a given quantum of energy which disappears from one place is bound to reappear in another. Jung used this rule, too, mainly for the purpose of understanding psychic phenomena, such as people's drives, wishes, affects, work performance and attention. When these shining qualities are subjected to darkening, they re-emerge in twilighty, ghostly, psychic phenomena, that is, in dreams and emotional reactions, accompanied by their vegetative side-effects. The so-called factor of extensity is also tied to this concept. It stipulates that the quantum of energy as well as the character of the psychic make-up extending into a new structure are preserved. In line with this idea, erotic passion may be transformed into "love of god." For Jung even the principle of entropy becomes a rule that is applicable to the psychological domain. The statement, according to which energy tends to pass from an improbable to a probable state, became evident for him in the development of schizophrenia. Here, a variable capacity of psychic expression is transformed into a relatively rigid, i.e. more probably symptomatology.

Medical experience has shown that all the laws on psychic energy cited by Jung are just as appropriate to an understanding of psychosomatic dynamics. They are quite as suitable for use in general medicine as they are in psychiatry, to wit: what has been done to some extent in Archetypal Medicine (see, e.g. 3,4,6).

These laws are equally eloquent when it comes to the somatization of the basic forms of human existence, which we discussed in the previous section. They enable us to conceptualize how these existential conditions acquire weight, how they materialize. This process also follows the principle of constancy and equivalence, as well as the rule of entropy and the law on the factor of extension. In the practice of psychosomatic medicine it is possible to observe, for example, how a burning passion is transformed in gastric hyperacidity with or without ulceration of the mucuous membranes of the stomach—in analogy to Goethe's lines, where he says: Nur wer die Sehnsucht kennt / Weiss was ich leide . . . / Es schwindelt mir / Es brennt mein Eingeweide" (W.J. Goethe, "Aus Wilhelm Meister: Mignon—Die selbe"); or, how reticence, parsimoniousness and stinginess express themselves in constipation and a tendency to experience outbursts of temper in the form of disorders affecting the cardiac rhythm, such as stumbling and racing of the heart.

However, these rules describe only part of energic pathogenesis, namely how certain forms of human existence change their substance; in other words, how the spirit Mercurius, in line with his fickle nature, may also encompass morbid metamorphoses.

Furthermore, with his love of polarities, C.G. Jung sees the above-mentioned basic forms of human existence as also being arranged along diametrically opposite lines. As a result, we are subject to archetypal conflicts throughout life.

Polarity does not mean equality. It also has a hierarchical connotation. We might therefore speak of superior and inferior forms of human existence, or dominant and recessive ones, echoing the idea that they are genetically ingrained.

Only the inferior forms of human existence are subject to the metamorphoses we mentioned, especially when the superior forms of behavior and the corresponding attunement to the world are overvalued, when they have become a matter of course and have acquired exclusive validity. In terms of the libido theory, we would speak of the excessive demand they make on psychic energy. The somatization of the inferior forms of existence is likely to take place when this overvaluation has reached its climax, or when it has gone on for too long a time. The extent of the illness, whether the condition is acute or chronic, depends on the depth of materialization, which borrows the energy it requires from the dominant value.

As was typical of Jung, the language used to describe this overvaluation was eminently visual: the superior forms of human existence are likely to "blind" us. We should not fail to add an epithet from the field of gravity, however; because in such states we are not only blinded, or dazzled, but usually we are also "carried away."

Moreover, when there is overvaluation there is, as a rule, also contamination from our "Persona," with its usual tendency to adapt to the outer world. Generally speaking, the superior archetypal modes of behavior with their corresponding attunement to the world are also those which define us sociologically in the desired positive way. While they induce the metamorphosis of our inferior mode of being, they are also visiting cards and enable us to live up to the social requirements. Quite obviously, this tends to happen particularly when we are hypnotized by them and in an in-flated, blown-up and therefore up-lifted state.

Finally, although the unconscious devaluation of our inferior being is habitually described as a "repression," we should realize that this concept does not refer to a refusal to take notice but something which is related to a movement of masses. In repressing something we ultimately weight it down as well and expedite it into the inorganic realm. To this end we use obscene language, which has its origin in morbidity, the dungheap, moral decay, sickliness and putrefaction.

To make the point more plainly, we would say that the very person—a farmer, for example—who operates with exaggerated purposefulness, who has to manage no matter what, will be the one to suffer most readily from lack of strength and elasticity of the connective tissues, from varicose veins, hemmorr-hoids and hernias. By the same token it will be the young man who carries his head high, full of idealism, who is as likely as not to develop Scheuermann's disease with a hunchback that obliges him to bow down humbly. And people who are hooked on their capacity for dry, sound reasoning will be the very ones with a good chance of becoming candidates for diabetes and an accompanying compulsion to staunch their thirsty existence.

We might also say that our so-called healthy areas are the very ones to make us ill. There is nothing more dangerous than resplendent health, the winged feeling of floating on air. Ultimately, we come to realize to what extent good health may actually be an existential emergency situation, and how public health policies promote somatization by adding fuel to the dream of "health for all." The more we exert ourselves to realize our ideas of health, the greater the likelihood that—following the principle of energetics—the archetypal pair of opposites falls apart and the inferior partner re-emerges in the form of material suffering.

ON THERAPY

In Analytical Psychology, therapy is a "talking cure," which is also conducted in the spirit of Mercurius, although in combination with other practices, often based on the reflective symbolizing of the material brought by the patient. For the mercurial spirit reveals itself not just subtly or materially, but also symbolically and figuratively in the archetypal modes of behavior, the corresponding attunement to the world and metamorphoses. As a rather hermetic science, Analytical Psychology relies on this possibility in contrast to the natural sciences with their rigor of method. The purpose is to induce the regression of the entropic pathological process and to throw light on the confining nature of the morbid symptomatology. The results are probably in line with the success rate of other psychotherapeutic methods, according to which roughly one-third of the conditions are generally cured and one-third can be improved, while about one-third remain unchanged.

In a way that is characteristic of Jung, this approach to therapy again carries the imprint of the primordial need for visualizing; or as it is usually put in Analytical Psychology, of becoming conscious. As a remedy for use in therapy, the symbols are therefore primarily intended to promote consciousness, i.e., to be luciferous. Their sublimating effect, as a means of taking us out of somatic sick(li)ness and into living the archetypal patterns, is considered to be of secondary importance. The successful use of the symbols depends, however, on the degree of somatization.

There are two kinds of symbols used in this manner: the first kind of symbol includes the images which show the overvalued forms of existence in our way of being, as well as those expressing our somatized conditions. They display a neutrality of value, which is characteristic of eternity, as it were. They may, for example, show the existential dryness of diabetic or at least pre-diabetic conditions, as well as those expressing unquenchable thirst. They would include images of stony and sandy areas, or the Gods of the desert and images from the realm of Dionysos.

On the other hand, the same applies to symbols of the second kind, those hybrid images, paradoxes and chimeric phenomena, which express the entire dialectics of our polarized forms of human existence. In the case of diabetes, one such image would be the alchemical hydrolith, the water-stone, which depicts the existential drama in question superbly and combines all its aspects.

Compared to the symbols of the first kind, we observe a dialectical compensation of energy, which is achieved here because everything that has been overvalued is degraded and everything that has been condemned to be somatized becomes pre-eminent.

If properly handled, both types of symbols are therefore capable of throwing light on the illness and of sublimating it. As Jung pointed out, symbols understood in this manner are genuine mediators, means, or medicines, which are used by the medical doctor to medicate in his medical practice. We note that all these expressions are derived from the Latin word, "medium," the middle. Quite obviously, this applies not only to psychiatry but also to physical medicine. Both kinds of symbols can take us back to what we described earlier as "forms of human existence that are lived," to at least a partial integration of the Dionysian, if we stay with the example of diabetic or pre-diabetic disorders of the sugar metabolism.

The setting we have for verbal therapy seems to be ideally suited for this approach. For most therapies are carried out in armchairs, facing each other, or even in an armchair placed behind a couch. You cannot even call it a "sitting-across-from-one-another," properly speaking. In many cases it would be more appropriate to speak of "lying-across-from-one-another." The business of verbal therapy is incubatory; and incubation takes place during the night while we are lying down.

Small wonder that this type of therapy presupposes that both the therapist and the patient have the gift of "light-magic," to put it in hermetic terminology. Some tendency to hypochondria or hyperchondria, as the case may be, is also a prerequisite, as is the gift of "gravitational magic," the art of levitation. What is also required is a certain awareness that one is NOT going to achieve shining wisdom and one will NOT escape either physical or mercurial gravity.

There is some solace in this: in the spirit of Mercurius, we do move through life with a certain clarity of mind, on the one hand, but also in the more or less "morbidic" consciousness of our physical dependency. Our occult and hermetic knowledge preserves us from the excesses of present-day utopian, scientific medicine. Although it may have fewer immediate and spectacular results to show for it than scientific medicine, it does make the incurable more meaningful and imbues it with a sort of "pistis et pax." However, the contention that scientific medicine is senselessly successful, while Archetypal Medicine is meaningfully unsuccessful is definitely a vast exaggeration.

ON INDIVIDUATION AND THE SELF

C.G. Jung considered that what he had to say started where treatment stopped. What he had in mind was the process of individuation, the development of psychic wholeness. In general, this process is compared to a tortuous path which may enable the person who takes it offset the typological splits, or even to integrate the contrasexual side of his personality. At least initially, Jung thought in terms of man's possible redemption, the reaching of a goal. The path was thought of as psychic development.

Later on, Jung became more skeptical. The question arises whether any Jungian ever proved that he actually reached this ambitious goal. In addition, we now have the experience gained in psychosomatics, according to which the archetypal realities of human existence may also be cast into materiality. It looks as though not only Analytical Psychology, but every other kind as well, reckoned on human life without considering the host. We might say that in the first half of life, people see the psychologist and psychiatrist with the same problems they submit to the internist in the second half, whereby they demonstrate yet again the existence of a mercurial spirit.

We all have the experience with the strange way our predisposition, i.e., our contradictory archetypal human condition, tends to decay and how many possibilities there are for our inferiorities to somatize and to turn into clinical pictures. There is not just the example of existential thirst materializing in the form of a disorder of the sugar metabolism, or even diabetes proper. I am also thinking of the way our tendency to become outraged and violent may bring about arteriosclerotic vascular changes with all they entail. Basically, even our heart attacks and cerebral strokes and many other things are part of the process of individuation.

More than anything, this path takes us down an "incline" which "gravitates" towards a wearisome old age. It is made up of cascades and partial remissions, a gradual falling off until we become a "case" and have our final downfall. The ultimate meaning of our mortality is the total transformation of our libido into materiality. Inasmuch as we are guided by the Spirit Mercurius in diagnosis and in therapy, we also have to consider the material forms of transformation as part of a "healthy" life. It is always a matter of life and death!

From this point of view, it is rather surprising to find how little solace people experience when they are faced with the prospect of ultimate materialization. It is as though our last abode was tinged by the same attitude of depreciation and condemnation we have in regard to the inferior dispositions which ultimately bless us with death.

Dissolution into the unconsciousness of matter is not much in demand, no matter how impressive the "hermetic" silence of the grave and the peace of the dead. Few are the visitors who find pleasure in strolling through the splendors of graveyards unless they are able to associate such strolls with an idea of life in a brighter and lighter beyond, in Nirvana, a heaven at the right of the Lord, or something of the kind.

Strictly speaking, even our ultimate materialization is not just "deadly." For whenever the mercurial spirit has materialized, therefore becoming more real, it is also potentiated from the energic standpoint. In dying, we are not just transformed into dust or "dirt," but also into "Erdkraft" (literally, "earth power"), according to Germanic popular belief. In other words, we become part of the earth's numinous forces, another aspect of the spirit Mercurius, as we pointed out earlier.

Something would be missing from our discussion of the Jungian "topoi" and their gravitational movement if we were to leave out the Self. For Jung, it was the center of human existence, although it was also rather elusive and shrouded in metaphysical darkness. For this reason, his attempts to describe it often led him to use rather vague, "dim" language, such as the "mediator of the opposites," the "ordering principle of our destiny." He also says that it is difficult to fathom its designs, but, as psychic wholeness, the Self is the goal of the individuation process, our self-realization. The concepts and images he uses to describe the nature of the Self are again taken from themes dealing with light. Basically, the Self appears to be for Jung the center of both the Conscious and the Unconscious, which means that it is also a manifestation of HIS mercurial spirit. This is exactly the point at which we would need a sort of "medical Self," a psychosomatic Self, which would reflect the theme of weightiness and become more kinaesthetic, as it were. For the Self is also the center of both lightness and heaviness.

This is, in fact, also the point where the Analytical Psychology in Archetypal Medicine comes inevitably close to mysticism of physical illness. The quasi-erotic feelings which Analytical Psychology nurtures for neurotic and psychotic symptoms are also at issue in Archetypal Medicine when it comes to the marvels of body pathologies. Considering that somatization addresses itself to the ultimate in human existence, body pathology is full of special microcosmic meaning. A bent for the mysticism of illness implies an alchemistic passion for finding the gold in the dung-heap of body morbidity.

When the hypochondriac nature of a psychosomatic adept does not include a natural inclination to have a mystic view of the Self in terms of weight, this perspective will hit him, as a rule, by the middle of life at the very latest, i.e., at a time when the gap between the psychic process and the miseries of the body becomes unmistakably wider.

At this point, we note the same kind of incestuous lascivity we mentioned in our discussion of the individuation process, an occult passion for Gaia-matter and her materiality. "Hic et nunc" she remains a constant factor in the way we experience ourselves. She is not only present in the form of darkness and perplexity, i.e., unconsciousness, but above all in our existential wearisomeness. Hence, even the psychosomatic Self has an innate matriarchal component.

Given that this Self reflects the Spirit of Mercurius and therefore the vision of an "ordo" and a womb, the experience of shelteredness associated with it must be largely "hypogaeic"—a term derived from the Stone-Age "hypogaeae," the Great Mother's underground places of worship on Crete and Malta, for example. This Self would therefore be much less "Marian," i.e., it would have fewer of the radiant characteristics associated with the Mother of God, traits with which Jung and the Jungians tend to endow it.

As we know, Jung's attempts to find symbols for the Self also took him into alchemy. To this end, the image of the "stone of the wise" seemed to be particularly handy. Despite the manifest unwieldiness of this symbol, it was useful for describing the peculiar, mystical interrelationship between the Conscious and the Unconscious. For Jung it remained primarily a psychic stone with all the implications of bright and dark sensations. It is, however, quite obvious that the stone also contains the motif of lightness and heaviness and that, everything considered, it is a psychosomatic, a medical stone.

It would be off the mark to say that all this "weighting" of the mercurial spirit had been the result intended by a consciously critical attitude for the purpose of establishing a more direct relationship between Analytical Psychology and medicine. Most of the shifts of emphasis followed a "gradient." The gravitational movement of Mercury's spirit toward Archetypal Medicine obeyed extrapersonal forces; it, too, was im-posed.

We can assume that the conditions of the times, namely those prevailing in the first part of the twentieth century as compared to those in the second part, played a decisive role in this development. Altogether, the century was one that began in a spirit of bright expectations and goals and therefore also in a spirit of humanistic chauvinism that was never questioned. Not everything was brilliant and visionary, however; a lot was boom and bluff. Along with darkness, heaviness of every kind was to be eradicated from the surface of the earth. The goal was a planet without gravitation. Ecological thinking became more plausible only under the impact of the de-pressing experiences in the second part of the century. Gradually, it became apparent that there were limits and an accumulation of debt to be paid.

There is no doubt that Analytical Psychology, with its sense of polarities, was ecologically predisposed from the outset. But as its orientation was mainly psychological, the ecological content remained just half real. Archetypal Medicine is more serious about ecology. Starting from the obvious premise that, in a limited world, there should be a balance between life and death, it goes one step further; health and sickness behave ecologically as well. This also applies to our liberalism and bias with regard to the laws of the inorganic world, which are experienced as alien. In this respect, Archetypal Medicine has a greater affinity for the ecological movement of the outgoing century than does Analytical Psychology.

REFERENCES

1. C.G. Jung, *SYMBOLIK DES GEISTES*. Verlag Rascher, Zurich, 1953. In Collected Works in English as "The Spirit Mercury."

2. C.G. Jung, *ERINNERUNGEN, TRAUME, GEDANKEN*, Verlag Rascher, Zurich, 1962. In English as "Memories, Dreams, Reflections."

3. C.G. Jung, "Ueber die Energetic der Seele," in: *UEBER PSYCHISCHE ENERGETIK UND DAS WESEN DER TRAUME*, Rascher Verlag, Zurich, 1948. In Collected Works as "On Psychic Energy" plus other sources.

4. C.G. Jung, *PSYCHOLOGIE UND ALCHEMIE*, Rascher Verlag, Zurich, 1944. In English as "Psychology and Alchemy."

5. Rafael Lopez-Pedraza, *HERMES,* Schweizer Spiegel Verlag, Zurich, 1977. In English as "Hermes" in Spring Publications.

6. Alfred J. Ziegler, *MORIBISMUS, VON DER BESTEN ALLER GESUNDHEITEN,* Schweitzer Spiegel Verlag, Zurich, 1979. English translation, "Archetypal Medicine" in Spring Publications, 1983.

7. Alfred J. Ziegler. "Die Schonheit der Pathologie" In *ERANOS JAHRBUCH,* 1984. Insel Verlag, Frankfurt a.M.

8. Alfred J. Ziegler. "Hydrolith" in *ARCHETYPAL MEDICINE.* Spring Publications, Dallas, Texas, 1983.

9. Alfred J. Ziegler. "Die dunkelgrune Gesundheit," Vortrag (lecture) Psychologischer Club, Zurich, 1985.

COMMENT BY SPIEGELMAN ON PAPER BY ZIEGLER

This "weighty" paper, filled with earth-spirit, is an excellent example of the kind of reflective, informed, "educated" work one often finds among European physicians, especially Jungians, but, alas, less frequently among American physicians more concerned with precision of diagnosis and technique. Dr. Ziegler, like many of our contemporary Jungians, found it necessary to go more deeply into "body," but he did so by re-linking to the physician's psychosomatic interest in a deeper way. Of the many beautifully expressed ideas contained herein, I liked the following best: "We might say that in the first half of life people see the psychologist and psychiatrist with the same problems they submit to the internist in the second half, whereby they demonstrate yet again the existence of a mercurial spirit." I was also struck by his reminder that even heart attacks, strokes, etc., which assault us in spirit and flesh, are also "part of the process of individuation." For these insights and directions, we can be glad, indeed.

I would ask only two questions: (1) Since somatic symptoms, like dreams, can be looked at either from the point of view of "compensation" or that of expressing the actual psychic situation, how is one to choose which is being expressed? (2) Could Dr. Ziegler say a few words about how he incorporates his psychosomatic approach in his daily work? Does he work in a medical clinic, or see people who come for medical treatment and not psychotherapy? And, in his analytic work, how does he comment on the somatic symptoms?

I, for one, look forward to hearing more about this direction of Dr. Ziegler, and think that Jung would be glad that his many second-generation followers take up the scraggly ends of all his own interests with energy and originality. Certainly Dr. Ziegler does so.

REPLY BY ZIEGLER TO SPIEGELMAN

(1) The answer to this question is inherent in the very concept of Archetypal Medicine, according to which, images of physical diseases represent forms of human existence that appear "mutated" in the body. Pathogenetically, it is

therefore a process which is compensatory to the patient's conscious attitude toward life in general and a specific existential situation in particular. It expresses an attitude toward these situations that is totally different from the conscious one. At the same time, the pathological syndrome also describes the nature of these situations, for they were the triggers of the pathology. Diffuse anesthesias of the skin would therefore be a compensatory somatization of a certain inevitable distance to life, while also describing conditions of life which tend to touch us too closely.

(2) I do not think it is so much a matter of how I make use of my psycho-somatic approach to what is essentially psychotherapeutic work, based on dialogue, but much more of how I integrate the themes cropping up in my daily work into my psychosomatic approach. For, as part of Archetypal Medicine or Morbism, my psychosomatic approach is not an arbitrary instrument but my WELTANSCHAUUNG. In accordance with certain European traditions, the subject, concept or vision takes precedence over the practical approach. The question which arises in practice is rather one of how the pathological syndrome, or the image of the disease—its pathogenesis, prognosis and psychotherapy—can be inserted into this WELTANSCHAUUNG! Even Jung's, and perhaps other psychotherapists' style of work can barely be distinguished from their particular attitude toward the problems of life in general. Ultimately, all their answers came from the mainspring of their innermost nature. While these had always been there, they merely became more consistent as life went on.

McNAIR'S RESPONSE TO ZIEGLER'S PAPER

Dr. Ziegler is a "man of vision." I enjoy and appreciate his point of view and capacity to see metaphor and psychological phenomenology. I feel acquainted with the "descending of spirit into matter" notion in those diseases I have had the opportunity to work with. I find it reassuring that Jungian Psychology can be brought so directly into physical medicine.

This paper had an immense impact upon me. I kept finding myself tangled in an intuitive web as I struggled to establish my own personal analog to his words. Thus it became a "weighty" piece to read. I had to read, and re-read, slowly. As always, time . . . and suffering, were inevitable. Ziegler's scope and precision made it days and months before I could adequately distill and digest what was being said to me. I looked up his book to see if that might help me. It did: not because of what he wrote, but what his translator wrote. He confessed that it took him over two years! I felt better; 10 months isn't so bad after all.

I have always felt best when I am the conveyer of this kind of intuitive spirit—the receiving end feels burdensome. This paper became a meditation for me; of an attitude, a perspective, of delight, of responsibility for my own physical space. I know for myself that I look upon physical disabilities or disease with a certain dread and anxiety initially . . . like coming across a snake on the path through the woods. The outcome is unknown until I become more related.

I like the perspective of the body as existential metaphor. It quite naturally appears that thoughts, feelings, moods, etc. have been more often the focus of metaphorical attention in Jungian circles. Consistent with Ziegler's thesis, I have not heard as much about physical symptoms during training. Yet when such a moment does arise, it leads to a sense of intimacy and kinship that I find gratifying. On the other hand, there lives within me an anxiety of being "caught in" and "dissolved by" Gaia-Mater and her materiality and thus into the "Erdkraft" state, for lack of consciousness. I must say the awareness of my own organicity—phantasies and sensations—increased tremendously doing this paper.

I appreciated reading about the change in Dr. Ziegler's psychology at mid-life, and the fundamental shift and differentiation from Jung's condition. Hearing about the nature of this sort of struggle has been very valuable to my own learning and struggle. Often enough, the experience is more valuable than the outcome—the product—since the human condition is a shared event, not the outcome that, to my way of thinking, is always idiosyncratic. What I am left with after all this is a much keener awareness of the body, the phenomenology within its physical space (as metaphor) and the interface with the physical space it inhabits at a given moment—the therapeutic session. I must borrow from Sartre for the notion of "existential imagination": we are forever caught in phantasy that we cannot see, yet within it have an imagination of ourselves nonetheless.

I sense that Ziegler has provided a map of an archetypal territory as a myth or fairy tale might do. With such a perspective one may grasp the existential imagination and the personal phantasy. If this be the case, then a tender empathy may arise to penetrate the isolating and alienating effects of a somatic state; not offering an escape or rescue, but a genuine human relationship.

(1) What existential theorists have contributed to the growth and development of your point of view?

(2) I would be very interested to know if any physical effect arose as you wrote this paper.

(3) What do you actually do with your vision? Do you share it, or hold and contain it?

(4) What suggestions would you have for body-work with therapy—or training?

(5) My capacity to comprehend and apprehend the "metaphor" in a physical process has come only after repeated incursions into its realm. Utilizing a pre-existing metaphor has not always been as beneficial. How is it for Ziegler after so much mapping? Does he set aside his histories to let the theme emerge anew each time or is it helpful to lead with it?

ZIEGLER'S REPLY TO McNAIR

The "vision" found its (representation) statement in "Archetypal Medicine" in English, and in German in "Morbismos." She shines in an unmistakable (obvious, evident) twilight and has her decidedly morbistic sound (not to be mistaken for the traditional "morbid") which can also be heard in the many existential theorists who seemingly are scattered over the whole European history of the spirit in an unconnected way. Yet I was not instructed (advised) by them; however I did find beautiful stimulus from them.

Under the philosophers are Pessimists like Schopenhauer, Cynics like Voltaire, Nietzsche or Oscar Wilde, Nihilists of the 19th century, and Existentialists like Sartre and Camus; under the poets and writers, you find German Romantics, the fatalists of Russian literature, the decadents of fin de siecle Paris and London and later, of course, in Thomas Mann; in other words, Vienna is a morbistic rejected chosen "homeland." Stimulation also came from the Christian religion, especially from the Mystics of "sorrow" from the Rhine and from the baroque "holy" mystics of the Spanish and Italian counter-revolution. Not to be forgotten is the Scandinavian theatre at the end of the last century with its propensity for gloom, the sickness operas of bel canto and finally the travesties of Fellini. Especially stirring were the morbistic painters, mostly the Florentine Mannerists, the Symbolists at the end of the 19th century like Kubin, Redon, Mouch and the Catalan surrealists. And finally, the early homeopaths also have said much—so as not to completely forget medicine—that is of the best, with which a Morbism can be thought through.

(2) In order to be able to answer this question, I would have to bring out the Diary notices of June and July 1985. In it is much about a wide and blue sky, flying phantasies and morning walks on the nearby Zollikerberg. On the other side, it was summer, nature stood still, the garden was luxuriant, great with summer growth, and the wild pigeons wailing from the nearby (cemetery) trees. The walks were not only in a lightly swinging vein, but often heavy and connected to heartache. The doodles of that time are contradictory: under the title of "the exit," a "cool" ("hip")-looking bird with pointed (jagged) plumage flies to the left; another time, a well-built negro woman, laden up to the shoulders with numerous ornamentally decorated breasts and a Fettsteis looks testily into the distance. Under that is written "Summer in Mombassa." Also is mentioned that the Chief Swiss Forest Ranger has calculated that by the beginning of the 90s the Bannforest of the Swiss interior will be destroyed by the emission of harmful materials.

(3) In psychotherapy, I speak of the morbistic vision quite often. You see, I am the vision personally. And many patients know of me beforehand through my books, articles and lectures. Most of them know whom they have before them. Often the theory finds its expression in certain core sentences like: What makes us successfull, kills us; health is dangerous, it makes us sick; Man is healthier if he is at least slightly sick, and so on.

(4) In conversation therapy, language is already body work! Or the other way round; when body work becomes speech, then it is displayed (manifested) within the therapy and education. Language is a psychosomaticum par excellence. It comes out of life itself and flows into it. It comes out of the organs and diseases and also leads to it. Mostly this language is the language operatoire of Science, but primarily it is poetic. For that reason, language (conversation) therapy demands a minimum of poetic talent.

(5) In the course of the years, a metaphoric body of thought has developed, which responded (matched) more and more the individual case, more empathetically and reflectively (pensive, thoughtful, contemplative, musing). Yet as individual as this may be, for the single sickness picture (plate, scene) it still circles (rotates) again and again around similar archetypal stereotypes that also, right at the beginning, can predict/announce the direction of the therapy. Franz Riklin, the late President of ISAP, already made an appropriate suggestion: one could in this way put together—build—an intrinsic (proper, true, real) atlas of a picturesque nosology.

The Impact of Suffering and Self-Disclosure on the Life of the Analyst

by

J. MARVIN SPIEGELMAN, Ph.D.

In the bathroom of my office hangs a poster portraying a life-size statue of a nude woman, before which stands a man wearing only a hat, coat and shoes, his back toward the observer. He bares himself to the statue, and the poster carries the inscription, "Expose yourself to Art." I have certainly been troubled by the issue of self-disclosure. Over the years, I have had any number of dreams of being in a public situation with either the wrong clothes or no clothes, and I have spent lots of time trying to sort out this issue of my persona in some decent way, without a huge amount of success.

One resolution of this issue, to expose to and for art, has resulted in several books of fiction I have written, and my style, even in scholarly articles, has been personal and often self-revelatory. In the following comments, I shall both reveal and conceal, for that theme, I maintain, along with suffering, is a chief feature of the life of the analyst, particularly in our work.

Patients come to us and reveal their secrets, their lives, their concerns, and we listen carefully, thoughtfully, and appreciatively, trying to be non-judgemental, if we can. Even if we can not, we have exposed our own shadows and secrets to our analysts enough so that we are less inclined, by and large, to condemn patients, if not each other.

This self-revelation of patients, we realize, is ultimately Self-realization with a capital S, since we understand that this exploration, thus begun and continued, becomes an arena in which the Self is gradually made manifest. Jung has taught us that it is not only the Self of the patient which is being revealed, but it is also the analyst's Self which is constellated and we are not only "in" the work with patients, but are required to reveal ourselves as well. For myself, I have found that what needs to be revealed are not facts and secrets about my life—which does not usually produce much of value therapeutically—but what I am thinking and feeling in relation to the patient, since the unconscious is mobilized in both parties. Therefore, the Selves are ultimately exposed, to one degree or another.

Not long ago, I added another little card, next to the poster I mentioned earlier, given to me by my wife for a birthday. On this card is shown a rather meek, elderly gentleman wearing a proper suit and carrying an umbrella. He glances rather startledly at a woman whose back is toward us. She is a fulsome creature, wearing a very luxurious fur coat, and she bares herself to this shy soul.

This card balances the picture. The two, together, express my views about the process of analysis being, ultimately, a mutual one, in which both parties are exposed to each other, and more importantly, to the unconscious itself. This fact, peculiar to our profession, has far-reaching effects upon us. I shall be noting these effects in the further course of this paper. Now, however, I wish to examine the second theme of the paper, that of suffering.

We can approach this theme, perhaps, by asking: What is it that makes the life of an analyst different from that of a chiropractor, astronaut, interior decorator or chef? The first thing that comes to mind is that we are connected with, fixed on, devoted to, suffering. We are totally and intimately confronted by the suffering of those who come to us, since they do not usually bring—at least at the outset—their joy, achievements and delights. This strange involvement with suffering already makes our lives different from the last three occupations, but not different from the chiropractor and, for that matter, from the physician, nurse, social worker or clergyman. These other healers, however, have quite a different outlook on human suffering. They are armed with techniques to alleviate pain or ameliorate the environmental strictures which cause or aggravate the pain. Physicians and nurses are skilled in the precise administration of drugs and procedures which cure or soften. Social workers and priests are allied with institutions which make life-in-pain more bearable. Clergy, further-more, have instruments and sacraments of belief and practice which give them direct access to helpful forces. Should these interventions prove unsuccessful, they do not consider themselves to blame, nor do their constituents.

Only "shrinks" can not shrink from nor evade the direct, powerless encounter with suffering. We are armed with our concepts, to be sure, and the strength resulting from endless years of training-analysis, but ultimately, as Jung has taught us, we are equipped only with our Selves. We encounter this suffering as both symptom and event, as condition and person, and our central question is always, "What are we—and they—going to do about it?" The answer for us is always individual, although the repeated encounter with this dilemma profoundly affects us. In order to understand the life of the analyst, we need to comprehend this endless confrontation with suffering, a feature which contributes mightily to our own "deformation professionelle."

How are we to approach this issue of suffering and what does it do to our lives? We all know that confession is good for the soul. We encourage our patients to fully and deeply express all that makes them suffer, to associate to it, to round it out, and together with us, to examine the causes and purposes of such pain. This work usually alleviates the suffering or ultimately provides meaning to make it bearable. It also can transform it. We are in the position of a caring and intelligent friend, but we are also knowledgeable and skilled in communicating non-judgementally and with some objectivity. Furthermore, as Jungians, we are committed to the view that the ultimate healer and authority lies within the person. We address our efforts to link this sufferer with his inner world, and we try to read the messages of the Self of the patient, in dream and fantasy, which leads toward healing and understanding.

But what does this repeated exposure to suffering do to us? Particularly when our efforts, understanding, and compassion are insufficient? We, too, are infected, as Jung pointed out, and our own suffering inevitably comes into the picture, both induced and activated, both similar to that of the patient and different. Finally, it is or becomes our own.

Could this fact account for the high suicide rate among psychiatrists? Perhaps it underlies the common wisdom that those who work in the area of mental health do not generally possess much of it themselves. We try to fend off such suffering, of course, both consciously and unconsciosuly, but the resultant rigidity and closed-offedness, as described by Guggenbuhl in his *POWER AND THE HELPING PROFESSIONS*, is not attractive either. In short, the issue hinges on what we call the transference, seen by many of us as not just the projections of the patient on the therapist, but as the unconscious co-mingling of the psyches, in which the archetypes are constellated and the analyst is affected as well as the patient. All this we know from Jung, who also told us that there must be some reason for us to have chosen such a dour and bleak vocation, that our psyches must need it. Indeed, we are all very much aware of the proferred image of the "wounded healer" and that we even heal from our own wounds opened up in the work.

I have never been happy with this image of the "wounded healer." I am aware that I am, indeed, continually wounded by patients and their psyches, that I help in the healing by finding my wholeness in the face of the fragmentation and distress which patients bring and which divides me, even splits me. The image is too dark and heavy, however, and leaves out the healing effects of joy and laughter.

We will remain with the issue of suffering, however, and examine how this effects our lives in a number of areas. I will address eight of these, and then return to our general themes of suffering and self-disclosure and the myths which underlie them. The areas which I have chosen are anxiety, depression, aggression, sex, money, alienation, community and religion. A large handful, naturally, and perhaps too much to include, but I shall be offering reflections rather than essays on these issues. I can venture to offer these reflections on two grounds: First, I have always had a number of patients who have been therapists, so I speak not only idiosyncratically. Second, my own suffering as a result of forces external to the work has been relatively mild, compared to many other people. So I think that I can speak of the suffering of the therapist which is a consequence of the work itself and of the personality of the therapist who, by either fate or choice, is immersed in such a vocation. Indeed, since my subjective impression is that I have suffered a lot in this work, I wonder how some of my colleagues, less blessed than myself in the areas of relationship and security, survive the assaults on the soul which our work brings.

ANXIETY

The first step in our eight-fold path of examination of the suffering of the therapist is that of anxiety. My own experience of anxiety, outside of the therapeutic hour, has been that of it being attached to other topics of my chosen list, namely aggression, sex, money, alienation, community and religion. I have only rarely experienced—outside of analysis—what we called in my Rorschach days "free-floating anxiety," or the nameless dread of which Kierkegaard speaks. Yet I have had patients, of course, who have suffered from this condition, and such a dread has indeed frequently manifested in the work. Jung believed that anxiety was associated with the numinous: dread and awe are the necessary concomitants of facing the gods. I recall Madame Jolande Jacobi, in a course at the Institute in Zurich in the late 1950s, solemnly intoning that such anxiety arises as a consequence of not being in touch with one's shadow. If your shadow is with you, providing the earthy grounding of its instinctiveness, for example, your anxiety will change to a specific fear, a realistic apprehension of present danger. A true statement, this, and one that we unconsciously assent to when we encourage patients to "go with the anxiety," to see where it leads and to what it refers. Name the god, as it were, and accept the fear, and we are half-way there. Yet what about our own anxiety, awakened during the analytic hour? Are we alert, we rightly ask ourselves? Are we connected, doing the "right thing"? Is this patient going to be all right, will he/she quit or commit suicide? Now, as I contemplate this anxiety of my patient and experience my powerlessness to alleviate it, to interpret it, even cope with it, my own anxiety arises by induction. As I experience this, I think, shall I reveal that I, too, am anxious, powerless, helpless? Will this self-disclosure aggravate the patient, make him/her feel even more helpless and also feel that I can not assist or even cope with the nameless fear? Or if I do reveal my own anxiety, will this be beneficial, alleviate the condition by a sharing, by an indication that I can stand it, endure it? Or, if I do disclose, will it be the feeling of anxiety itself, or will I also reveal that I am afraid that I can not help, that I will be abandoned by the person who, perhaps, is feeling the very fear of abandonment which is now assaulting me?

In my own analytical stance of "mutual process," in the belief that the archetype is now constellated between us, I will likely reveal any or all of the above and wait for the reaction. And the result? Sometimes very helpful, sometimes not. Sometimes this self-disclosure on my part leads to a deepening, a capacity to move onward and more meaningfully, with a therapeutic effect. Sometimes, however, I am greeted by—and I think now of a particular patient— a look at me from previously downcast eyes, with non-understanding, a further dread and a sense that I, too, can not help him, just as no other therapist could.

So, with this patient I am powerless and even the confession of our mutual powerlessness makes things worse. I then suggest that we both ask or pray together for the source of this dread to reveal itself here in the room. And now, this rationalist who has been successful in his life but in his sixties is nearly broken and defeated, is so fearful of praying together and, probably, finds this erstwhile rational therapist to be a superstitious and dangerous fool, that he wants to bolt. Yet he also has a little hope and wants to please me. I feel the same thing, I say, in a further orgy of self-disclosure, and the hour ends. Soon, not in that session but in several more, he terminates the therapy, and I feel like the fool. Now, many months later, as I write, I feel the need to telephone him and find out if what I said above was true for him. So, I call and he is delighted to hear from me. Yes, he is still surviving, just the same as before, only just barely. He is with a previous therapist, one who gave him drugs. Yes, I was right that the demon was just too much and that he was even more terrified of being together in prayer. He feels that he should have stuck it out. But that is not why he left. He ended because there was just too much gloom and doom in our relationship, nothing upbeat. No, it isn't better now; the demon of which he was afraid is still there, it neither leaves him nor kills him. We share a few words of mutual appreciation and hang up. So, here I am with my paper, once more, my own anxiety alleviated by a connection with him and by the healing power of self-revelation. The demon-god, dark and unforgiving, relents for one moment and my ex-patient is grateful for the care and contact and I am grateful that I need not feel guilty for the failure, nor feel abandoned. So, whose therapy is it? For whom do we do this work?

I turn now, to my colleagues, toward whom I direct these words, and acknowledge that it is the self-disclosure which seems to be at issue here, whether successful or not, whether it assists the patient or not. I conclude from this that what is mobilized in such events is, indeed, the god itself, which we dread. It is the darkness of the dread, and the dark side of the Self which is being revealed. The self-disclosure about which we are ambivalent as professionals is actually disclosure of the Self (capital S). This is what is at stake in our work. We reveal and conceal, just as the Self is revealed and concealed. Our struggle is to find the right attitude with which to address this revelation. The Self-manifestation of the images of the divine, which usually remain in the background for others, haunt us. The aspects of totality which want to be seen and incarnated also defy all our efforts at approach, whether we placate, command, cooperate or submit. Ultimately, I think, with each patient, if we go deep enough, we discover aspects of this god of Self, and anxiety is just such a condition for its encounter.

I wonder, then, if my other anxieties, apart from the therapeutic vessel where it is induced, are also manifestations of the god? Is the god which I fear out there in the world the same one? When I am anxious over money, over abandonment, over performance, do I experience the self-revelation of the god? The same demon that plagued the patient with whom I failed? Am I, too, merely hanging on, surviving the onslaught, neither relieved nor dying? At times it seems that way. But I also find, unlike my patient, that my capacity to kneel to the higher power, to regard it as Other and greater, to do all I can with my ego, but also to surrender this ego is what brings relief, meaning, continuity. Do I teach this to my patients? I suspect that I do.

What is the difference between anxiety considered in the therapeutic process and that encountered in the workaday world? Everyone suffers anxiety about money, performance, security, and we all dread the unknown. But how we handle it alone and with friends and loved ones is a different matter than how we do this with patients. With the latter, we are participatory, we are induced, we are willing victims. We are part of that stoked alchemical process which even heats up the feared and rejected content. Some colleagues, mostly Freudians, want to increase anxiety, turn up the heat, providing motivation for greater and more sincere work. I do not share that view. The god comes of its own accord. Just work away and the unconscious, if so inclined, will appear. The hard part, as it was with my anxiety-ridden patient who had positive dreams and deep dread, is to integrate it, to endure it, to survive it.

And that is how our lives as analysts are different from others: we are partners in the plague. We submit to the darkness, to the "emotional plague" as Reich called it, willingly, with consciousness, even gladly, because this, we think, will heal or transform or bring more light. What is more, we do this because it is our calling, our vocation, our life. This does make us strange in the eyes of the world, and makes it difficult for us to communicate what we do, how we are. This makes us, too, like scientists and prostitutes, not ordinary. And, as with the vocations just mentioned, we are admired and despised, sought after and feared.

DEPRESSION

This psychological condition is, in my experience, the most typical and frequent form of psycho-pathology found among our fellow therapists. Most of us experience down-goings and despairs in the course of the work, and more than other professionals do. Witness: the high suicide-rate among psychiatrists. Witness: the later works of Freud, Adler, Reich, and in a more profound and worked-out way—as for instance in *ANSWER TO JOB*—Jung. Pessimism and the problem of evil is the lot of the advanced worker in the vineyards of the soul. So, too, has this been my own most typical psycho-pathology, particularly since the age of forty. How many mornings have I awakened in darkness, gloomy and distressed! Everything seems laden with uncertainty and pain. Why is this so? I remember telling Michael Fordham that his work was certainly brilliant, but it usually left me feeling depressed. He responded, heartily, that he thought this was a good thing, since I was too high up in the air and needed to be brought back to earth. My fiction-writing, for example, was unfoundedly optimistic. Well, he had read only my first psycho-mythology book, *THE TREE*, which is surely upbeat, but he had not read my book called, *THE FAILURES*, a story of an unhealed healer, an unpublished writer, an empty teacher, and an unfrocked priest, all of whom go for healing to a powerless magician.

Yet Fordham had a point. Many therapists, Jungians particularly, tend to be intuitives or intellectuals and we are, indeed, high up or in the head, not enough connected with the body and the earth. But, then, what about the most important body-therapist and theorist, Wilhelm Reich? He ended up with a very pessimistic attitude, as shown in his book *REICH SPEAKS OF FREUD*, if not downright mad. And what of Freud and his feelings of "discontent" and "disillusion"? Non-Jungians are bleak, too.

One reason for this depressive and disillusioning condition is to be found in what our colleague Robert Bosnak, of Amsterdam and Boston, has discovered in our images of inferiority. Starting with Freud's first "Irma" dream—the archetypal beginning of the work of analysts—Bosnak shows us that it is the analyst's image of inferiority, defeat and incompetence which dogs us endlessly in our work. His paper was the first I ever read which spoke to the condition I have usually had, not so much in therapy itself (although I do occasionally experience it there also), but whenever reading Freudian-style work. Feelings of inferiority, failure, and incompetence come with that reductive attitude, I believe. It is, all the same, true. We are archetypally conditioned to experience this lamentable condition. But the writings of Jung, I find, with its synthetic attitude toward darkness, provides the necessary complement to the reduction. Not only is the analyst's anima, as in Irma, badly treated, too much for us, and sick, she is also, as in Jung's anima of his doctoral dissertation, a medium for the depths, fascinating and revealing.

However we conceive of this depression which dogs most of us, how do we deal with it? Following the Jungian procedure, we go down with it, we let it speak, we folow the movement of the soul into the depths. But many of our patients can not or will not do this. It is not their way, especially in the earlier years of the work. So, then, what do we do, or suggest to them? Well, we burn it out, in the American method, through activity: jogging, swimming, exercise. Here the image of coping with the "nigredo" is to burn away the dankness and heaviness of Saturn, which sometimes works, sometimes not. How different, say, from the attitude toward depression taken by the Asian! One Japanese psychiatrist who worked with me told me that the treatment of choice for depression in his country was rest, to be quiet, to retreat and to allow nature to restore energy and wholeness. How different from us! I am reminded of the poster suggested by an American monk to contrast the western and eastern viewpoints. It said: "Don't just do something, the Buddha said, stand there!"

In my own experience, all of these methods—rest, activity, active imagination, and consciously moving away from the dark moods—do help the condition. All are right at times and are ineffective or inappropriate at others. How do we know which and when, and how do we know when to ask our medical colleagues for help with drugs for those patients with whom none of these is effective? Well, we don't know, although there are books about depression and increasing knowledge about its physiological concomitants and antecedents.

What we do know is that we therapists experience more of it than do other professionals. Is this through the induction I have spoken of? Or the initial condition of our psyches which attracts us to the work in the first place? Or the necessary compensation to our heights and intuitive soarings? As it is with all the treatment modes, so are all the explanations true. Furthermore, we seem to experience more failure than do physicians or lawyers, more frustration in achieving goals of wholeness and creativity. We are willy-nilly tied to extreme ambiguity and uncertainty in our work. Very little is certain and even that is always relative to that particular individual who enters into our offices and our psyches. The blessings and curses of individuality, like that for art, depend on the soul and its achievement. But how do we gauge the latter? Are we like van Gogh, geniuses who produce great work and are not recognized, or like Boucher, precious and talented, successful but shallow? How many of us look to highly recognized or more successful colleagues, particularly those from other schools, and see them as shallow, or catering to the public triviality?

That competitive and envious shadow is to be solved, I discovered, by sacrificing it, abjuring it, consciously, in the outer world. Give up the competition and embrace the simple life. I suspect that many of us have come to such a solution privately. We go to work, come home to family and friends, read our books, write papers, tend our gardens, look forward to those weeks of vacation in the mountains and seashore, and are content. Work and Love, said Freud, and resolve competition that way. Yes. In this, we are like many other people, yet we come to this, I think, out of the heat and drama of our work, the deadness and vitality of the analytic process, in which the alchemy is secret and contained, for we can not even talk much to others about what we do.

No wonder we are inferior and superior, and no wonder so many of us opt for the simple life outside, to compensate the complexity and uncertainty of the inside—that is, the inside of our offices and the inside of our souls. We are specialists in the darkness of the soul, and in that we can join no other vocation that I can think of, not even that of most clergy. We are more like monks or hermits in that regard, but we are neither totally alone nor in groups, as they are. We are with an "other" and with each "other" who appears. What a profession! What a blessing and what a curse! No wonder we seem strange, and no wonder the simple life is so attractive to many of us.

The answer then—or, at least, my answer—to the depression evoked in our work, is the simple life. Brought down from ambition, greed and competition, to joys of the simple life. Brought down, too, to the divine darkness which enters into our work and wants to be included in our lives, lived as an undercurrent to our simplicity.

AGGRESSION

We move, now, as a depth psychologist might be expected to, from depression to aggression. Have we not been told that the former is a repression of the latter? And that the expression of anger and its concomitants is the cure of the same? Well, yes and no. We do know, from Reich, that anxiety and sexuality are mutually exclusive, physiologically and psychologically, but I am not at all sure that depression and aggression are in the same polar connection. I have spent lots of time on a Reichian couch, yelling and hitting, which has been relieving, but that, in itself, did not "cure" depression as much as the "simple life" has. Nor do I generally have much trouble being in touch with my own aggression and being able to verbalize it or visualize it in fantasy. These capacities to imagine and verbalize, however, have been only partly effective against what I conceive as my greater problem, that of muscular tension.

Muscular tension, in turn, in my opinion, is very much a consequence of our work. Sitting there, day after day, attending to the psyche of the other, is certainly "contra naturam" and requires lots of physical exercise and non-concentration on others as an antidote, but even that unnaturalness is not the cause of this stress. Rather, I think, that which produces stress is the endless alertness required of us, the perpetual attention to what is happening in self and other, so that mere relaxation and unconsciousness is a luxury indulged in all too rarely. Furthermore, the poison of the process seeps into us; the unacknowledged rage and aggression of our patients is what claws at us from below and from behind, bombards us hourly, daily, weekly, yearly. After some years, I found, our bodies, so assaulted and alerted, become tense, rigid, inflexible. Tennis and running won't do it, although they help. Even Reichian therapy and conscious connection with the body is not enough either, although very helpful to me.

I really do not know any remedy for the stress and muscular tension, although we each have many methods for coping. But what are we to do about the restraint of our natural aggression? Not that we need to hit patients or yell at them, but we might need to say to passive-aggressive folks, "Wake up and acknowledge your negativity and hostility, damn it!" And even if we did, it would not help much, even though it could conceivably be consciousness-bringing for a particular patient. No, the poisons which seep into us go deeper, and our constraint against running away, or against natural reactions—fight or flight—even if we allow ourselves verbal expression in the hour, are such that we can never overcome the "analytical stance." That analytic stance, unnatural in the extreme, is full-attention, alertness, care for the other, and restraint of our natural reactions and movements, all in the name of compassion and consciousness.

Nor would we have it any other way. That "contra naturam" is what we do and what we teach. Our releases come from insight and union of soul. They also come when we can effectively be natural and whole with our aggression with the patient. But still, what do we do about the body and this unnaturalness? Luckily for most of us, analysts are not by nature inclined to be particularly aggressive physically or even strongly athletic. Most of us are contented with our week-end tennis, swimming and walking. We add to that by going into nature when we can, and being healed of these poisons of the soul by the Great Mother Herself, as we hike in Her precincts, smell the trees and revel in the silences.

But the tensions persist anyway and Jungians, in contrast to Reichians, are said to be insufficiently "in the body," or are even seen as "dead." At some conventions, alas, I have seen what they mean. But I have also been at a Reichian convention or two and I am not impressed with what I have elsewhere called a "P.E." approach to life.

The reasons for this persistence of tension, as I have said, are not only the restraint and alertness of the therapist, but also the endless taking-in of the poisons, via the unconscious in particular. Transference does indeed "absorb" us, and we are absorbed into this endless "nigredo" and mercurial poison, no matter how much we are aware. I think that we do rather well, by and large, considering the extent and nature of our work. Those of us who have worked a long period of time in a mental hospital will know what I mean. The poisons of the soul infect the atmosphere to the extent that one can hardly tell patient from therapist in such institutions after a few years. Nor is this limited to the insane, in my opinion. The darknesses of the psyche revealed every day in the newspaper and confronted on the freeways of social intercourse are compounded in our rooms by perfectly decent people, including ourselves. The devils provoke our consciousness; our consciousness provokes the devils. The cure is in the process, but is never fully effected. When one speaks of the "wounded healer," I think of it as residing in my tense muscles, rather than in unhealed complexes, and I think that I am not alone in this. Perhaps the muscles are where the complexes reside.

Mars, then, is insufficiently served in our work, since we can only accept him in the soul. We do not jump, fight, yell, run away; nor do we sit in a sweat box, sleep—or most of all—turn off consciousness in those intense daily hours. Intensity without activity, and poison without antidote: those are the deformations that really count in this baleful work, a field more dismal even than economics.

I am still working on this problem which, for me, is to be even more aware of the body in my work and even more conscious of what is happening therein and to attend to it. I try to bring in my aggressive reactions, verbally, as much as possible, and to be "natural." I seek mutuality in the work with aggressive energies. Still, I search for new answers. I have weekly deep-tissue Ayurvedic massage, have experimented with bio-feedback. Colleagues do other things, such as Feldenkrais, as well as stretches (as I do) and running.

Women therapists seem to have less of a problem with this matter than men do. Maybe they can relax better or are less aggressive by nature or by role. I would be glad to know why. Perhaps this is one compensation for them for the centuries of oppression by that same masculine aggression and why they have lived longer and, by and large, happier lives.

However we view the issue of "dealing with the poisons" on a personal, subjective basis, the implications of the transference and the resultant alchemical work with patients can not successfully be denied. Ultimately, we need to confront ourselves and our patients that these poisons are being extruded "into the room" and are shared as an alchemical "third" between the two partners. My own response to this dilemma, which Jung recognized in his book, PSYCHOLOGY OF THE TRANSFERENCE, has been to embrace what I call "mutual process"—the recognition that ultimately both partners are effected by the archetype and they work consciously and openly together to transform these poisons and gifts of Mercurius. The word used by Joe McNair for this process is "metabolize" and I think it is appropriate. This archetypal element arises from and goes into the very cells of the body, particularly since we are committed to a work of the soul and spirit and deal in image and word. The body gets it, and it is, in my opinion, only when we acknowledge and share these bodily reactions that there results a mutual "metabolization" of these transpersonal poisons and gifts.

SEXUALITY

When we turn from aggression to sexuality, we have to say "more of same" to all that we have already said about aggression. It seems that we male therapists suffer more from this general inhibition against acting-out than do our female colleagues. We are stimulated and restrained as well. We are seduced and become seducers. We are privy to all the sexual secrets and are challenged beyond wits end. If Mars is frustrated by analytic work and makes us pay the price in muscular tension, Aphrodite is both worshipped and denied, and she is compelled to submit to being appreciated in the form of her son, Eros. We serve soul and spiritual union, not the flesh.

Furthermore, when we discover that we suffer more from the unexpressed, indirect form of aggression manifested by our patients than from open hostility, we also recognize that it is the silent seduction and stimulation that goes on in the therapeutic relation which causes havoc. If I am "turned on," as they say, is it because I am feeling and experiencing something in the patient or in myself alone? And, if I acknowledge this openly, am I going to be misunderstood as making an overture to sexual acting-out, or am I being unconsciously seductive? And, if the patient opens up desire, lust, and love, may I react honestly and directly with what I experience—verbally, of course—or should I interpret, or merely acknowledge. Most of these possibilities (except interpretation) occur in non-analytic relationships, it is true, but in analysis they are heightened, carry more weight and implication.

My own resolution of the dilemma is to be open about not only the stimulation and arousal, but to present the accompanying fantasy, with the expressed intention of offering these as reactions, and inviting the patient to report his/her reactions and fantasies. With my viewpoint of mutual process, I believe that body reactions, including aggression and sexuality, are usually archetypal responses and, if I am open and show the way of dealing with them by example, I am aiding in the direction of integration, rather than repression, evasion or acting-out, I preface such self-revelation with a statement of the nature of our analytic commitment to consciousness and enhancing the capacity to love—not to acting-out, nor to love affairs, etc. When the limitations of the work are mutually accepted, then both parties can open up to what the unconscious brings in when it is, indeed, mutual. It is in this way, in my experience, that the poison of the unexpressed, unresolved sexual and aggressive fantasies can be fruitfully worked on and transformed.

But one is always in danger of misunderstanding. I think, now, of a woman I worked with who had a very negative father problem. I liked her, but did not find her particularly attractive. After a time, however, I became aware of sexual feelings about and toward her. I hesitatingly told her so, and she was utterly startled, since she had no such feelings toward me. She reluctantly accepted these things, however, and, in time, I thought of this as a kind of ambivalent Eros coming through me which would repair the damage done by the father's disregard and rejection of this woman when she had reached adolescence. I was both bringing up the rejected and repressed and teaching her how to deal with it by listening to and expressing her own honest reactions. At times, however, I felt like a dirty old man.

One day, at the time of the notoriety of some child-abuse cases in our area, I had such feelings again, and then I said, "Perhaps I should open up a nursery school!" We both laughed uproariously. It was not long after that when a memory of her being abused as a child returned and the dissociated sexuality made perfect sense, both as a "return of the repressed" and as a "healing of the wound (of rejection and invasion) of the father." This was a healing event. Would this have occurred if I had kept my mouth shut? I do not know. But that is our dilemma.

My own experience of the analytic work is that I am soon divided into my opposites by the patient and what he/she brings to the sessions. I often feel as if my "left hand" is open to the taboos of the soul, my own included, and my "right hand" maintains the protective, parenting, connecting energy, with both "hands" being necessary. My advantage is that I sit in the middle of these and can move toward or report either of these directions or fantasies, and not be possessed by nor identified with either of them. I continue until wholeness is achieved. I have to add, however, the word "usually," or one of Jung's favorite Latin quotations, "deo concedente," for such is our need and trust when serving the healing god, the Self, as manifested in the analytic work.

What sort of life is this, for the analyst to talk about, stir up and express, though limitedly, this lustful and tabooed aspect of the psyche every day, with many people? Are we not secret Don Juans, or dirty old men? Yes, certainly, for these are "rejecta" of the psyche which intrude themselves into the work as the darker aspects of Eros, clamoring to be accepted, healed, integrated. And they must be included, but deprived of their destructive violating aspects. Spirit and flesh, morality and desire are thereby re-united and the initial splitting effect of the patient, mirroring his/her own split, becomes healed in the relationship we call transference. Poison, once more, is included and dissolved through a healing connection.

This is strange work, is it not? Here we are, rather ordinary-looking men and women, engaged in a secret sex and aggressive life, like our brother and sister hustlers, prostitutes. Perhaps we are like the "enlightened one" in the last of the ten Zen Ox-herding pictures, consorting with wine-bibbers, butchers and other rejected ones and, as the commentary to the picture says, we and they are "all converted into Buddhas." No wonder we are secret heroes and heroines, as well as secret hustlers and "devils," because, indeed, we aim to be secret Buddhas, or at least to serve such divine images.

I find it difficult to understand how those colleagues of ours who do not have a religious attitude deal with these upsurges of lust, desire, and violence, as they bubble up in the "vas," the vessel of the analytic work. If we did not have a religious attitude, how could we (I) possibly do this work? Badly, I would imagine. But then I don't know what other gods are being served, consciously or unconsciously, by colleagues. I am personally convinced that some god is being served, whether one is aware of it or not, and we are compelled, all of us, to find out which one and how.

Again, what strange work this is. Not even clergy are required to do this! Now, does it suit us? I think so, since we not only redeem the psyche in this work, we are ourselves continually redeemed thereby. But to whom but you, my colleagues, can I say this? It sounds so inflated. Yet it is clear that we are quite ordinary, all the same. Another paradox to accept.

MONEY

Money is a topic for us which may be even more charged and filled with taboo than sexuality and aggression. Everyone knows, of course, that we charge entirely too much for our time, that all we do is listen, that therapy has little effect. Besides that, are we not caretakers of the soul? Should we not be generous, loving and giving, a kind of Dr. Christian of the psyche? If not, we ought to be.

Now, such a collective image of what psychotherapists are or ought to be is bad enough for us, but if we add the suffering of patients about money, then we are in further trouble. How many of them feel cheated or deprived by unloving parents or a hostile world? And how many of these believe, somewhere deep down, that somebody—namely, the therapist—should make up for these lacks and deprivations? To charge for our time is understandable, but we should be non-mercenary, unmaterialistic, and self-sacrificing.

How is an analyst to deal with these images and expectations? First, we try to make them conscious. Even when they are made conscious, does that settle the matter? I remember working with a psychotherapist who told me that throughout his previous long Freudian analysis he had the mildly subliminal hope and belief that his analyst was saving up all his checks and would give them back to him at the end of the work. With me, his image was more that of an insurance policy. If he came and exposed his weaknesses and failings with me, then these would not destroy him in the outside world. The issue became, how much was he willing to pay for that service, and when would he get these things fulfilled elsewhere for less money? This financial attitude toward therapy came from a capable, generous, very conscious man. Just like me. We, too, are just as generous, caring, socially responsible, and devoted to service as was my analysand, but are also just as frightened, insecure, envious and greedy as the next man. We have worked at these things and are conscious, but money itself is such a charged and ambivalent symbol that one could write a psychology with that as a center as much as with our more usual Eros and Thanatos psychologies.

We all share the consciousness of money as a symbol of security, value, prestige, personal worth, power, love, and even connected with the Self. But why do I become so enraged when patients not only do not pay me, but do not even apologize for not doing so? Why am I driven to murderous thoughts by such cheating, when with other losses I can be more philosophical? And why, too, do I worry when my practice drops, get chagrined when I hear that former students and colleagues have fuller practices or get more for their services than I do? Is this only the usual envy and competition? Am I alone in such emotional financial intensity? I don't think so.

Surely we analysts, like our patients and everybody else, suffer the usual problems of money, such as the need for security or power that I mentioned above. We also suffer from the unreal expectations of patients and the collective. I am of the opinion, however, that we Jungians have an additional suffering in this area just because we believe that we are serving the Self. I have discovered that in this belief of service, I welcome each new patient as, somehow, sent by God. I am there for his/her development as well as my own, and the problems that are presented are just the ones that I need to deal with at this time, even if I don't like it. That, of course, makes my working life and each patient quite meaningful for me. Jung said that this was a good attitude for us to have. The other part of this belief, I have discovered, is that somewhere I have the expectation that the Self should take care of me. Since I am devoted to doing the work of the Self, both within my psyche and "in the world," then patients should be provided who can pay me enough for the livelihood of my family and myself. If the Self wants me to do this work, it should see to it, by golly, that I survive in it! If not, then I, like fallen-away priests and nuns, have lost my "vocation"!

No wonder, then, that I am so enraged when patients do not pay, and don't even acknowledge that they owe me. They are denying the Self for me. The imagined penalty for that, in my mind, is death! Is it a wonder, then, when they—less conscious than I—expect me to work for nothing? Should I not be father and mother, even an agent of the Self for them, too? What to do, then, with this painful insight?

I am reminded of a dream I had some years ago, which still lies in the back of my mind about many things, including money. In this dream, I was walking across a bridge to a futuristic city when a crippled beggar, bodiless and seated on a sort of skate board, comes to me and announces that he is God. I nod and offer to buy him a drink at the kiosk there. As I acknowledge him, this self-proclaimed God-figure grows a body and is quite whole. After we toast each other with wine, he holds out his palms to me, from which flow a huge number of gold and silver coins from every country and time. End of dream.

This, then, is how I understand the complexity about money: The Self is both a beggar and a provider; it wants to incarnate into my life and needs my recognition. When I do so and share a relationship of spirit, then all the values and achievements of the ages—God expressing Himself/Herself throughout history and life—are vouchsafed me. But I can never forget that God is beggar as well as giver and that I, as a carrier of such an ever-incarnating content, am also beggar and giver. I can not escape this dilemma, but perhaps the insight can make me less murderous on the one hand, nor destroyed on the other.

A curious thing just happened. As I was writing the foregoing lines, a patient called and announced that she did owe me money, although in the last session she denied it. She was going to send the check by mail today. God does provide! But I also need to remember that one of the most common lies told is, "the check is in the mail"!

ALIENATION

This word was more popular among intellectuals and students in the 1950s than it is today, along with the concept of "organization man." Perhaps the reason it is less popular today is that alienation is more widespread. Movies and the arts no longer glorify and console the man who is different from the crowd, who goes against the pack. Instead, they look to virtues and values of the past, of the community of the faithful farmers, the shared communion, ethnic solidarity. We are shown that communion because we lack it so much. Almost everybody feels alone in a hostile, uncaring world.

How does the analyst figure in this? We were always alienated and still are. We are "strangers in a strange land"; even the old word for our profession as healers of the mentally ill makes us "alienists." Jung told us the following, when he wrote about alchemy: the one who embarks on the individuation process finds himself alone, isolated, different from his surroundings and in possession of a secret which keeps him apart. He must work long and hard and deep to once again find his link with that collective world outside, and he must find it by going to equivalent lengths to the collective world inside.

We are, then, strangers, but friends to the patients who come to us, who themselves feel like strangers in the world. And how does this endless befriending of the stranger who comes to us effect us in the world? We are more strangers than ever, unable to engage in small talk. We often are rotten group participators, awkward and suspicious in social gatherings, guarded with our colleagues. Perhaps I paint too dark a picture and describe only myself and some others; but I venture to predict that not a few of those who see or hear these words will recognize themselves in the description.

Why is this so? Is it because of the individuation process? Or because our profession is a peculiar one and kept apart by projection and agreement? Yes, this is true, but other people are embarked on individuation and belong to peculiar professions without being especially alienated, such as astronauts, deep sea divers, and oil-well cappers. The reason, therefore, lies elsewhere. I believe, once more, that it lies in our concern with suffering and our play of self-disclosure. The person who is endlessly involved with hearing secrets, telling secrets, guarding secrets, being open and being closed, endlessly reflecting on what is going on in the background, is bound to be a peculiar fellow and one who is shunned as well as courted. Shamen have few friends.

How many times I remember going to parties and when the usual questions as to my occupation came up there were snorts and jokes, petitionings for advice, opening up of problems in a corner, or not-too-subtle hostility. That was years ago. Nowadays, along with the alienation of everybody, everyone also has been to a psychotherapist or is going to one, so the novelty has worn off. It is not the ordinary fellow in other fields who is alienated from us, it is we who are alienated from him. And this just because we do this strange work of reveal-conceal, of suffering, and it effects us in the ways that I have mentioned. Since we serve the mentally ill, so are we seen as mentally ill. And, if our patients are not particularly mentally ill, still we are branded with the label. Who can listen all day to such stuff? Who listens? We all know the jokes and stories, like these, and we all know how impossible it is to share what we really do and how we are, even amongst ourselves, let alone with other citizens.

What, then are we to do? Jung's answer, of course, is that the deepening connection with the collective unconscious at first alienates us, but later finds us once more not only connected with our fellow humans, but also to plants and animals and stones. Sometimes, however, we analysts are better connected to plants and stones than to social life, and are better nourished thereby. It was Jung, too, who said that after thirty-five every man is like a lonely ship who blinks to other ships, but goes about on his own voyage. He was connected deeply, but not too personally, I think, except with a very few. It is probably not different for us. Jung had his outer collective, however, as few of us have, and even our Swiss colleague, Adolf Guggenbuhl, has addressed this isolation and alienation among us, espousing friendship as an answer to it.

For myself, the answer lies partly in friendship, but also in being more open in the analytic work, in enjoying and appreciating family, in spending lots of time in nature. Many answers and no answer, because this alienation problem leads directly to the next item on our eight-fold path of the issue of the suffering of the analyst, namely Community.

COMMUNITY

Carol Shahin has aptly described the Jungian community as a "village for people who could not remain in the village." That remark goes a long way to account for the fact that Jungian groups often split, that internecine squabbles and power plays are just as prevalent among us as in any political party. One might have thought that our penchant for integrating the shadow would have made us less quarrelsome or mutually rejecting. And for those of us who have even less invested in the Jungian or any collective, as such, there is apartness, "ships passing in the night." I have discovered that such a community-denigrating attitude is even built-in among Jungians generally.

Since I returned to membership in the Los Angeles Society a few years ago, I have found that almost every new graduate goes through a final darkness and frustration with the administration or some authority and comes out with the feeling that he or she would do just as well, or even better, by not being a member at all. Not only is this an unexpected outcome, but it seems to be even a desired one in some ways. In the background is the dictum, "Don't project the Self onto the Society," or any society for that matter.

Now, who can fault this advice? Certainly not I, who has had rough treatment from a Jungian collective in the past, and treats the current reconnection as an opportunity to work out my own shadow in relationship to social life. This distrust exists for most of my colleagues. Many have expressed to me their frustration and disrespect for our Society life, yet all somehow try to do what they can. My own experience is that I can find some satisfactory mode of connection with almost any member of our group on an individual basis, but as a collective, this is most difficult and frustrating. My chats with Jungians from other communities, by and large, reveal something similar.

What a paradox! All these individuation-pursuing and self-realization-promoting people have a difficult time being with each other, except on an individual basis! It would seem that we lack, on a group level, the kind of vessel that analysis itself provides, whereby consciousness, truthfulness and relationship are deeply served. Nor are we likely to find it very readily. Group therapy will not do it, as attested by the experiments of analysts and trainees from various places and times. Nor is there much desire to find or create such a vessel, since Jung thought it hopeless, really. The Jung Club of Zurich, for example, was seen as a "battlefield," according to Franz Riklin, a place to encounter your shadow, but one goes home to work it out. I have been forced to conclude that he and Jung were right about groups, in general.

But what about community, and what do we analysts do about it? The answer is, not much. There are professional meetings and, as the number of Jungians increases, there is more variety and possibility of intellectual sharing, but kinship—such as it is—reduces still further. That is a fact, I believe, and one to further the suffering of the analyst. Where are the causes to serve, the parties to support, the truths to espouse? Mostly in the inner work, in the analytic structure, and in one's requirements of personal process. At best, we discover the "ecclesia spiritualis" of like-minded people, apart from collectives.

We discover our membership in the hidden community of seekers. If we are lucky, we find our compensations in a more greatly appreciated marital, family and friendship life. Yet we are deeply alone, making our link with the depths of the inner collective and looking for ways to manifest or connect in the world. Jung was both fortunate and capable in having sufficient depth and complexity to "give back" to the outer collective what he received from within, and to find, even in his lifetime, a sufficient resonance to enable him to go on. The rest of us have to do with less, although we also do not have to undergo the kind of hell he underwent, for example, in writing his *ANSWER TO JOB*.

Each of us carries his/her own process, but we do not have a communal vessel of equivalent value for further work in the transformation of our collective darkness. Yet the condition of the world obviously requires such a thing. If Jung is right, the only answer for collective darkness is for the individual to work on his own, and to suffer the splits and lacks as incarnated by the Self in her/his own soul. That we must do anyway. In the future, however, with the increase in the number of extraverts who are attracted to Jungian psychology, there may be some creative contribution to our dilemma which will show a way of collective work which does not violate the individual, yet values group work, too. We who could not stay in the village find that the village we have joined is hardly a village at all!

RELIGION

The step from the issue of community to that of religion is a short one, indeed, and very much parallel to it. How many analysts are active members of a religious community? How many even attend services of any denomination with any regularity? About as many, I would suppose, as are active in community life! We are as introverted and atypical when it comes to religion as when we face community.

I used to think that this was a good thing; I shared the usual banalities about not being interested in "organized religion." By the time I had completed my training and had gone much deeper into the psyche, however, I changed and felt that it was important to have some connection with my religion of origin, that the "given"—as van der Leeuw had put it—was just as important as the "possible." I had concluded that the chief transition events of human life—birth, initiation, marriage and death—were all social phenomena, requiring ritual and a link with the community and religion of my inheritance. I fulfilled this precept for myself, my wife and children. I even added further "observance" of ritual for the chief holidays of the year (national as well as religious), as well as our regular Friday night prayers and family service of ushering in the Sabbath. All this was important just because my personal myth was ecumenical and transcended the religion of my birth to include several others, as well as being a religion of the psyche. I suspect that most of my colleagues have felt something similar, since even those who were clergy to start with end up being more therapist than spiritual counselor.

Yet, since most of us are far from immersed in community religious life, just as we are estranged from general community life, we suffer this apartness. Our individuation offers us symbolic understanding and even appreciation, but we are lacking, all the same. We do not, by and large, share the sacraments or behavioral laws which provide our fellow institutionally religious the succor and satisfaction of enactment and fulfillment. Our religious life comes from our relation to the Self, an ongoing dialogue within, which is sometimes shared in outer events and with others, but it rarely can sustain the kind of mutual worship that is the rightful inheritance of humanity at large.

The loss is severe and causes a suffering which sets us apart from how humanity has always been. We are almost as non-observant as agnostics, yet we are at least as religious as the most intensely devoted practitioners. Few of us can abide being a member of a congregation. Our discrepancy militates against it.

Some of us, for example Edward Eddinger and, before him, Esther Harding, think that Jungian psychology is itself a "new dispensation." And most of us think that Jung has indeed ushered in a new consciousness which is a "quantum" leap over the past. But we are not, luckily, like the members of a new sect who have found the "truth" and want to foist it on others. We are too well aware that we endlessly struggle to find and live our own truth and we respect others need and right to do the same. But the alienation from community, and particularly religious community, is a serious suffering for us.

For the past several years, I have been leading what I call a "psycho-ecumenical group" composed of clergy who are also therapists. They include rabbis, priests, nuns and ministers, all of whom have had Jungian analysis. We have met to give papers, to demonstrate rituals, to discuss issues, to share in religious holidays. Some in this group have even said that it is easier to share certain religious doubts and struggles with each other than with the clergy of their own community. I find this group, which meets about eight times a year, to be a very important one for me. It gives some outer form to my own inner ecumenical myth, as well as helps me maintain connections with friends I might otherwise not see. This has been one resolution of my dilemma of lack of community.

Another resolution of this lack has been to attend high holiday services at a local hospital, rituals led by a rabbi who is also a psychologist and a good friend of mine. I therby keep my connection with tradition and maintain an individual relationship. These, plus family observance, make me a most fortunate person, I believe, yet I still feel that gap, that lack of organic connection with community and community religion which, I think, is part of the alienated condition of our time. M.L. von Franz has been of the opinion that the Self wants us to be strong enough to stand alone, and I think that she is right. Yet we suffer this deprivation, since the Self is also a deeply manifold being and process which yearns for kinship connection on an outer collective level as well.

In the section on Money, I related a dream I had in which the Self appeared as a crippled beggar, gradually taking on body as I acknowledged him and our relationship. During the same week that I had that dream, another one came to me in which I was informed that God's body constituted the entire universe, that it was like a worm biting its own tail, that its organs were composed of all the galactic systems and planets, and that all life constituted the cells of This Being. Furthermore, I was told that this Being breathed in and out in a vast harmony, and that those cells (or beings) lucky enough to be located at the places where this breathing occurred had mystical experiences.

My dream said nothing new about the apprehension of the divine. It has been frequently noted that we are all One, and that God is One in that multiplicity of existence. Yet the difference was that I dreamed it, it happened to me personally, and it compensated that other image of God that I had, earlier in the week, which emphasized my particularity. I think that the second dream, the more collective one, made a truth real for me, but did not indicate how this was to be lived. I also think that this is the problem of "the many," that of multiplicity of images, to be resolved in the next five hundred years perhaps, the time that Jung told our colleague, Max Zeller, it would take to form the "new religion." That "new religion," I believe, will not replace any of the older ones, any more than Christianity has replaced Judaism, or Buddhism has replaced Hinduism. Yet one hopes that a balm will then be provided which our suffering souls need so badly. This will not happen for us, of course, who live now in that transition time, but we can still rejoice in having a glimpse of what is to come.

DISCUSSION

The foregoing reflections have revolved about two themes, as I mentioned at the outset. These have been self-disclosure and suffering. To round out our discussion, I think it valuable to see these issues from an archetypal perspective and for this purpose I have selected, from among other possible choices, the relation between Teiresias and the Goddess Athena for the theme of nakedness and self-disclosure.

Teiresias, you will recall, was a true prophet and visionary among the Greeks, being the one, for example, who warned about the violation of the incest taboo and prophesied several aspects of the Oedipus tale. He gained his prophetic capacity, it is related, as a consequence of inadvertently glimpsing Athena unclothed. This Goddess of culture and consciousness, born out of the head of Zeus, was deeply offended at being seen naked by Teiresias and blinded him. She recompensed him, afterwards, by giving him inner vision and the capacity to hear the gods. This same Teiresias had also been party to another event which he did not seek, when he chanced to see two snakes coupling. Attacked by them, he slew the female and was turned into a woman. After seven years, during which he lived as a harlot, he again saw snakes coupling and was attacked by them. This time, he slew the male, and resumed his masculinity.

Our seer, the mythographer Kerenyi tells us, "saw things one does not normally see," and was both honored and punished thereby. He saw the nakedness of the Goddess, her secret Self, the naked truth that lies behind the bringing of culture and consciousness. Athena, we remember, was the one who assisted Prometheus in achieving the divine fire. She is on the side of civilization, to be sure, yet to see her true nakedness—the secrets which lie behind the advancement of consciousness, as we see them in our consulting rooms—is to be blinded to the outer world as others know it. The recompense is to have increased powers of intuition and to see into the depths. We, like Teiresias, witness the breaking of taboos and the nakedness, not only of the human psyche, but also of the gods, as revealed in our work.

We also witness the union of the snakes—that symbol of divine healing—and, more than most people, we are compelled to experience our inner contrasexual opposite, male and female. For this, too, we are handsomely paid. In all this, we are serving the divine in a feminine aspect, that of the expansion of consciousness and the advancement of civilization. We do this, I believe, like

Teiresias, just because we happened to "be there" when the Goddess made her appearance. We surely do more than this—which is to say that other aspects of the divine principle, such as Aphrodite and Eros, are being manifested—but it is the nakedness which is of concern right now. I would add that even though the Goddess punishes Teiresias for the hubris of seeing her, she also desires this exposure, since she is so kind to him, giving him her best gift. Even Zeus and Hera look to him for authority, when they demand his expertise to resolve their quarrel as to who has more pleasure in sex, male or female. I hope it is not disrespectful to suggest that here is even a root metaphor of marriage counseling!

I would conclude from the foregoing that the gods are ambivalent about us humans, both wanting us to see and punishing us for this. Here, perhaps, lies the deeper reason for the theme of self-disclosure, which is so central in our endeavors. I would say that what is disclosed in our work is the Self, both that of patient and therapist, but also transcending both. The Self is being incarnated and disclosed, and the aim, just as Athena supports, is the advancement of consciousness. We are honored and punished thereby.

This leads to our second theme, that of suffering. An archetypal basis behind this theme, one that I choose to discuss here, comes from a dream and vision that I had a few months after beginning my own analysis at Christmas time in 1950. In it, a divine child was being born, and was attended by three new wise men, but these were a Jewish rabbi, a Christian priest, and Buddhist priest. I did not know it then, fortunately, but this anticipated birth of the "anthropos" would be accompanied for me by these three images which are deeply related to the theme of suffering.

The Christian image, of course, that of the crucifixion of Christ, is centrally concerned with the suffering of God and man as the Self enters into the human condition. Jung has been his most profound, perhaps, in describing this event in ANSWER TO JOB. The central tenet in Buddhism, Duhka, the condition of suffering or dis-ease, is to be overcome by following the eight-fold path of right living, leading to the experience of the Self. And, it is no secret that Judaism, while not espousing the path of suffering as the way to the divine, has been a chief recipient of such agony during its entire history.

My dream and vision reported these attendants to the birth and now, thirty-five years later, I can acknowledge that this has been my fate—to cope with the suffering of my patients and myself as this ecumenical birth of the "anthropos" is ushered in at the end of the Piscean aion. All three views—of the incarnation of the divine, of the endurance and transcendence of the opposites, and of the personal relationship with God as both an inner and outer fact—have permeated my own analytical work. I venture to suggest that some variant of these has affected my colleagues as well.

So, then, our suffering, perhaps, is not in vain and is itself the kind of penalty that Teiresias and Prometheus, to say nothing of Jesus and Buddha, paid with so dearly. In Judaism there is a tradition that there are, at any one time on the earth, a number of "just men," "Melamed Vovnikim," who suffer particularly because they carry the burden of the god-head. It is even greater suffering that some of them do not even know that they do this. I believe that the twenty-four men of that tradition are being added to in increasing numbers during the present generations and that we Jungian analysts are better off if we consciously realize that even to see the divine in manifestation is to be party to that suffering. The rewards are of greater consciousness and the realization of being co-creators in the vast evolutionary process which we glimpse with such awe. It is no wonder, then, that we are so burdened and uplifted by what goes on in the ordinary little rooms in which we conduct our analytic work.

COMMENT BY FORDHAM ON SPIEGELMAN'S CONTRIBUTION
Dear Spiegelman,

Your paper has arrived. I eagerly read it and read it again. I respect the way you struggle with your conflicts and problems and wish you good luck with them but they are not mine: I do not suffer much with my patients and many of my patients do not suffer much either, indeed if they can do so productively I think that the analysis is drawing to a close. Nor do I find disclosure a problem. Let me describe an occasion when I did disclose something. I have a patient who has changed his time from 9 a.m. on a Monday morning to 8:15. Twice I had expected him at 9. On each occasion, I was in my dressing gown when he arrived and he saw me thus attired. I let him in and dressed in about five minutes. When I came down he was silent but we succeeded in doing some work on that; he felt neglected, not wanted and so on. At one point he said he thought I should be on the couch and start my analysis by him. He changed the subject but towards the end of the interview I said that I did not think my failure was related to him so much as my age and difficulty in getting up in the morning. Nothing very grand about that disclosure.

What you do seems to me not so much analysis as confrontation therapy. I think most of your disclosures would have got digested and given the form of an interpretation.

But these discussions are much too brief to assess our agreements and differences over technique and it would be possible to get down to brass tacks only by submitting each other's cases to supervision by the other. Alas, not possible.

I do think it important not to get competitive and think each of our methods is the right one. I do think that what you do is sincere and I respect it, and I wish you well with it. But as far as myself, I would not act as you evidently do, sometimes at least.

With best wishes,
M.F.

REJOINDER BY SPIEGELMAN TO COMMENT BY FORDHAM
Dear Fordham,

Many thanks for your honest response. I liked your example, but it is, as you recognize, a far cry from what I would regard as "self-disclosure." Our differences seem to reside in what we consider important to analyze. You think of my work as "confrontation therapy"; I think of yours as dominated by the child archetype. On my side, what I analyze are dreams, and the relationship, as manifested in mutual reactions. You analyze the person. I believe that our differences represent not only personal variants but, like the "founders," we represent different analytic attitudes which could, maybe should, be more carefully compared. Alas, we can not, but perhaps someone, reading our material here, will be motivated to go further with such comparisons. Actually, many other comparisons can also be made from the contributors to the present volume. Our differences are softened, I think, in the mutual appreciation of the sincerity with which we approach the work, and our mutual respect, as well. Many thanks for your contributions to our field and to this book.

Sincerely,
J.M.S.

COMMENT BY ANDREW SAMUELS TO SPIEGELMAN'S CONTRIBUTION

Spiegelman is exposing the wound that drives him and showing how, after considerable distillation, his experience and suffering during the course of an analysis can be put at the service of the patient's individuation. We have tended to split conceptions of analysis as a two-person interaction from versions of it which stress the inner journey. My feeling is that this is a pity and this paper approaches the paradox of oneness co-existing with boundary in analysis; how "I" am only constellates in relation to "you." I was also struck by the way Spiegelman returns again and again to the centrality of the body in the analytical experience.

Marvin Spiegelman has asked me to add a brief paragraph about myself. In spite of a background in the theatre, I formed the desire to be an analyst very early—in my late teens. The reason I became a Jungian is rather unedifying. All the other training bodies to which I replied rejected me as being too young. The Society of Analytical Psychology was the only one not to reply at all. One day, while taking a stroll in central London, I "found myself" in Devonshire Place, the street in which the SAP's headquarters were then located. Not knowing the number, I asked at one of the houses and then knocked at the SAP's door. The office staff found my letter; they were not particularly surprised that nothing had been done about it. I was in the process of asking them what to do next when a voice piped up from the corner: "I'm on the professional committee—if you've got an hour to spare I could see you now because my consulting room is upstairs." I had, she did, they accepted me.

I was 12 when Jung died.

REJOINDER BY SPIEGELMAN

I specifically thought of Dr. Fordham as a potential critic for my paper since my views are rather far from his and I believed that he would give an objective and thoughtful opinion. I was not disappointed. I thought that a second view, from someone in the younger generation of analysts, as Andrew Samuels is, would also be helpful. When he said that he thought I had a "dynamite paper" I was especially pleased, since I was under the impression that my style might be more compatible with the newer generation of analysts. Samuels, as one of the "lights" of that generation, has not disappointed me, either, and I am grateful to be understood, as he succinctly demonstrates. His story of how he came to be a Jungian is altogether delightful and much in keeping with our erratic profession. Jung only died physically when Andrew was 12—it is altogether apparent that his spirit lives on in the variety of "Jungians."

Reflections on Professional Deformation

by

ROBERT STEIN, M.D.

C.G. Jung was still very much alive and vital when I began my analytical training in Zurich in 1956, even though it was toward the end of his life. In preparing this paper, I realized that many of my present concerns about depth psychology were already constellated in the few contacts which I had with him at that time.

I remember my first visit with Jung. We had hardly sat down in his study when he plunged into a lament about the medical profession. Perhaps he did this because he knew that I was a physician. "Why," he said, "doesn't the medical profession understand me?" Even though he smiled and had a mischievous, knowing twinkle in his eyes, he still seemed pained that his ideas were not as understood and received by the medical establishment as were Freud's. I had an incredible session with him as we sat facing each other with our knees almost touching. I said very little even though I had a list of things to talk about. Jung seemed to be in an expansive mood and, as he rambled on, I was amazed that he was speaking about all of the issues that concerned me, as if he had seen my list. I left elated and overwhelmed by this contact with the Great Man.

Another memory of Jung involves a seminar in which he spoke for almost two hours, primarily in response to a question which I had sent him. Of course, I was very flattered. I don't even remember the question, but once again Jung seemed to have a direct connection to what he himself called The Great Man. He was fantastic in the humility he demonstrated as he made it come alive before us. He talked of the importance of not identifying with The Great Man archetype, of not losing our humanness as the archetype speaks through us. I had a numinous experience as Jung spoke because I seemed to anticipate every word he said before it came out of his mouth. I thought I too must also be tuned into the words of The Great Man, just as Jung was. Needless to say, the experience was too much for me. I was unable to maintain my human boundaries with this direct connection to the archetype. As a consequence, I experienced an enormous inflation which was followed by an inevitable depression lasting many weeks before I could integrate the experience.

At another seminar, Jung talked about the demands which depth analysis places upon the analyst. He talked about the importance of the analyst being himself/herself—natural, spontaneous, open, vulnerable and unprotected by the professional persona—particularly once the individuation process becomes central. When Jung finished, he lit up his old pipe and asked for questions. One of our Italian trainees stood up and said, with obvious concern in his voice, "But

Professor Jung, if we are open and natural as you suggest, won't the shadow also enter?" Jung's instantaneous response was, "Well, of course!" For a few moments, a great still came over the room until we all caught on and began to chuckle over the foolishness of the question.

I had another meeting with Jung when I returned to Zurich to take the propaedeuticum exams after having spent six months in the London training program. My reason for deciding to do some of my training in London was largely because of my feeling that transference work was being neglected in Zurich. For a number of reasons, things did not go well for me in London and I finally decided to leave their program. I knew after my first meeting with my control analyst that there would be conflict. He and I clashed immediately over the issue of ego-directed versus self-directed psychology. He insisted that the analyst needs to rely on his ego, not the self, in order to establish boundaries, maintain consciousness and protect the patient from the destructive, shadow aspects of the self. I said to him that his view seemed to be in opposition to Jung's position. His response was, "Well, Jung may be able to trust the self, but most of us have to rely on our ego." In more recent talks with this same analyst, we have both changed and are not so polarized, but at the time I was very shaken by my London experience and I talked with Jung about it. With great passion I told him of my fear that the London school was moving regressively back into traditional Freudian ego psychology. He was very supportive, reassuring me that there was nothing to fear because in time the Self would win out.

Toward the end of my training, I had one unpleasant encounter with Jung. For over three years I had experienced enormous support from the Zurich Jungian community as well as from the living presence of Jung, which enabled me to become deeply immersed in my own inner process. My connection to outer reality was often so tenuous that if it were not my good fortune of having to attend to my relationships to my wife and small daughters and my analysands, I am not sure I would have made it. The profound psychological changes I experienced had moved me away from the ego-centered world I lived in toward a total commitment to serving the life of the soul. I was deeply concerned about how I would be able to make the return journey to a world that had so little respect for the soul and so few viable containers which support the soul's development. The fact that I was returning to such a success-oriented, extraverted, materialistic culture as the United States did not help matters—this was before the sixties revolution.

My question to Jung at this seminar was essentially as follows: Professor Jung, how can an individual carry this new spirit of individuation back into a world that has no adequate vessels to contain it? Do we not need, as Jesus said, new bottles for the new wine? For some reason, Jung was obviously upset with my question because he responded irritably and cruelly by saying that I would not have asked such a question if I had understood the concept of the Self; and, for good measure, to really put me in my place, he made sure to let me know that in Biblical times they used wine-skins, not bottles. Apart from this put-down, what he said essentially was that the Self points the way toward new forms and rituals and that by remaining true to the inner process, changes in the outer world will emerge spontaneously. I don't know why he reacted so strongly to my question, but I was devastated and also damn angry at him. To this day I continue to struggle with this issue and I have many questions about his point of view, which I think he expresses clearly when he says that "Relationship to the Self is at once relationship to our fellow man . . . " (*PSYCHOLOGY OF THE TRANSFERENCE*, 1954).

Since the Self's vision of the world is cosmic, transpersonal, timeless and eternal, it does not necessarily take into consideration individual human limitations or how the spirit of the times may make it impossible for the Self to be received and realized. Unless the ego informs the Self about these matters, I believe that the latter, knowing that the truth of its vision will ultimately be realized, is not particularly concerned about space-time limitations. What I am suggesting is that while establishing a connection to the Self is basic to individuation, the creative process of giving form and expression to the Self in relation to other people demands an ongoing dialogue with the other as well as with the Self. My disagreement with Jung and many of his followers is in this tendency to believe that changes in relationship to the outer world will automatically occur once we get into a right relationship with our inner world (the "Rainmaker" model). I have no doubt that a right relationship to the Self and creative outer changes do go hand in hand, but I think it leads to elitism and inflation to think that my inner work will automatically effect great changes in the outer world.

Jung's emphasis on inner reality and inner connection has been very much needed by our Western culture, but the shadow side of this has been the Jungian tendency toward viewing our outer involvements as important mainly for furthering the individuation process by giving us the opportunity to experience and withdraw our unconscious projections. I think this overemphasis on the withdrawal of projections can lead to a de-souling of the outer world.

Looking back at these encounters with Jung, I can see that I was already deeply involved with most of the issues that I will be touching upon here: (1) the conflict bewteen an ego-centered and a soul-centered psychotherapy; (2) the importance of the analyst being himself/herself—open, vulnerable, spontaneous and not fearful of revealing his/her own shadow; (3) the polarity between being and becoming, between the soul's need for intimacy and its need for development; (4) the importance of the kinship community for creating new and viable containers to support the individuation process. I believe a truly soul-centered psychotherapy can only develop if it is grounded and contained in a kinship community.

Recently my wife asked me why I have always seemed so negative about psychotherapy in spite of my deep involvement and commitment. It made me think. My first thought was that I must have had some expectations about Jungian analysis that have not been fulfilled.

From early childhood I have been driven by a sense of mission to change this mechanized, power-dominated world into one where love and the life of the soul are the ruling principles. Contributing to this obsession, I am sure, was my deep sense of painful isolation as a child, which was certainly not helped by my strongly introverted tendencies. My reasons for entering analysis were the break-up of a primary relationship and the collapse of my belief systems, particularly my conviction that our industrialized, capitalistic society had alienated man from his true nature and that the evils of the world could be corrected by right thinking minds, vegetarianism, and a socialist society. Jungian analysis was both a humbling and freeing experience for me. Forced to face the limitations of my ego and reason, I was opened up to a profoundly religious experience in which I first saw myself as no bigger than a grain of sand encompassed by a vast universe. Almost at the same instant, I had a vision of a numinous moonlit night in which I experienced all the plains, forests, mountains and streams of the continent, of the world, entering into me and becoming one with me. I experienced myself totally insignificant and powerless, but at the same time filled with all the powers of a universe in which microcosm and macrocosm are one. I realized that whatever I did or said was determined not by my little will, my little ego, but my relationship to higher and greater powers.

This transcending experience lifted me temporarily out of my own personal little misery. Having been raised an atheist, this experience, early in my Jungian analysis, was like a conversion. I was able to let go of my crumbling Marxist dialectical materialist belief system and turn to my new-found belief in a higher power for salvation. I was filled with the hope and expectation that I had found the right path for fulfilling my destiny. Since the concept of individuation also held out the promise of my eventually becoming a more open, spontaneous, whole, loving person, capable of having and maintaining deep, intimate relationships. I was soon totally committed to the process.

I believe that I have become much more connected to and accepting of my true self, and that my capacity to relate empathetically and deeply has become highly developed. But I also feel that the analyst's habitually reflective and emotionally detached attitude has, in many respects, diminished my capacity for intimacy. Perhaps because of this and age, I have found myself less and less interested in relationships. I much prefer doing things alone with myself, open and receptive to my own soul, as I am at this moment. It seems much easier for me to reveal myself in writing, even though I feel somewhat ashamed about what I have just exposed about myself. But, if I am an example of what happens to a Jungian analyst who has been dedicated to working on his own individuation process for almost forty years, and working to help others for thirty years, it would be a sad commentary on our profession. I would like to believe that what has happened to me has little to do with my profession, but my impression is that as time progresses many analysts tend to move in a similar direction.

On one level, I am not surprised about what has happened to me. I saw it coming many years ago, and that realization has been responsible for much of my negativity toward the traditional psychotherapeutic process and structure. Why should I be surprised, if after years of developing the capacity to be detached, objective and always reflective so that I do not contaminate my patients with my own complexes, that I have become deformed in my capacity to relate naturally, spontaneously, primitively, unconsciously, humanly?

"How self-disclosing should I be with patients?" is one of the most frequent questions I hear from graduate psychology students and candidates in analytical training. To me this question reflects a basic fallacy in the modern psychotherapeutic endeavor. In my book, *INCEST AND HUMAN LOVE (Spring* Publications, Dallas, 1984), I touched upon this issue. This paper is an attempt to explore further some of the basic assumptions underlying the prevailing models of psychotherapy which require the therapist to withhold his/her spontaneous feelings and reactions, and to maintain distance and objectivity in this and in other ways.

Why this fear of self-disclosure in a therapeutic system designed to attend to modern man's neglected soul? How can a discipline which trains therapists not to reveal the spontaneous, unreflected movements of their own souls help others who are themselves so alienated from and fearful of the soul? What is the basis of the notion that intimacy and emotional involvement is oppositional to objectivity and detachment? And what is the basis for the notion that a spontaneous, unreflected reaction is potentially more detrimental than a reaction which is withheld, reflected upon and used primarily as an instrument for increasing consciousness? How essential is the experience of equality, intimacy and communion to the therapeutic process?

Traditionally, the transference has been used primarily as an instrument for helping to make conscious the unconscious and to resolve or alter developmental complexes. One tends to speak of the psychotherapeutic relationship in terms of positive or negative transference, neither of which have much to do with promoting the experience of mature intimacy, which can only occur between souls that feel free and equal. While analysis cultivates the exposure of the vulnerable soul, its structure is oppositional to the experience of communion between equals. Since the traditional analytic model requires the therapist to carry the responsibility of consciousness and to not contaminate the analysand's process with his/her own needs, not only is intimacy between equals not possible, but the situation tends to evoke all of the fragmenting fears of intimacy associated with the incest taboo. Rather than helping us develop our capacities for intimacy and soul-connection, the analytic model teaches us how to contain this fundamental human need and to further strengthen our ego position so that we will not be overwhelmed by the so-called id drives. In my view, the claim that depth analysis helps us develop our capacity for intimate relationships is basically false. If anything, it presents us with a model for ego-distancing rather than soul-connection.

If I accept the limitations of the analytic structure, I can certainly acknowledge that it has facilitated the development of my capacity for self-acceptance and for experiencing a connection to the directing intelligence of a higher power. I feel my commitment to the individuation process and the practice of psychotherapy has been invaluable in helping me to recognize and accept the soul in all its multiple aspects, and it has certainly helped me maintain my faith in a benevolent Deity, even at those times when I have felt totally cut off from God. So, although many of my expectations have not been fulfilled, I have become much more accepting of what is, of myself in all its inadequacies and failings.

Nevertheless, I feel that I am still caught up in the need for change, for improvement, development, progress, becoming, and I tend to lose sight of the Being pole of the process. However, I think that something in Jung's system and philosophy has helped perpetuate these expectations, namely the emphasis on change, development and the goal of wholeness. Also, Jung's emphasis on work, on the ego engaging the unconscious in active imagination in order to transform the PRIMA MATERIA into the LAPIS PHILOSOPHORUM, helps to perpetuate the fantasy of becoming a superior, enlightened soul who lives in complete harmony with himself and the cosmos. Depth analysis (Jungian and Freudian) has always been more concerned with change, development, Becoming, than with acceptance and Being.

Why do people stay so long in the analytical situation if it is not out of the expectation that they will attain a healing resolution of old wounds or complexes, change old patterns of relating and generally improve the quality of their lives? If the goal were limited to self-exploration for the purpose of coming to soul and self-acceptance, I think profound changes in attitude and structure would follow. Even though we know psychologically that change and becoming needs to be grounded in acceptance of being, the overwhelming emphasis in psychotherapy is toward change. Our patients certainly don't pay our high fees in order to just "be" with us, although unconsciously this is often the case. Most of us feel uncomfortable about being paid for intimacy and relationship, but we feel fine about using the soul's need for relationship as a therapeutic instrument for understanding, interpreting, and working through transference.

What I am getting at is that the prevailing notions about therapeutic responsibility, about what it means to do a good job, are all highly critical about the therapist losing his/her objectivity and becoming emotionally involved with his patient. Yet if the experience of being with another person involves equality, intimacy, communion, how is this possible unless the limitations of the traditional therapeutic model are transcended? So even though we know better, I think we have moved so heavily into a growth and becoming orientation because communion and being are so threatening within our current structure.

I think the notion that intimacy and emotional involvement are oppositional to objectivity and detachment is largely responsible for the direction psychotherapy has taken. A truly soul-centered psychotherapy would never have fallen into this type of polarization. Such a notion has its roots in an ego-centered psychology which does not recognize the archetypal origins of therapeutic distance and objectivity, even though modern physicians still swear an oath to far-shooting Apollo. Not for a moment am I arguing against the importance of detachment and objectivity, but rather for the awareness that when the ego identifies with this function and feels responsible for carrying this type of consciousness, it is soul-splitting and communion is not possible. When objectivity enters through the Healing God, through Apollo, when the Great Man speaks as he did through Jung, the ego is no longer burdened with the inhuman task of having to carry this archetype.

I now see the analytical ritual as a temenos designed primarily for the purpose of connecting to soul and evoking healing powers. I find that anything, such as the alchemical model (in spite of its metaphorical value), which emphasizes change, development, progress, becoming, working on the process, tends to perpetuate our cultural neglect of soul and acceptance of being. Thus, in the therapeutic interaction my main emphasis is on *acceptance of what is and of honoring the needs of the soul in the living moment.*

For example, I have been seeing a very successful creative man who came to me because of "burn out" and depression. He plunged into the work immediately, keeping a journal, writing his dreams, etc. But his resistance, which was also there from the beginning, soon gained ascendency, and I found the work hard and tiring. I knew that much of his resistance was related to the pressure to perform, which was also constellated in the transference. But an important aspect of the pressure, which we had both missed, was revealed only after the following experience in a 90 minute analytical session: Soon after he sat down, he appeared somewhat out of it, which was not unusual. I asked him what he was feeling and he said, "I'm feeling like I want to go to sleep." I suggested that he listen to his feelings and go with it, which he did. Lying down on the couch, he went immediately to sleep and I soon dozed off with him into a very pleasant dreamy state even though I had not at first been sleepy. We slept for about a half hour, both of us awakening feeling very nourished by the experience.

I had often felt very sleepy with him and sometimes suggested that we both close our eyes and sink into the unconscious in order to see what images appear, but this was the first time that I had risked just going to sleep without any purpose. It was a bit difficult at first because I felt guilty about not earning my money, but I soon let go of that. From this experience, he realized that he had been coming to analysis only in order to overcome his creative block so that he could return to his successful career, and not primarily to connect with the needs of his neglected soul. For most of his life, this man had been under such inner pressure to live up to his mother's heroic animus that what he is most needing now is recognition and acceptance of his essential being. One usually experiences this type of acceptance in the beginning of analysis, but the demanding, negative parent archetype and our cultural work ethic soon appear, recreating the family pathology. Of course this is inevitable and essential, but I believe that a therapeutic model which emphasizes the "Celebration of Being" rather than growth is much more aligned to the needs of the soul in our times.

I feel I have moved much closer to living up to Jung's dictum about the importance of the analyst being open, vulnerable, spontaneous and not afraid of exposing his/her shadow. I place great emphasis on cultivating an awareness of the body's sensations and emotions in the therapeutic interaction. While dreams continue to serve as an important source of connection to the psyche, I have come to view everything as a dream and imaginal experience, so that I am no longer so dependent upon dreams as the royal road to the unconscious. I have also become much more aware of the value of a number of other modalities such as (1) Gestalt techniques, but viewed from the archetypal perspective; (2) use of the couch to direct the analysand's attention inward toward greater emotional-bodily-imaginal awareness and away from the interactional field; (3) focused visualization and other types of imaginal work during the hour; (4) working with the mutual projections occurring in the therapeutic relationship in order to move the psyche and to become aware of the nature and power of the archetypes; (5) Couples therapy has become for me an invaluable aid to the inner anima/animus work; (6) Lastly, I have found group therapy of great value.

The task of a Jungian analyst is hard, demanding superhuman consciousness as well as a highly developed capacity to be open to the experience of intimacy in relationship. I think our profession has failed abominably in the latter. An underlying reason for the failure, I believe, is that the development of consciousness has been emphasized to the detriment of Eros, the uniting principle of relatedness. If the sharp separating light of consciousness is essential to expose the deep splitting wounds to the soul, then the diffuse unifying light of Eros is necessary for their healing. An important aspect of this healing process is the experience of communion with another human soul.

SPIEGELMAN'S COMMENT ON STEIN'S PAPER

As I read Stein's "Reflections on Professional Deformation" and as I sit now, at my Swiss Hermes typewriter vintage 1956, I recall with pleasure and nostalgia our days together at the C.G. Jung Institute in Zurich in the last half of the 1950s. Stein, Jim Hillman and myself were affectionately called "Sons of the Prophet," but it was Robert Stein who was clearly the most courageous, confrontative, and passionately involved in all aspects of Jungian psychology, willing to risk and question, both as a student and as experimenting analyst-in-training. Even his going to London out of criticism of Zurich's lack of attention to the transference was just such an act of courage. He was received back lovingly and it was just his honest spirit, I think, that enabled him to be at least a bit outrageous at times, but appreciated. It is, therefore, sad that he reports here his distancing and detachment.

His observations about the detachment of the analyst and its effects upon his/her personality, however, can hardly be denied. Yet I wonder if this can be laid so completely on the need to be responsible for consciousness-raising, for reflection and for not bringing in the analyst's own needs and complexes. We now know full well, as Jung so said so long ago and as Stein reports, that we can hardly do otherwise than bring in our complexes. I would suggest that the deformation might be at least partially attributable to another problem, namely the necessity of endlessly focusing on the "other," the analysand. We are unnaturally attentive, every minute of every work-hour, on what is happening with our patient, no matter how much we also attend to what is happening in ourselves or in the conjectured "third" of the relationship itself. This focus may be a good exercise for us, since we are mostly introverted and, therefore, can use such outer-object attention, but it can lead to the lamentable condition that Stein describes. Each analyst must cope with this dilemma and resolve it somehow. I, with my "mutual process" conception, have emerged, I think, less "detached" in my therapeutic work, but I am quite deformed when it comes to group life generally, and in ordinary social encounters. Quite useless am I, really, and often painfully inadequate, in contrast to my effectiveness in one-on-one connections or teaching or inner work. I am less effective now than I was in my twenties. That deformation, I think, comes from the analytic focus and my inner focus, as well.

The question then becomes: Does not each orientation in life, from work or personality, result in some kind of deformation or one-sidedness, and that this can not be helped really? Can we not, as Stein suggests, even accept our inadequacies resulting from this orientation and somehow embrace our "Being," as he also suggests, thus softening our failures, if not transforming or overcoming them? Or does he recommend some way of changing? It would seem that his shift to spontaneity and focus on connection rather than consciousness has been useful to him, but has not solved his "detachment" problem. What, then, is to be done? I think that acceptance is a key, as he suggests, and if aging itself contributes to this detachment, its virtues of ultimate serenity and objectivity, perhaps, can compensate the painful relational deformation that Stein describes and that we all suffer, in one way or another.

As a colleague and friend, I thank him for his honesty, then and now. It is just this sort of presentation, I think, that can be helpful to both students and practitioners, for it makes us more conscious about our craft, its effects upon us and, perhaps, brings us closer together in an understanding of a shared suffering.

STEIN'S RESPONSE TO SPIEGELMAN'S COMMENTS

Let me first thank my old friend Spiegelman for his kind words and praise about my courage, which for me always seemed much more of a necessity for survival than courage.

Spiegelman suggests that the deformation may rather be owing to the necessity of endlessly focusing on the "other," the analysand. I failed to mention this important aspect of the psychotherapeutic relationship because I felt it was implied in my remarks about the analyst having to maintain an observing, reflective position. But I think Spiegelman is right to make this point, because the unnatural pattern of habitually focusing one's attention on another person's needs or process can certainly be deforming, even if one does not feel responsible for carrying consciousness.

Spiegelman suggests that his method of "mutual process" has enabled him to be less detached in his therapeutic work. When an analysand is ready to assume responsibility for entering into a mutual process with the analyst, I can see that this certainly would free the analyst from feeling that he must carry the sole responsibility for maintaining boundaries and consciousness. In any deep analysis, I believe the analysand's awareness that a mutual process is at work is essential. Nevertheless, as long as the analysis continues within the same ritual, including the payment of a fee, I believe that only a limited mutuality is possible and that the focus still remains primarily on the analysand's process and development. So I would once again suggest that Eros would be best served by a therapeutic model which emphasizes communion and acceptance of Being rather than Growth and Becoming.

McNAIR'S COMMENTS ON STEIN'S CONTRIBUTION

Bob's paper offers me some solace for the shadow of this profession. I have often been wary of the cost I have had to pay in doing this work. One outstanding theme stays with me after reading his paper several times: The personal struggle of "An Analyst." Starting with a comment on Jung's Lament, his meeting with Jung, the inevitable vacuum that followed, and then a lifetime's search, Bob put me in touch with the struggle which goes beyond "what does one do?" The question then becomes: "How do I stay with it?"

My own start with ego-psychology led me to seek out Jung for a larger cultural context. Unlike the London example for Bob, my encounter with Jung helped quench my thirst for more substance. Having thought I found a new home for my psychological interest, I instead discovered my own vacuum, in the wake of Jung's expansiveness. I appreciate Bob mentioning his "tenuous moment" and subsequent dependency and support from his family and work. I have often found it difficult to realize that my work and not my personal/social reality is often my most reliable and dependable source of validation and affirmation.

At this point in the paper, for me, Bob departs upon his own personal unresolved conflict. Likewise, at this point, I began to produce pages of reactions and responses to what Bob said. Obviously, my own complexes came into action . . . and some focus. Suffice to say, for myself, I am much more allied with the Rainmaker Model, having had no success, to date, in establishing a safe and prosperous kinship with a "communitas group." In fact, I have suffered my most damaging and debilitating injuries at that juncture.

Bob's paper does yield a certain pathos that touches me and reminds me of the personal struggle and suffering one must go through. I have no problem with his critique of Western Methodology of language, Lacan notwithstanding. It is not where I can stay very long. Mother Nature is an aspect of my life which I have come to rely heavily upon. As Jung claimed, it has an intrinsic reliability. I see it to be another end of the pole that I contend with so as to stay centered within my own psychology. Hence, I spend a lot of time in the mountains. Coming back from Zurich year after year, with my infusions of Introversion and Nature, helped me build my internal residence—a secure place. Although I shared the same fear as Bob with regard to extraverted Los Angeles, I can only say that depth psychology has helped me develop a better capacity for intimate relationships.

A note of appreciation: When I entered the training program in Los Angeles, I came with the same attitude as I had in Zurich—separated, isolated, within my own commitment. At a certain point, estrangement began to outweigh a dread of social life. Bob suggested that I meet with my fellow trainees at their weekly dinner. It proved to be very meaningful in the end. It helped me to "stay with it." The struggle remains.

The feeling in this paper, for me, is one of affirmation in Bob's relationship to himself, yet a difficult life beyond therapy. There is a real tension in this paper . . . of unresolved conflict. Mine or his? Bob has made me aware of just how much I owe to the mountains; they do for me what nothing else can; help me digest the physical effects of this work.

STEIN'S RESPONSE TO McNAIR'S COMMENTS

I am pleased that my paper helped Joe feel affirmed in his own struggle with psychotherapy. I am also pleased that Joe feels that depth psychology has helped him develop a better capacity for intimate relationships, but he does not speak precisely to the issue that I have raised about the deforming effects which the practice of psychotherapy has upon the therapist. I, too, feel depth psychology has been invaluable in helping me to develop my capacity for intimacy, but I still insist that while the traditional analytic attitude may initially create an environment which enables the analysand to safely reveal herself/himself, this is not to be mistaken for an intimate relationship. Furthermore, I can not imagine any psychotherapist escaping the deforming effects of this unique perspective from which he/she habitually views the soul in daily practice, no more than I can imagine the actor, doctor, lawyer or engineer escaping the deforming effects of their chosen professions.

How I Do It

by

JOSEPH B. WHEELWRIGHT, M.D.

(The following are selected excerpts from Dr. Wheelwright's book, *St. George and the Dandelion: 40 Years of Practice as a Jungian Analyst*, published by the C.G. Jung Institute of San Francisco, 1982, 109 plus xiii pp. Grateful acknowledgement for permission to reprint here are extended to the author and the publisher. Page numbers of the original book are given for those who might wish to pursue the original for greater detail.)

(On how he chose to become an analyst. He had been ill and feverish.) The fantasy went like this: Jane and I were driving along in a car, and suddenly a tire blew, or something happened, and the car went off the road and down a cliff end over end. Somehow or other Jane was unhurt and she dragged me—all mashed up, legs wrapped around my neck, squirting blood in every direction—out of this mess and nursed me back to life. Well, in Firenze, with a temperature of 106, I did better. I went over a cliff as usual, only this time I was the one who pulled HER out of the wreck, and I was the one who nursed HER back to life. Now that may not sound like anything to sway the Empire State Building but for me it was the turning point. From that point on there was never any question in my mind about what the Good Lord had in mind for me to do, and what I wanted to do, and I could do. (pp. 5-6)

My own focus has tended to be on the earlier part of Jung's work which I find quite compatible with Frieda's (Fromm-Reichman) and quite compatible with Erik's (Erikson). It is worth mentioning that back around 1915 or 1916, Jung made the statement that the analyst was in a peculiar position because he found himself at the same time subject and object of the therapeutic process, and Frieda agreed with me that this was equivalent to Sullivan's formulation of the analyst as participant-observer. Also Jung's concern with ego development in the first half of life is very compatible with the whole trend of ego psychology, especially Erikson's, so I feel no conflict there at all. However, Jung's notions about the task of the second half of life are something else again. (p. 8)

In therapy it often seems unfruitful to make a head-on assault on a complex, especially one that is of common occurrence. For instance, it may be assumed that all men have mother complexes and castration complexes, but not necessarily ones that interfere with their lives. To deal effectively with complexes that are troublesome, however, it is essential to establish a general attitude apart from the attitude of the complex, that is to strengthen the ego point of view. The complex can then be brought into consciousness and assimilated. (p. 16)

(On the teleological nature of neurosis) Nature seems principally concerned with growth, and to achieve this end, she inflicts pain on her victims, those who falsify their true identities or fail to live up to their full capacities. Out of the catastrophe comes new hope and new life. The phoenix-from-the-ashes motif nicely symbolizes a successful analysis. (p. 20)

(Young analyst with a strong-willed patient who was seen as a Goddess, but wanted, unconsciously, some "rough stuff") One night she had a dream that shocked him (analyst) to his senses and showed clearly that he unconsciously had been acting out the masculine role that she unconsciously wanted for herself. She dreamed that he had small horns and a pointed beard, unmistakably Mephistopheles. He was striding up and down his consulting room, throwing her come-hither glances and saying, "Let's go out together. The Waldhaus Dolder is a nice hotel. Any night will do, any night." This jolted the analyst back into his own point of view; his ego took over again. For when he considered such a course of action, consciously, he knew he really had no desire for such shenanigans, quite apart from any moral or professional considerations. He liked her, but not that much! So he had to explain his real point of view to her and admit he had been guilty of leading her on, unconsciously to be sure; but most catastrophes in analysis occur through just such lapses of consciousness on the part of the analyst. And dreams sometimes make useful objective comments that nevertheless cause the analyst considerable discomfort. (p. 21)

(Question by Spiegelman: Is this not a shadow-animus union? How about the idea that the content belongs to both partners and analyzed that way?)

Analysis insists that one's consciousness must be a democracy. One must acknowledge the existence of disparate psychological elements and give them their value. In a highly collectively-minded country like ours, there is a great danger of identifying with one's persona, one's adapted side, thus denying the existence of the shadow. This is precisely the situation that leads to a "bouleversement," a reversal of the apparent personality. (p. 22)

I'd like to start off by saying that TYPES is really where I came in on the Jungian scene. (p. 53)

It is of interest that Jung worked out his type formulations as part of his lifelong attempt to understand what went wrong between him and Freud. (p. 55)

I never think of us in psychiatry as real doctors. In fact, I think the medical model is actually antithetical to analysis. (p. 68)

(Reports done by Bradway, K. and Detloff, W. using the Gray-Wheelwright type test) They found . . . that the Jungians in San Francisco and Los Angeles came out 90% introverted and 80% intuitive. I'm absolutely convinced, because I've spent a lot of time in psychoanalytic circles, that the opposite is true in the Freudian scene, that their members are predominantly (I would guess about 80%) extraverted and sensation types. They're very consistent in these two aspects. Jung had arrived at a similar conclusion with regard to himself and Freud; namely that Freud was heavily weighted on extraversion and sensation and he on introversion and intuition. (p. 57)

For some strange reason the subject of types seems until recently to have been very neglected in Jungian training centers. Perhaps this had to do with the fact that Jung moved on in his later years to a passionate exploration of the collective unconscious. In so doing, he left types behind, except incidentally, and most of his followers moved with him. Being atypical, I have never been able to forget them even for a day. (p. 76)

In one of his seminars, Jung made a very felicitous statement to the effect that if one has discharged one's debt to one's genes and to society, one has lived oneself out of life. I thought that was beautiful. (pp. 84-85)

It seems to me that if one is truly going to make it in marriage, one has to be immensely hooked on the growth process. I look upon this not as any great virtue nor any great "unvirtue." It seems to me that some of us are just stuck with it. I get terribly resentful sometimes when I'm driving along and see a farmer working his fields. I think, Goddamn, wouldn't that be nice! All there is for him is the wind and the rain and the sun, and here I have to go back and have more analysis, and I am 70 years old; to hell with it!" And yet I just can't help it, you know, it is just too damn bad about me. And it's too damn bad about all of us Jungians. Really we are just stuck with it. (p. 86)

To sum up these two periods of life, in youth the body orientation ties one to outer physical events for life's rewards and psychological events. This implies the important task of disidentifying from outer things. I would in fact define maturity as the degree to which a person has withdrawn projections upon persons, places and things. It appears to me fortunate that as catabolism of the body increases, there appears to be a release of energy producing the effect of increasing anabolism psychologically. More simply put, the less energy is demanded by the body, the more energy is available for psychic growth. (p. 93)

(Quoting Jung, more or less) Freud and Adler and I are not exceptions to this rule (that you must not generalize your own psychology, but everybody does), so our concepts are really personal confessions. We have generalized them, we have abstracted them, and we produce lots of documentation so it will appear that we based these notions upon an overwhelming body of evidence we had amassed through years of clinical practice. Don't let that fool you for a minute. What surprises me is not so much that none of us has the whole truth, but that there are so many people who find our value systems and our attitudes and our truths congenial to them. (p. 98)

(Postlude) The range of voice and goals possible for Jungian analysts never ceases to amaze me. I think it fair to say that the heart of the process for most of us is the emergence of potential growth in consciousness. We are primarily oriented to health and growth, not to psychopathology. This is reflected in our terminology. Jung often said that one of his biggest debts to Freud was that he explored psychopathology so exhaustively that it left him, Jung, free to explore health and its limitless possibilities.

For most of us, our only goal is for the patient to be what it is in him to be. We try not to have bright ideas about our patients. When I start work with a person,

I am always reminded of a statement of Michelangelo. He said that David was in that shaft of marble and that he must be very careful in liberating him, so that he—David—could emerge unscathed. Jung said the same of HIS sculpture. We are blessed in having no system, no set way to go about analysis, no beginning, middle, or end. This permits us to find our own way and to function according to our temperaments. The interesting thing is that we all get reasonably good results as long as we remember that there is no RIGHT way for us, only a right way for each one of us. (pp. 103-4)

ATTITUDES AND VALUES (pp. 26-35)
Screening:

I suppose that one of the most important things I do as a therapist occurs before I do any therapy at all, namely screening. I consider myself really fortunate to have been able to pick and choose whom I work with. I haven't done this on an elitist basis; I've done it because of my own limitations. The very fact that I have certain gifts means the price of admission is that I have certain "ungifts." If somebody comes along who needs the kind of stuff I have only on my ungifted side, they'd be better off if they went to the movies. To me it's arrant nonsense to think that every therapist can be equally good with all kinds of people. I just don't think it's true.

So I usually have two or three preliminary interviews with prospective patients in order to give us a chance to size each other up, and unless all the little green lights go on inside my cranium, I suggest they go to one of my colleagues. For my part, I want to make sure in the first place that we can communicate, speak a language that seems to make sense to each other; in the second place, I want to make sure that there can be mutual trust; and in the third place, I want to be sure that I can actively believe in whomever I work with. I don't think it's enough just to accept people passively. I suppose if a one-legged, pea-green man came in and announced that he enjoyed cohabiting with sheep, I could probably sit there and not be too upset about it, even smile blandly at him. But it's got to be more than that; the person actually has to be important to me.

Patient Fees:

An interesting thing happened with Jung about prices. He said to me, "Now about charges . . . "

I said, "This is very embarrassing, very awkward, because I . . . to tell you the truth, I am just about broke. We have been living in a basement on $150 a month for the last six years and my nest egg is pretty well dried up; there isn't much of it left."

"Well, I'll tell you what I'll do. In spite of that funny sort of British-sounding way you talk, you are an American, aren't you?"

"Yes, yes, it's just that I come from what I call the 'incest group' in Boston. (They all marry their cousins; it's the only place I know of outside of New Guinea where first-cousin marriages are not only permitted but even encouraged.) They all talk this way because they don't know they are Americans; they think they are British. I just never outgrew it." Jung thought that was pretty funny.

"Well, there you are," he said, "you really are an American."

"Yes, I suppose I really am an American."

"Well, okay then, you're rich."

"I have just been telling you that I am not rich."

"Oh, everybody knows that all Americans are rich, so I tell you what. If you are a doctor, I will charge you half price. But I don't recognize all that M.R.C.S.L.R.C.P. stuff you talked about. What does all that mean?"

"Well, it's the equivalent of an M.D."

"I thought you were a doctor; I thought you had really done it. You said you were going to."

"Yes, I did it."

"Well, then you are a doctor, and so you get half-price. Instead of 15 francs, that makes it 7.50. Now, let me see, I'll just send you a bill every month. I know you can't pay me, but I want you to take it seriously. I don't want you to throw these bills away or burn them up or give them away to friends for souvenirs; they are real bills. What you do is take these bills and keep them and save them up. Then you pay me when you are rich the way all Americans are supposed to be."

"Okay, I'll pay you when I am rich."

I didn't feel that I was really rich enough to pay him until about the middle of the war, and I had a difficult time getting money through to Switzerland, but I did. One of the first things I said to him when I saw him again in 1951 was, "I hope you got that money. It wasn't half enough, but I hope you got it." He laughed and said, "I told you that you would be rich someday."

That experience had a very profound effect on me because, of course, in psychoanalytic circles, a great deal is made of money. There is a great deal of what I consider hypocritical cant that goes on about your analysis not doing you any good unless you financially bleed and die, and therefore, "I am only charging you this much for your own good, you know." Anyway, I think that one's experience in analysis conditions a great many of the things one later does as an analyst. I am sure this experience with Jung had a lot to do with the fact that I have always seen many patients for reduced fees or played "banker" for them. People say to me, "But you can't do that; they will feel guilty and inhibited, and you won't get a real analysis." It hasn't turned out that way. If patients have problems about it, it is just grist for the mill, something more to discuss. Actually, it has worked very well.

Jane and I settled something between ourselves at the beginning of our practices, and I am sure that it had something to do with Jung's attitude. We decided to settle for making as much money between the two of us as I could legitimately make by myself. This meant that we could take on many people who couldn't begin to pay the going rates. In fact, I don't think we have ever turned down patients because they couldn't afford it. This isn't intended as a boast about generosity. It is really selfishness in that it has meant that we have been able to screen our patients and to work only with those people we thought would find us meaningful and, because of our temperaments, more useful to them than other equally good analysts down the street. So, it has been an indulgence. We have made less money, but we have had very rich professional lives. I attribute this largely to the attitude that Jung had on this subject, and I must say that we have lived comfortably, eaten and drunk well, and traveled widely. We have not been sacrificial lambs.

Analyst-Patient Relationships:
From the foregoing, it will be obvious that for me the interaction between myself and the patient is the crucial thing, and I struggle hard to try and describe what in heaven's name it is that I do. This is very difficult indeed, but one way I have of putting it is that when I am working with somebody, I hook one of my legs very tightly around a leg of my chair, dispatch myself into the skin of my patient, hang around in there for a while, pull myself back out again, and try to figure out what seemed to be going on while I was inside the patient's skin. That's one way I could say it. Or I often think of it as plugging in with absolute concentration.

Something else that's important for me is to be no different in my consulting room from the way I am with my family or friends. Well, I don't make love to my patients, but I may laugh or cry, and I'm certainly more focused on the other person than I might be when I'm with a friend. I don't have the feeling of dispensing knowledge to swine who come in kissing my shoes. Nor do I use any sort of facade, any sort of technique. If ever I should, you can be absolutely certain I'm doing it not for the patient's sake but for my own, because I'm going down for the third time. That is, when I find myself falling back on technical devices, it is usually a defense to cover my own anxiety or feeling of inadequacy in the situation.

In other words, I've learned to treat therapy as a relationship, a process, and I try very hard to keep my theories out of this process because I don't want anything interfering with my immediate experience, my immediate contact with the patient. All that theory in my head isn't so important. Too much conscious concern with it tends to distort my observation and experience of the patient's quality. What is important—the indication of a successful therapy—is that both parties change, are touched by each other and grow.

Diagnosis:
In the same vein, I would like to comment that I think diagnosis is a terribly dangerous thing. I'm enormously opposed to it in the field of therapy because if I start disgnosing people, all the things I've read about anxiety states, or hysterical conversions, or schizophrenia, or manic-depressives, or whatever it might be, immediately come flooding into my head. It's as if I'd pushed a button, and all this knowledge pours through the floodgates and gets between me and the person

I'm working with. I used to say that before I'd start work with a patient, I'd rush in and grab an eraser off the blackboard and scrub my cortex absolutely clean, so there would be nothing preconceived between me and the patient.

I feel it is desirable to establish a relatively informal setting and to minimize the implications of authority inherent in the therapeutic situation. In this connection, I recall a day I spent with Jung in 1951 at his country place in Bollingen. It was the first time I'd got back to Switzerland since the war; I'd left in 1939, about 13 years earlier.

He said, "I hear that you are doing all right." I beamed from ear to ear and then he added, "in spite of the fact that you are an M.D." What he was talking about was one of these archetypal things that we Jungians (including Jung himself) are enormously focused on: the whole tradition of the shaman, the healer, and the danger of identification with it. This happens when you think you're a cross between Mahatma Gandhi, Red Grange, Joe Namath and Siegfried: quite a galaxy of heroic material. I don't find this very good for patients.

The hero archetype is a particular pitfall for me, and I think it is for many if not all psychiatrists. Mine took the form of St. George. When you're working with patients and realize that their needs and the place they're moving around in are very frightening and require a total mobilization of yourself in order to meet them and to accompany them and to match them, you often become not quite sure that you have it in you; maybe you could do it with about THAT much left over. It's a really scary thing. Well, at that point, sometimes I find myself being taken over by the St. George image. Mind you, I don't exactly look in the mirror and see myself in a suit of armor galloping across the fields after the dragon, but it gives me a kind of jolt; it's like a squirt of monkey glands. It gives me the ability to do a lot of things and to have all sorts of strength and courage that normally I don't have. But it is also a very fearsome thing; it's a little bit like putting a Porsche motor in a Volkswagen; you know, the chassis isn't quite up to it. So usually I have to go back and have another spin with my favorite analyst.

One thing that favors a reality-based relationship between analyst and patient, and implies rapport and reactivity on the part of the analyst, is more frequent use of the vis-a-vis arrangement as opposed to the couch. In London, the Jungians all seem to have slipped around the corner and bought a couch; but in this country and in Zurich, this is not so. I have bootlegged a couch, but I don't use it all that much, and my criteria for using it are certainly not the same criteria a psychoanalyst would have. I tend to use the couch when a patient has such verbal constipation that we both just sit there breathing for quite a long while. I think that is very expensive—after all, the patient is paying for the hour—and besides, it makes me very uncomfortable. A couch does help a bit, I think, in instances like that. But when I do use it, I'm likely to sit at right angles to the head of my patient, so that the patient can look at my beady eyes if he wants to, and if he doesn't want to, he can peer at the rubbing from Ankgor Watt, or he can peer at the wall. Not infrequently I will walk around the room; I've been described by one of my friends as a running analyst, in contrast to a sitting analyst.

The avoidance of anonymity seems to me to highlight one of the principal differences between the Freudian and Jungian schools. Jung has described the therapeutic relationship as an intensely personal one in an impersonal framework, personal but not intimate. It seems to me essential to establish a reality-based relationship. I am using the word "transference" to indicate projection of any unconscious contents. These include not only the unresolved infantile feelings and attitudes, but also contents that have remained "in potentia" and can only be assimilated into ego consciousness via the analyst. In my experience those things that need to be projected will be, without the therapist's forcing them by playing an anonymous role.

I feel that a large part of the effectiveness of therapy stems from reality-based interpersonal exchange between analysand and analyst. This means that the two people in the transaction are partners jointly engaged in a struggle to dispel the neurosis and explore the growth urge that afflicts the patient, including resolution of the transference. Therapy involves making an alliance with the healthy aspects of the patient, and until this has been accomplished, my primary focus is on health, not psychopathology. This is not an either/or, but a matter of emphasis.

An important implication of this approach is my belief that the healthy aspects need to be activated and encouraged throughout the therapeutic procedure. Erik Erikson once said that he thought one of the reasons Jung left Freud was that he could not bear Freud's unrelieved pessimism. While I recognize pain as a necessary concomitant of growth, it seems to me that neglect of the positive, healthy part of the patient overemphasizes the painful side of the procedure, even to the point of extolling it as a virtue. As the "reductio ad absurdum" of this tendency. I am reminded of the London navvies and charladies I used to treat during my medical training. Any attempt to give them palatable medicine was vigorously resisted; they used to insist on "the good stuff, Guv'nor, that nasty, 'orrid black medicine that mykes yer gag." In contrast to this and to balance the books, Frieda Fromm-Reichmann described her analysis as a joyous experience, and when I asked "You mean a liberation?" she agreed.

It seems to me important to hold theory in abeyance so nothing can interfere with the immediacy of contact or will stand between patient and therapist. An overly conscious concern with theory tends to distort one's observation and experience of the patient's quality. This attitude implies a minimizing of techniques. As I said, when I find myself falling back on technical devices, it is usually a defense to cover my own anxiety or inadequacy in the situation. But I am speaking only for myself, not prescribing the "right" way to do therapy. There is no "right" way to do therapy; each analyst must find his or her own style.

Jungians principally use dreams rather than free association to get access to unconscious material. Of course this emphasis brings up the question of attitude toward dreams. Does one take a dream as being in fact a distorted wish-fulfillment? If so, one is going to have to cope with the latent and the manifest content. Or does one only work on a dream reductively? Or does one, as I think Jung does, take a dream as a statement of how certain things are down in the basement at a given moment in time and space? Jung disbelieved in the idea that dreams are tailored by a censor and felt that if a dream was not understood, the failure was attributable to the analyst and analysand.

In contrast to the systematic approach of Freudian analysis, which may be said to have a beginning, a middle and an end, the Jungian process is non-systematic. A deep Jungian analysis is really a kind of controlled psychosis, a sort of guided tour through psychosis analogous to Virgil's trip with Dante. In other words, from the Jungian point of view, if you become psychotic, you're sloshing around in the primordial slime of the collective unconscious, rubbing shoulders with archetypes, and in a deep Jungian analysis this is what happens. The nearest Jung came to formulating a system was when he made the statement that analysis consists of four stages: catharsis, explanation, education and transformation. But this is a general formulation and does not blueprint the clinical operation.

Finally, a basic Jungian attitude toward neurosis should be briefly stated: neurosis may be viewed as a challenge, an attempt by the organism to promote growth, as well as an illness. In short, neurosis has a purpose as well as a cause.

Training Analysis:
I think there are times when a man therapist is indicated and times when a woman therapist is indicated. I don't care how good a mummy I try to be, I'm just not as good a mummy as a woman is; and I don't care how good a daddy a woman is, she's not going to be as good a daddy as a man is. These are very arbitrary and provocative statements, perhaps, but that's the way it seems to me.

When I was first beginning to work with Jung, he said, "I suppose you're going to talk an awful lot about your mother. You've got the look of a mother-drowned man somehow."

I said, "Yes, I suppose so; yes, I expect so. In fact, I know of course I will; doesn't everyone?"

"No. And all that stuff just bores me to extinction. For forty years I've been listening to people talk about their mothers, and I can't stand any more of it. Now my assistant, Toni Wolff, tolerates it very well. So I tell you what you do: you go and talk about your mother to her. She will do very well with all that shadow business. Then when you have some archetypal material, something that's really interesting, we'll talk about that."

"Well, all right." I felt more than a little dubious about this arrangement, but actually it worked out very well. I saw Toni Wolff maybe three times a week and Jung once or twice a week. Curiously enough, there was remarkably little overlapping.

I've had my psyche tinkered with, I guess, by about seven different analysts since 1931, when I started down the road, and it's been about even, male and female. There's no question, as I see it, but that working with a female analyst activates things in my psyche—everyone's psyche—that working with a man does not and vice versa; each activates, mobilizes, different aspects of the psyche. For just this reason, I have always been very keen on trainees being patients, somewhere along the line in their training, of both a man and a woman.

Another point about training is that in our Jungian training centers—and in the psychoanalytic centers as well—there is something that strikes me as awfully difficult and troublesome about the custom of casting the training analyst in the simultaneous roles of judge and therapist. To my mind these two roles are mutually exclusive, and this practice bothers me a great deal. If I could have my way about this, the training analyst would actually be disqualified from having anything to do with the promotion of the candidate.

I should also like to put in a plea for the encouragement of dissidence in the training centers and institutes. I find that things tend to move toward conformity, and in this way things tend to get crystallized into law and go dead.

Then, of course, there's the perennial chestnut which I think should be included in these remarks about the training situation. I will not be invidious about my colleagues, only about myself, in saying that when I was a young fellow, one didn't go into analysis only to get trained to be an analyst, at least this analyst didn't. I went because my psyche was in disrepair; I wanted and needed therapy. Most of us older people tend to react rather negatively when candidates present themselves and say, "Well, I'm perfectly willing to submit to analysis, you know; after all, I realize it's part of the training and everything; but of course I don't feel that I really need it." You can see the training analysts making black marks in their books about these people. But if a candidate comes in and says, "Of course what I am really after is the therapy; I'm having some tough problems and difficulties, and after I've worked these through, I hope to become an analyst," then they're very tickled. It's rather tricky; one has to be neurotic enough, but not too neurotic. I don't know how this is going to develop, how it's going to be handled in the future. It's my impression that most of the candidates who are applying nowadays are in far less hot water than most of us were when we were young.

Lay Analysis:

One thing that Jung and Freud did not disagree about was the question of lay analysis; they were both very strongly in favor of it. I happened to be having lunch with Anna Freud once, and I thought it would be interesting to hear her comments on the subject. So I said to her, "You know, Jung and Freud never thought about this, but what do you think about the M.D.s grasping psychoanalysis to their bosom and plunging down the football field with it?"

And she replied, "Well, your metaphors are a little peculiar. I don't really understand them quite, but I do get the gist of your question, and to tell you the truth, I am outraged by the whole idea."

"Oh, good! I know why I am; why are you?"

"Well, my father devised psychoanalysis as an investigative instrument. And those M.D.s with all their therapeutic zeal, have perverted it almost beyond recognition." And then she went on to cite one of the reasons I'd also had for feeling the way I did about the importance of lay analysts: psychoanalysis and therapy in general simply can't be contained in the medical discipline, or in any one discipline, and they have suffered enormous deprivation from the loss of enrichment by anthropology, religion, philosophy, law and all the other areas that used to feed them.

COMMENT BY SPIEGELMAN ON WHEELWRIGHT

The excerpted material from Dr. Wheelwright's book gives a rather full picture, I think, of this flexible, successful analyst who has managed to be friends with the eminent ones in both the Jungian and Freudian camps. His credentials as a Jungian, in both training and attitude, are impeccable, yet he is an avowed extravert among the introverts, a feeler amongst intuitives. He is a physician who sees the goshawful limits of the medical model. He is a patrician who welcomes the poor, in spirit and finances. He is deadly serious about the work and its importance, yet he is an arch-supporter (no pun intended) of humor and wit. In short, as is shown even in the title of his book, *St. George and the Dandelion,* Dr. Wheelwright has grasped Jung's central principle of the opposites and lived them.

I am reminded of an incident early on in my experience of him. The time was in the spring of 1960, at a meeting of the Los Angeles and San Francisco Jungian societies. A friend of mine, newly returned from the training in Zurich (I had been back about a year), was in pain, despite his air of triumph at the meeting. When we chatted with Wheelwright, I half-jokingly said to Jo, "My pal, here, is in pain; help him doc!" Wheelwright immediately responded that he would lie down on the couch himself since he was in worse shape than either of us. It was just the right thing and made us laugh, for we were feeling inadequate back in America, here with all these well-personaed types (we were mystics, of course). Wheelwright instinctively broke the projection and made us realize that all of us were suffering, inadequate, human, "shrinks."

But what of the man behind the humor? One senses that introverted side, and it certainly impregnates his remarks here. Some questions occur to me. How did he react to Jung's apparently flippant attitude at times, and how did it feel to be the "strange extravert" in that high-powered crowd of Jungians in the '30s? And what does he think about the apparent lessening in the passionate devotion of many new analysts now, in contrast to his generation, and mine, too? Is it like it was with the mystic Bal Shem Tov: the fire lessens with succeeding generations?

Other questions: How did his Freudian friends view his informal Jungian style? And did they become interested in Jungian psychology, too? (I must say that I enjoyed reading both Fromm-Reichmann and Erikson more than most other Freudians; Wheelwright had good taste!) What would he advise contemporary candidates to pursue? He suggests the importance of the humanities, arts and social sciences. What else might he recommend?

Finally, I wonder about Wheelwright's experience of suffering in the analytic work. I talk about it in my paper for this volume. I wonder what he would say, since he heard a summary version of it in Boston in October 1985. Is that where the introversion has a big voice in him, in contrast to the ready humor? One imagines that his candidates could say a lot about that.

COMMENT BY McNAIR ON WHEELWRIGHT

The Wheelwright article is perplexing for me. This is a common reaction for me with extraverted psychologies. I find that his response to stimulus items is so in contrast to my introverted one that by the time mine sinks and surfaces I'm two paragraphs behind him! I spend a lot of time making the adjustment to this contrast in my own work. I can get polarized into all those "senex" qualities easily. I can only wonder what it was like for him amongst the "80% introverts"? Reflection? Identification? Tremendous ego for survival!

He does confront me with my own one-sidedness. And he exposes the dexterity of Jung's psychology which I find reassuring. I also find my puer-wit trying to get into this paper.

I felt comforted by his deliberate screening attitude. I'm never quite sure about mutual trust at the beginning—it's a wish, but I can't imagine it being substantiated until a major encounter with negative transference has been survived, somewhere down-stream. I appreciated his story of the leg-wrapped-around-chair technique for getting into his patient. Again, my reflex is precisely opposite. I stay still and let the patient's condition "get under my skin"—directional empathy, I suppose. I do agree with his notion of techniques, etc. being a defense posture. However, if I do feel the temptation I may actually play it out so as to uncover the cover-up.

I do find an inverse relationship between clinical language and personal-experiential disclosure. My experience in Zurich the past summers has shown that the American contingent associated to "diagnostics" whereas the Europeans tended toward humanities. That may change, however, with licensing becoming a greater issue, and "credits" displacing (replacing?) experience as the learning "product."

I enjoyed his story about eyeing the "farmer"; when I feel envious of the farmer it's because the "farmer" in me has been neglected. Likewise, I'm unclear about his anguish of "it's too bad about all us Jungians."

I liked hearing the idea of shift of libido from the physical growth as life progresses. That is becoming more evident to me at this stage in my own life.

There is a definite up-beat, kinetic quality to my image of Dr. Wheelwright's attitude—humor, wit, sarcasm, a certain amount of "athletics" appear to be crucial here. It is reassuring that after all is said and done he feels it to be a "rich professional life." Next time I need to go for a "spin with my favorite analyst" I'll try it at 78 RPM!

I found myself wondering if (or how) his body became part of his "Jungian" career vis-a-vis his initial phantasy. And, since he appears to be rather kinetic in his reactions, how does that dimension bond itself to his work? What role did his sense of humor play throughout his work? I find that humor is a delicate spirit—Wheelwright seems to react with it, or employ it generously. What has it revealed to him?

The allusion to Fromm-Reichmann's statement that her analysis was a "joyous experience" stunned me. Again my senex attitude was exposed! I would not normally think of it that way. Most often people come in suffering pain and anxiety—and it only gets worse for a time. A few, and only a few, came "knowing" that there is more to (their) life and want contact with it. For them, perhaps, it is liberating and joyous. For myself—I never cease to delight in the insights and way of the unconscious; however, the trade-off has been to acquire a greater capacity for suffering, ergo, more.

REJOINDER BY WHEELWRIGHT

Thank you for your generous reaction to my un-book. When people ask me about it I say it's distinction is that in the field where the thinkers predominate I dare them to find an idea in what they call my book. Actually, I did sneak in a few ideas which you, with your perspicacity, responded to. I shall make a stab at answering your questions, but do not expect too much.

First, what about Jung's flippancy? Well, I always enjoyed it and felt it to be a welcome compensation for his incredibly serious pilgrimage—with and without patients. As for being the lone extravert, it was hard, especially in Zurich. I think I included my encounter with Barbara Hannah on this subject in my book. She liked me but was horrified also. I had an Anima fit at Esther Harding's 80th birthday celebration. In my paper I left my script to blaspheme against having to cope endlessly with the unconscious. She and von Franz and Riklin, sitting in the front row, were stunned at a man who didn't long to spend more time splashing around in the primordial slime. However, there was a saving grace: I became the bearer of the extraverted flame, thus relieving the others from having to develop their own extraversion. At one level I became the group mascot, and at a deeper level I became the court jester. This last, of course, gave me license to be outrageous. (I had an enthusiastic assist in those days from Mary Bancroft, which she mentions in her Centenary tribute to Jung.) Actually, I fulfill both roles with the Freudians, only with them I carry the Jungian flame instead of the extraverted flame.

I have never gotten away from the idea that to be a Jungian analyst is a calling—not a professional choice. I am shocked when I find candidates who have less than total commitment to their own psychic growth and to the people they work with. When I give lectures or seminars, I ignore the changing times, and by my own passions aim to activate their passions. Sometimes it works. And I always look askance at analysts who consider money their primary motivation.

My Freudian friends found my style a relief, their own rules of behavior being so rigid. I used to say to them that the Golden Rule was to sit behind the couch denying relationship so that the patient, in desperation, projected everything but the kitchen stove on the analyst, being very careful to keep their mouths shut and their bowels open. Usually they laughed. Only a court jester could get away with such behavior. I would add that if one couches interpretations or reactions in a humorous way one can get away with saying things that would ordinarily be considered "lese majeste," or worse, statements that would stimulate violent defense reactions.

Yes, a lot of Freudians did pick up Jungian attitudes and concepts, though they didn't give us a by-line. As for me, and our group in San Francisco (who are friendly with the Freudians and vice-versa). We have learned from them. Our shocking failure to explore the early years—the reductive bit—is being corrected by some Jungian analysts. Bill Willeford, for instance, has a book in press focused on nothing to two and a half, and we have joint meetings with the Freudians and benefit by their focus on nothing to five. And many of them now work vis-a-vis their patients. My cliche is that Jungians suffer from the lack of Freud and vice-versa.

It is my prejudice that the effectiveness of an analyst suffers unless she or he have a long term love relationship which is central to their life and development. I would add that living in various cultures and participating in them can be enormously helpful.

I should ike to add an interesting and perhaps shocking comment, namely: during the 30s, when I was going through medical school, Jung used to tell me that I had the ability to be a good psychotherapist. However, it was not until I went to Einsiedeln and saw the Black Madonna that I got started on a long deep journey with Isis. This immersion in the collective unconscious, which the man in the street would have called psychosis, delighted Jung. It told him that I could live and work in depth, and for the first time he said I would make a good analyst, and wrote me a letter of recommendation.

I've always thought that Yahweh could have devised a better ingredient to promote growth than suffering. However, I have stopped fighting City Hall and am resigned to this fact. But, unlike the Puritans who brought me up, I do not enjoy suffering for its own sake. (My Grandfather used to say that if you're hurting you can be sure you're on the right track.) But I am reconciled to the value of suffering for a purpose, namely what the Hippies called the growth and development trip. For me, the rewards have so outdistanced a great deal of suffering, that I cannot in good conscience complain to the management.

Epilogue

by

JOE McNAIR, Ph.D.

Once upon a time, in October 1985, Marvin asked me if I would be interested in playing the role of the archetype of the student. It sounded like an interesting project: simple enough, just respond to these papers. As is often the case with creative projects, the spirit takes on a life of its own and, in the end, I became a "willing victim" of its labor.

This has been an immense venture for me personally; writing is not my long suit. It was as though I was in a long dream with a new character coming forward periodically to present his or her truth and wisdom from a life lived deeply. Some responses came easily while others took many months to accomplish a conscious perspective that was creative and honest.

It was much like an active imagination, with an ongoing dialogue within myself and connected with the particular author at the same time. There was a process of circulation and metabolism before a final distillation would lead to a creative image/response. I only knew that each one was completed when there was a calming sense of understanding and relatedness. It was read and re-read, write and re-write. Consequently, my process enlarged and refined itself over the course of a year and a half. I am sure that there is a qualitative difference between my first effort with Dr. Dreyfuss and my final one with Dr. Beyme. Imagery is my natural medium, not the word. Hence my struggle was to translate my images into their linguistic analogs. I hope that I was able to do this adequately.

It is with a profound sense of appreciation and gratitude that I wish to express my heartfelt thanks to those who wrote papers and responded to my comments and questions. As is most often the case with creative works, I am the one who is transformed, while the book is free to have a life of its own.

I believe that these papers represent some of the most sincere testaments from within the realm of "being an analyst" that a student such as myself could ever hope to read. It was a very special feeling to be part of it. Thank you, Marvin.

As others have said, there is a feeling of being exposed and vulnerable when writing personally. It is true. Yet it is this very condition which we inevitably invite upon ourselves to be together in our aloneness.

Joe McNair
2 February 1987, Groundhog Day, Candelmas

Autobiographical Notes and Contact with Jung

Dr. Med. Fritz Beyme — Switzerland

Born in 1918 in a mountain village of the Grisons in Switzerland, my schooling took place in Switzerland and north Germany, alternately, with high school adding northern England, as well. Medical studies in Lausanne, Zurich, Rome and completed in Zurich. Post-graduate study in Child Psychiatry in Solleures, Leyden and Basel, with specialist's diploma. Psychiatric training interrupted by four years in Davos with lung Tbc. Diploma from C.G. Jung Institute Zurich in 1957. Private practice since then in Basel.

Contact with Jung came in 1945, my first year in psychiatry. When treating— with eidetic imagery—a stuttering high school boy, I came across symbols of alchemical transmutation and wrote Jung a letter asking for analytical training. He answered that illness precluded more pupils and recommended Dr. C.A. Meier, with whom I worked from 1946 onward, interrupted by the Tbc. After resuming analysis, I entered training at the Institute in Zurich and had a first audience with Jung in Kusnacht. His estate and the seignorial ritual of admission to his study impressed me, especially since I descend from a family in reduced circumstances that had lived on a manorial level for generations. The huge library reminded me of my grandfather's. Jung talked about his time with Bleuler and Freud. He also said that psychopathology in his time was so poorly founded that the residents used to look suspiciously at each other, trying to guess whether the colleague had discovered some symptom in one's self. The second personal talk took place after I had completed training and Jung signed my diploma. He told me about his first voyage to the USA and how Freud faced the sky-line of New York saying: "If those over there knew what we are bringing to them!"

When I completed analysis with Dr. Meier, I continued on with Mrs. Jung, since it was recommended that training should be undergone with both sexes. In her warm-hearted and unpretentious way, she did everything to make one feel at home. Her consultation room reflected this attitude and sharply contrasted with the library-dominated offices of Dr. Meier and Professor Jung. I retain a pleasant memory, 35 years later, of harmonious cooperation between analyst and analysand.

Dr. Phil. Gustaf Dreifuss — Israel

Because of a strong dissatisfaction in my work as a chemical engineer and a religious problem as well, I began analysis. After three years in analysis, I decided to study at the C.G. Jung Institute in Zurich in order to become an analyst. I graduated in March 1959 and left Switzerland for Israel in September, together with my wife and two small children. We settled in Haifa where I began a private practice. Since 1970, I have been teaching and training, supervising students of the Postgraduate Section of Psychotherapy in Tel Aviv University and later also in Haifa Medical School, in addition to the Jungian group.

My contact with Jung was not very extensive. It was around 1950, when Jung was already 75 years old, that my analyst suggested that I bring a dream to him. I had two sessions with him and was very impressed by his lucidity and knowledge. His amplifications of my archetypal dreams were full of wisdom and enlightenment.

Michael Fordham, M.D. — England

I was a pillar of the establishment at a public school. I went to Cambridge and won an exhibition in Natural Science at Trinity College. I went to Saint Bartholomews Hospital with a Shuter Scholarship in anatomy and physiology. Graduated in medicine and wanted to become a neurologist which lack of cash prevented. Later, I escaped from Psychiatry by winning a Fellowship in Child Psychiatry at the London Child Guidance Clinic. Obtained the following higher degrees: M.R.C.P., M.D. (a thesis degree above the United States M.D.) Later became a Founder Fellow of the Royal College of Psychiatry and was given an honorary Fellowship of the British Psychological Society.

I met Jung in 1933 and after World War II was in regular contact with him, partly through being an editor of his Collected Works and partly out of personal inclination, until his death.

Dr. Med. Adolf Guggenbuhl-Craig — Switzerland

Studied theology at the University of Zurich, philosophy and history in Basel, medicine at the Universities of Zurich and Paris; rotating internship in Providence, Rhode Island; residency in Omaha, Nebraska and at the University Clinic of the Burgholzli in Zurich. After being certified in Psychiatry and Psychotherapy, began private praxis in Zurich. Personal analysis and control work during residency in Psychiatry in Zurich.

I met Jung at lectures and seminars, especially during psychiatric training, but also at official or half-official social occasions. I never worked with him analytically.

Baroness Vera von der Heydt — England

(See detailed listing in reply to comments.)

Dr. Phil. Mario Jacoby — Switzerland

Born in Leipzig, Germany in 1925, I spent my school years in St. Gallen, Switzerland. Studied music in Paris and London and was for some years a concert-violinist and music teacher. Began training at the C.G. Jung Institute Zurich and at the University of Zurich in 1956. Doctorate in Pedagogics, Philosophy and History of Religion in 1964; Diploma at Institute in 1965.

Worked for several years as a psychotherapist in a psychiatric hospital, also at the Jungian Clinic at Zurichberg. Currently I am an analyst in private practice, training analyst, lecturer and member of the Curatorium of the C.G. Jung Institute Zurich. My main publications appearing in English are *THE ANALYTIC ENCOUNTER* (Inner City Books) and *LONGING FOR PARADISE* (Sigo Press).

As to my contact with Jung: I never had a personal encounter with him at his office. On one occasion, Dora Kalff and I gave a little concert for him at the Psychological Club. We played some baroque music which he seemed to enjoy— so he said at least. One other incident I never forget, seemed to me typical for his kind of humour. On the occasion of his 85th birthday, there was a large gathering at the Dolder Grandhotel. The president of the Club, a well-meaning lady, began her opening address by announcing that, due to the delicate health of Professor Jung, nobody should smoke. She added that if somebody needed to smoke, he should be kind enough to do it outside the hall. After she had said this, one heard somebody leaving the hall to smoke a pipe: it was Jung!

Joe McNair, Ph.D. — USA

Education: Ph.D. in psychology from University of Southern California, 1974; Work and study at C.G. Jung Institute Zurich in the summers of 1980-1985; in Jungian work since 1975; analyst-in-training, Los Angeles, since 1983.

Private practice in Sherman Oaks, California for fifteen years; taught at California State University, Northridge for 12 years.

Andrew Samuels — England

(See comment to Spiegelman's contribution.)

Dr. Phil. Sonja Marjasch — Switzerland

Education: Ph.D. from the University of Zurich, where I studied English and American Literature, Sociology and Journalism from 1939-1945. Graduated from the C.G. Jung Institute in Zurich, after four years of training, in 1958. Since then, in private practice. Training Analyst and lecturer at the Zurich Institute. Occasional papers at meetings of professional societies.

I had no personal contact with Jung but remember being twice part of a group of students who went to his Kusnacht home for a "control seminar." It really was a monologue by Jung on some dream or picture presented by a student. Once this took place in his garden which, in retrospect, strikes me as very important since it was the only time in my training that psychic work was done out-of-doors.

J. Marvin Spiegelman, Ph.D. — USA

Ph.D. in Clinical and Social Psychology from the University of California, Los Angeles in 1952; Diploma from the C.G. Jung Institute, Zurich in 1959; Diplomate in Clinical Psychology, American Board of Professional Psychology, 1959.

My experience of Jung was limited largely to hearing his public lectures and some seminars for advanced students at the Institute in the last half of the 1950s. I had one final meeting with him, upon my graduation, wherein I sought

his "blessing." This was of overwhelming importance. I have described this in
the little book, *REMEMBRANCES OF JUNG*, produced by the C.G. Jung Club of
San Francisco, 1983.

Robert M. Stein, M.D. — USA

I have been in the private practice of Jungian Analysis in Los Angeles since
1960, having received my Diplomate in Analytical Psychology from the C.G.
Jung Institute Zurich in 1959. Before going to Zurich in 1956, I practiced general
medicine for six years. I received my M.D. degree from U.C. Irvine, College of
Medicine. My undergraduate studies were done at the University of Maryland.

My contact with Jung was discussed in my paper. All in all, I attended three of
his seminars and I had two individual sessions with him. In addition, I attended
several gatherings at which Jung appeared, including the first meeting of the
International Association for Analytical Psychology in 1958. Jung received a
standing ovation at that meeting and was also honored at the closing banquet at
the Dolder Hotel.

Arwind U. Vasavada, Dr. Litt. — India

I obtained a Master's degree in Eastern and Western Philosophy and
Psychology (1934), followed by the D. Litt. in Philosophy (1945) from the
Benares Hindu University, Varanasi.

Later on (1954), I went to the C.G. Jung Institute, Zurich on a scholarship
offered by the Government of India and obtained the Diploma in 1956. Being
the first Indian student to study at the Institute, I had the valuable opportunity
of meeting Dr. C.G. Jung, who took a personal interest in me and guided me
during some critical stages in the journey of Individuation. In Jung, I met a Guru
in the west who initiated me into the western path of Self-realization.

Joseph B. Wheelwright, M.D. — USA

Education: Milton Academy 1920-1924; Harvard College 1924-1927;
St. Bartholomew's Medical College, London 1932-1938.

My first contact with Jung was in 1932 (I was on my way to Vienna to see
Freud, but changed my mind!) I worked with him for several months and then
left for England to do medicine. Each year I went back to Zurich for one month's
intensive work. In 1938-1939, I was qualified and my wife and I lived in Zurich. I
saw Toni Wolff three times per week and Jung twice per week. When I returned
in 1951, I saw him quite a few times but not as a patient. None of us had formal
training, except our own analysis and the weekly seminars. There were other
analysts for me in England and America. Freud said a responsible therapist
should be re-cycled every five years. I have religiqusly followed this dictum from
1939 until five years ago.

Dr. Med. Alfred Ziegler — Switzerland

I was born in Lucerne, Switzerland in 1925. My University studies took place
in Geneva, Vienna and Zurich. During the period of my assistantship in

psychiatry and internal medicine, I trained at the C.G. Jung Institute in Zurich. Training and control analyses were undertaken with Jolande Jacobi, K.W. Bash, Franz Riklin and M.L. von Franz. Since 1960, I have been in private practice as a psychiatrist and psychotherapist in Zurich. Simultaneously, I have been a lecturer, training and control Analyst at the Jung Institute.

I had personal contact with C.G. Jung during the late part of his life at patient colloquia, lectures and official celebrations. Psychosomatic problems continue to be my primary concern and, meanwhile, this passion has led to the development of a "philosophy" of psychosomatics which is my own and which I call "Archetypal Medicine" or "Morbism." Its premises are unmistakably Jungian. At the present time I am preparing an anthology of lectures and articles which is to be entitled: *IMAGES OF A SHADOW MEDICINE* (transliterated from the proposed German title).